THE NATURE AND STRUCTURE OF CONTENT

The Nature and Structure of Content

JEFFREY C. KING

OXFORD
UNIVERSITY PRESS

OXFORD

UNIVERSITY PRESS

Great Clarendon Street, Oxford OX2 6DP

Oxford University Press is a department of the University of Oxford.
It furthers the University's objective of excellence in research, scholarship,
and education by publishing worldwide in

Oxford New York

Auckland Cape Town Dar es Salaam Hong Kong Karachi
Kuala Lumpur Madrid Melbourne Mexico City Nairobi
New Delhi Shanghai Taipei Toronto

With offices in

Argentina Austria Brazil Chile Czech Republic France Greece
Guatemala Hungary Italy Japan Poland Portugal Singapore
South Korea Switzerland Thailand Turkey Ukraine Vietnam

Oxford is a registered trade mark of Oxford University Press
in the UK and in certain other countries

Published in the United States
by Oxford University Press Inc., New York

British Library Cataloguing in Publication Data

Data available

Library of Congress Cataloging in Publication Data
King, Jeffrey C.
The nature and structure of content / Jeffrey C. King.
p. cm.
Includes bibliographical references and index.
ISBN-13: 978-0-19-922606-1 (alk. paper)
ISBN-10: 0-19-922606-7 (alk. paper)
1. Proposition (Logic) I. Title.
BC181.K56 2007
160—dc22   2006103218

Typeset by Laserwords Private Limited, Chennai, India
Printed in Great Britain
on acid-free paper by
Biddles Ltd., King's Lynn, Norfolk

ISBN 978-0-19-922606-1

For Annie, my favorite thing in the world . . .

Contents

Acknowledgements

Because I have been thinking about the issues discussed in this book for a long time, I owe lots of people thanks for helping me think through them. Inevitably, I will forget to thank some folks. If you are one of them, please forgive me.

It was conversations many years ago with my then colleague Michael Jubien that first got me thinking about issues concerning propositions. The many excellent discussions I had with Jubien on these and related issues early on profoundly affected the way I think about them.

I began writing the book, or at least thinking about writing it, shortly after I arrived at USC in fall of 2004. Conversations with Jim Pryor and Alex Byrne on visits to USC that year were extremely helpful and allowed me to begin to see the shape of the book I was to write. Somewhere around that same time, I had a long email correspondence with Matthew McGrath on the topics covered in the book. Matt's relentless and excellent questions and criticisms were crucial in moving my thinking forward at that point. Then in spring of 2005 I taught a graduate seminar on the metaphysics of structured propositions at USC. I thank all the participants in the seminar for their helpful comments and suggestions. I especially want to thank Scott Soames, who sat in on the course and provided numerous helpful suggestions and criticisms. I spent the summer of 2005 and much of the fall producing a first draft of the book. In winter 2005–06, John Hawthorne visited USC for several weeks to give a series of talks. While John was at USC, he, Jim van Cleve, David Manley, Scott Soames, and I had a reading group on Chapters 2 and 3 of the book. I cannot overstate the importance of those meetings. Afterwards, I had pages and pages of notes containing incredibly difficult objections and incredibly helpful suggestions. I spent the next several months rewriting central parts of the book in light of these objections and suggestions. Chapters 2 and 3, and in general my views on the issues raised there, are considerably different and better than they were prior to the meetings. So a very grateful thank you indeed is owed to Jim van Cleve, John Hawthorne, David Manley, and Scott Soames.

I have to single out John Hawthorne, David Manley, and Scott Soames as the three philosophers who had the greatest influence on the book. After the reading group meetings just mentioned, I had several multiple hour meetings with John and numerous discussions with Scott and David. The book is much better than it would have been as a result of these meetings and discussions.

In spring 2006 I gave part of Chapter 2 as a talk at the Logic and Language 2006 conference at the University of Birmingham. My commentator Dominic Gregory managed to raise three excellent points in a five minute comment. (That has to be some kind of record!) One of them in particular altered my thinking about some very important matters. My thanks to Dominic and to the audience at the conference. I also had a very useful email exchange with John Collins (who was at the conference) after the conference that very much helped clarify my thinking on a number of issues. Finally, just before sending in the final version of the manuscript, Mark Schroeder provided very helpful comments and suggestions.

I was fortunate to have had two very diligent anonymous referees. Each sent me pages of helpful comments and I am deeply indebted to them.

For several years, Jason Stanley urged me to write something like this book. I have discussed my views on the topics the book addresses with Jason more than any other philosopher. His influence on my thinking has occurred over a period of many years now and it has been profound.

Peter Momtchiloff was quite simply a fantastic editor. Since I first discussed the book with Peter, he has been encouraging, incredibly patient, and wonderfully efficient. I also wish to thank my excellent copyeditor Joy Mellor for the wonderful job she did.

Finally, I must acknowledge the role my lovely wife Annie, to whom I have dedicated the book, played in its production. I had the good luck to have married a woman who is incredibly smart and whose sound intuitions are untainted by philosophy. The price she pays for this is that she is subjected to calls interrupting her own work in which I ask her things like: "What's an example of a gesture that gives an instruction?" or "Is the following sentence intuitively true: 'Jeff owns more surfboards than Napoleon'?" She handles this with remarkable grace and humor, while providing excellent answers. In addition, while I was working on the book, she bent over backwards to do things for me that would allow me more time to write at crucial junctures. This even before we were married! And finally, the love and support she gave me while I worked on this book were of incalculable value to me. My friends say she is too good for me. They're right.

Introduction

I first began thinking about the issues addressed in this book, various issues concerning what one might call the metaphysics of structured propositions, in the early 1990s. Since that time, these issues have never been far from my mind. Indeed, the vast majority of my work since the mid-90s has been in one way or another connected to my thinking about these issues. Even my book on complex demonstratives (King 2001) had its roots in a paper on the metaphysics of structured propositions, (see King 1996: 501 and 509–11). In the few papers I wrote on these topics in the nineties, I was never able to fully develop the view or to consider its implications. Further, my views on these issues have evolved since then in certain ways. Because of these things, because of the centrality of my thinking on these issues to my overall philosophical orientation and because it seemed to me that others didn't see connections among views that I hold that are mediated by my views on these issues, I decided it was time to write a book on the metaphysics of structured propositions. The present book is the result of that decision.

Before diving headlong into metaphysical issues surrounding propositions, it would be wise to say a bit about why philosophers believe in propositions at all. Of course, belief in propositions has had a distinguished history in analytic philosophy. Three of the great founding fathers of analytic philosophy, Gottlob Frege, Bertrand Russell, and G.E. Moore, believed in propositions.[1] Many philosophers since them have shared this belief; and the belief is widely, though certainly not universally, accepted among philosophers today. What motivates the many friends of propositions to think there are such things? I think the answer is that there are a variety of important jobs that propositions seem capable of performing, where it isn't clear what would perform those jobs in their absence.

To begin with, pretheoretically it seems that sentences encode pieces of information and that distinct sentences may encode the *same* piece of information, as is perhaps the case with 'Snow is white,' and '*Schnee ist weiss*.' Further, what piece of information a sentence encodes (perhaps relative to a context) together with the way the world is determine whether it is true or false. If propositions

---

[1] At least they did at certain points in their careers. Of course, Frege called the things we think of today as propositions *thoughts*.

exist, we can identify them with these pieces of information and make sense of this. Sentences express propositions (relative to contexts), different sentences may express the same proposition and propositions are true or false depending on how the world is. Second, we think that some things are the possessors of modal features such as being impossible, possible and necessary. Our pretheoretical talk suggests that these are the same things that are true and false, since we talk of things being necessarily true, possibly false and so on. Further, it seems as though someone uttering a German sentence and someone uttering an English sentence could thereby attribute necessary truth to the same thing. Again, if propositions exist, we can see how all this would be so. Propositions are the bearers of modal features, and by uttering sentences of different languages people might attribute the same modal feature to the same proposition. Third, there are things we believe, doubt, and assume and again our pretheoretical talk suggests that these are the same things that are true and false and possess modal features, as when we talk of believing something that is necessarily true. As before, if propositions exist and are the objects of our attitudes, we can understand how this would be so. In believing something, I stand in a relation to a proposition and that proposition may be necessarily true. Fourth, when we attempt to formulate a semantics for a natural language like English that contains modal locutions and verbs of propositional attitude, invoking propositions produces a nice, neat semantics. Expressions like 'Necessarily' operate on propositions. A sentence fronted by 'Necessarily' is true just in case the proposition expressed by the embedded sentence exhibits the proper behavior when evaluated at different possible worlds. Sentences containing verbs of propositional attitude, such as 'Rachel believes that Frege is smart', assert that individuals stand in relations to propositions, in this case that Rachel stands in the believing relation to the proposition that Frege is smart. Further, if we invoke propositions, in cases like that just considered and many others as well we can hold that that-clauses designate propositions and are used to attribute properties to them or assert that they stand in relations, as when we say that it is true that snow is white, that Shane believes that snow is white, that logicism entails that arithmetic is a branch of logic, and so on.[2] Perhaps there are other jobs that propositions can perform as well, but I believe that friends of propositions all believe they can do the jobs just canvassed.

I think it is fair to say that most advocates of propositions have come to believe that propositions must be more fine grained than sets of metaphysically possible worlds. For it seems possible to believe that $2 + 2 = 4$ without believing that first order logic is undecidable. But since that $2 + 2 = 4$ and that first order logic is undecidable are true in all metaphysically possible worlds, on the view that propositions are sets of possible worlds, it would not be

---

[2] In Chapter 5, I discuss how to understand the claim that that-clauses *designate* propositions. As I say there, it may be that that-clauses sometimes designate things other than propositions as well.

possible to believe one and not the other.[3] For this reason, most advocates of propositions favor accounts of propositions on which they are more finely individuated than sets of possible worlds. I'll call these *fine grained accounts* of propositions.

To summarize, advocates of fine grained propositions are primarily motivated by the fact that such propositions can fill the roles discussed to this point. Perhaps there are other ways to perform the jobs discussed. But I think it can be claimed that other ways of doing this are likely to be less neat and more problematic than having propositions perform these jobs. For example, there isn't any widely accepted, well worked out alternative to the semantics of verbs of propositional attitude that eschews propositions and that can claim to be as neat and unproblematic (the existence of propositions aside) as an account that invokes propositions. Given these facts, it seems to me that the only reason for *not* invoking propositions to perform the various jobs discussed is that they are thought to be in some way problematic. And certainly, many philosophers have thought that this is so. I believe that for the most part this is what motivates philosophers who try to get by without propositions. That is, in general it isn't that foes of propositions think they can do things *better* without them. Rather, for one reason or another they think propositions are problematic and so they feel *compelled* to do without them.

The present book is addressed to both friends and foes of propositions. With most of their friends, the present book will assume that an account of propositions on which they are structured entities with constituents and so are individuated more finely than sets of worlds is desirable. The primary purpose of the book is to formulate and defend a detailed account of the metaphysical nature of propositions of this sort and to show the account to have many virtues. In so doing, it will attempt to engage at least some foes of propositions as well. For it will be argued that on the view to be formulated, there is no mystery about what propositions are, given rather minimal assumptions it follows they exist, and we can begin to see how and why they manage to have truth conditions and so represent the world as being a certain way. These points will address at least those foes of propositions who are such because of claiming not to understand what propositions are, or claiming not to have any reason to think they exist, or claiming not to understand how they could represent the world as being a certain way.

More specifically, given the motivation for invoking propositions I've outlined, my idea is that if (i) there is an account of propositions according to which there is no mystery as to what they are; and (ii) there is good reason to think they exist; and (iii) the account sheds light on the central feature of propositions (i.e. that

---

[3] Further, Scott Soames (1987) has argued persuasively that relaxing the requirement that worlds be metaphysically possible and allowing propositions to be sets of virtually any sort of truth supporting circumstances runs into similar difficulties.

they represent how the world is); and (iv) the account doesn't have problematic consequences; and (v) arguments against propositions can be defused, then we should adopt that account of propositions. The structure of the book reflects this idea. Chapter 1 formulates the main question to be addressed in the first three chapters of the book, the question of what holds the constituents of propositions together, and considers the answers Gottlob Frege and Bertrand Russell offered to this question. These answers are rejected, motivating the search for a new answer. In Chapter 2, a new answer is sketched that yields an account of what propositions are. It is argued that on this account (i)–(iii) just mentioned are true. Chapter 3 takes up consequences of the account sketched in Chapter 2, focusing on consequences that might be thought problematic. It is argued that there are no problematic consequences, and hence that (iv) is true. In Chapters 4 and 5, arguments against structured propositions in particular and against propositions in general, respectively, are considered and defused. This suffices to establish (v) above. Hence Chapters 1–5 constitute an argument that the account of propositions sketched should be accepted.

Above, I suggested that two jobs propositions play are being the objects of attitudes like belief and doubt and being the things operated on by modal operators such as 'necessarily'. However, some philosophers have mounted vigorous challenges to this claim. In particular, these philosophers have argued that there are a number of sentential operators in natural language, such as tenses (e.g. the past and future tense) and location expressions such as 'somewhere' and 'everywhere', that appear to operate on the same things as modal operators. If this is so, the things that modal operators, tense operators, and place operators operate on are too impoverished to serve as the objects of the attitudes. This is a serious challenge to propositions, since if successful it would show that no one thing can perform the jobs I've claimed that propositions are to perform. And this would in turn to some extent or another undercut the motivation I have given for propositions. In Chapter 6, I address this challenge by arguing that modal operators are distinctively different from tenses and place expressions, in that the former operate on propositions and the latter do not. Finally, Chapter 7 shows that the account of propositions I defend can be used to resolve the paradox of analysis and related difficulties.

A few final comments on the argumentative strategy of the early part of the book may be useful. In Chapter 1, I assume that we are only interested in fine grained accounts of propositions for the reasons I've outlined here. I claim that the best fine grained account is bound to be one on which propositions are structured and have constituents. Any such account that is credible, I claim, will have to answer the question of what it is that holds the constituents of propositions together. I then reject the answers Frege and Russell give to this question. Here for the most part I write as though I am assuming structured propositions exist. But that pretense is dropped in Chapter 2, where I claim that a *plausible* answer to the question of what it is that holds together the constituents of a proposition must give us good independent reason to think that propositions exist. The account I sketch there does so, or so I claim.

The lack of an account of exactly what structured propositions are, an account of their metaphysical nature, has made even friends of propositions uneasy and has probably inclined many to be foes. The present book attempts to put their friends at ease and to win back their foes.[4]

---

[4] Thanks to an anonymous referee whose comments and suggestions helped shape this Introduction.

Tuples

1

The Primary Question and the Answers of Frege and Russell

As I indicated in the Introduction and for the reasons given there, I'll begin by assuming that we are interested in fine grained accounts of propositions. Of course to say that propositions are fine grained is not yet to say what sorts of things are constituents of propositions, nor even whether propositions have constituents. I mentioned in the Introduction that I think that propositions *do* have constituents. This is mainly because I find the idea of "simple fine grained propositions", fine grained propositions without constituents or parts, mysterious. What would make such a simple proposition be about, say, Paris as opposed to Santa Monica? In virtue of what would it have the truth conditions it in fact enjoys? I cannot see that these questions have answers if propositions are held to be simple and fine grained. But it seems to me they should have answers.

Because of such considerations, I also will henceforth assume that propositions have constituents. As to what sorts of constituents propositions have, even this question is not my *primary* concern. Still, in order to address the issues that *are* my primary concern, it will help to adopt a view about what the constituents of propositions are. Hence, I shall adopt without argument a view of these matters to which I am sympathetic. Nathan Salmon (1986), Scott Soames (1987), David Kaplan (1989) and others, all influenced by the seminal work of Saul Kripke (1972), have articulated views according to which certain linguistic expressions (perhaps taken relative to contexts) contribute individuals to propositions. In the wake of this work, it is widely held that proper names, indexicals ('I', 'here', 'now', etc.) and demonstrative pronouns (taken relative to contexts) contribute the individuals they designate (in those contexts) to the propositions expressed (in those contexts) by the sentences in which they occur.[1] Such expressions are generally called *devices of direct reference*, the term 'direct' alluding to the fact that these expressions don't contribute some entity to a proposition that at a

---

[1] It is usual to include demonstratives, both simple ('that') and complex ('that woman who lives on the second floor'), in the class of expressions that contribute individuals (relative to a context) to propositions. I leave them off because I argued in King (2001) that complex demonstratives, and perhaps simple ones as well, are quantificational.

circumstance of evaluation determines an individual distinct from the entity. Rather, the individual itself gets contributed to the proposition.[2]

Because I think there is much to be said for this view, and because I have found what the above authors have said convincing, I'll adopt the view here. So I'll assume individuals occur in some propositions. However, we will see that making this assumption is not necessary to raise the main question I wish to address. The natural next step is to assume that (syntactically simple) n-place predicates contribute n-place relations to propositions (where 1-place relations are properties). I'll take that step. So I'll assume that propositions are entities that are more fine grained than sets of possible worlds and contain individuals, properties and relations as constituents.

Propositions fitting this description, often called *structured propositions*, are sometimes represented in a certain way. The proposition that Annie likes Carl is sometimes represented as follows:

1. <Annie, liking, Carl>

That is, the proposition is represented as an ordered triple of Annie, the liking relation and Carl. Could the proposition actually *be* that ordered triple? I believe there are reasons for thinking that it cannot be and more generally that propositions are not ordered n-tuples. The first problem is a Benacerraf style worry.[3] There are a number of distinct n-tuples, all of which seem to be equally good candidates for being the proposition that Annie likes Carl. For example, in addition to 1, there are

1a. <liking, Annie, Carl>
1b. <Annie, Carl, liking>
1c. <liking, <Annie, Carl>>

It is hard to see why any one of these should be the proposition in question, while the others are just non-proposition ordered three-tuples.

Worse, to this point I have been implicitly assuming the standard definition of *ordered pair* (in terms of which ordered n-tuples are defined) due to Kuratowski.[4] Holding that definition constant, any number of three-tuples, which are

---

[2] Sometimes the claim that a term is a device of direct reference is understood merely as the claim that the term doesn't contribute some descriptive or conceptual material to a proposition that at a circumstance of evaluation determines the term's referent by means of the referent satisfying it, (see Salmon 1986). On this way of using the term 'direct reference', to claim that a term is directly referential is not yet to make any claim about what it does contribute to propositions. Those who use the term 'direct reference' in this way often understand the claim that a term is *Millian* as the claim that the term contributes only its referent to propositions, (see Salmon 1990). I'll understand the claim that a term is directly referential here as including Millianism so construed, since these issues are not my primary concern.

[3] Benacerraf (1965).   [4] $<X,Y>=_d \{X, \{X,Y\}\}$

just certain sets on this definition, are equally good candidates for being the proposition that Annie likes Carl as 1-1c make clear. But of course there other ways to define ordered pairs (and so n-tuples). And on these other definitions, ordered pairs will be *different* sets from the sets they are identified with on the Kuratowski definition. So we now have as apparently equally good candidates for being the proposition that Annie likes Carl the sets 1-1c are identified with on the Kuratowski definition of ordered pair (and hence ordered n-tuple), as well as the sets 1-1c are identified with on other definitions of ordered pairs (and hence n-tuples). It is just impossible to believe that there is one of these candidates that *is* the proposition in question. What in the world could make it so?

A final difficulty for the view that propositions are ordered n-tuples concerns the mystery of how or why on that view they have truth conditions. On any definition of ordered n-tuples we are considering, they are just sets. Presumably, many sets have no truth conditions (e.g. the set of natural numbers). But then why do certain sets, certain ordered n-tuples, have truth conditions? Since not all sets have them, there should be some explanation of why certain sets *do* have them. It is very hard to see what this explanation could be.[5]

On the basis of these difficulties, I conclude that propositions cannot be identified with n-tuples of their constituents. This leaves us with the view that n-tuples such as 1 are properly understood as *representing* propositions. Now that we see that ordered n-tuples are not propositions but are merely used to represent them, I can raise the primary question that I want to address in the first part of the present work. The question is, simply, what do the corner brackets and comma in 1 represent? That is, 1 as a whole represents the proposition that Annie likes Carl, and so the corner brackets and comma must represent some feature of this proposition. We can of course give a provisional answer to the question of what feature of the proposition that Annie likes Carl the corner brackets and comma represent. Presumably, they represent whatever it is that holds the constituents of the proposition that Annie likes Carl together and endows the proposition with a certain structure. But now our original question resurfaces in a new form: what is it that holds together the constituents of the proposition that Annie likes Carl and imposes structure on it? In general, propositions must have something that does this. Clearly, somehow the constituents need to be held together for there even to be a proposition. If there are no propositions, as some suggest, the constituents of alleged propositions nonetheless exist. So to have propositions in addition to their constituents, something must bind the constituents together in the proposition. Further, there seem to be propositions with the same constituents. For example

---

[5] Note that refusing to identify ordered n-tuples with sets, perhaps taking them to be *sui generis* entities, won't help with either of the difficulties I have raised for the view that propositions are n-tuples. First, we would still have no reason to identify the proposition that Annie likes Carl with one of 1-1c as opposed to any other. And second, we would still have no answer to the question of why certain n-tuples have truth conditions and others (e.g.$< 1, 2, 3 >$) don't.

the proposition that Carl likes Annie and the proposition that Annie likes Carl appear to have the same constituents. So the difference between them must be how those constituents are arranged or structured. Our question, then, is: what is it that binds together the constituents of propositions and imposes structure or an arrangement upon its constituents? This is the question that will occupy us for the first two chapters.[6]

Note that the question of what binds together the constituents of propositions and imposes structure on them is at least to some extent independent of the question of what the constituents of the proposition are.[7] That is why in discussing what the constituents of propositions are above, I said that I was not primarily interested in that question. Still, I have adopted what I view as the most plausible account of what the constituents of propositions are. But I wish to emphasize that those with other views about what the constituents of propositions are should still be interested in the question that is my primary concern and that I will subsequently address.

Before attempting to answer the question of what holds together the constituents of propositions and imposes structure on them, it would be wise to consider answers others have given to this question. Recent structured proposition theorists, including those mentioned above, have been surprisingly silent on this subject. Indeed, though one often finds propositions depicted as in 1 above in the works of recent structured proposition theorists, there is generally no indication as to whether the theorist in question takes the proposition *to be* an ordered n-tuple or rather takes the ordered n-tuple to *represent* the proposition. Further, if the latter is in fact the case, there is no indication as to what *the proposition itself* really is and what binds *its* constituents together.

partly logical

[6] As an anonymous referee pointed out, if propositions are just mereological fusions of their constituents, there need be nothing that binds the constituents of propositions together. Presumably an advocate of this view would hold that mereological composition or fusion is unrestricted (any group of things has a fusion) and that there is no unique fusion of given parts (in order that one has distinct propositions with the same parts). Further, an advocate of this view is likely to view unrestricted composition as ontologically innocent and "automatic": commitment to the parts just is commitment to their fusion. (Thus Lewis (1991) (who does however embrace uniqueness of composition): 'But given a prior commitment to cats, say, a commitment to cat-fusions is not a *further* commitment. The fusion is nothing over and above the cats that compose it. It just *is* them.' p. 81—I am of course not attributing to Lewis the view under discussion according to which propositions are mereological fusions of their constituents. It is because the composition is automatic and innocent that nothing would be required to bind together the constituents of propositions on this view (nothing holds the cats together in the cat-fusions because they are nothing beyond the cats themselves). Though I don't consider this view in any detail in the present work, my main problem with it is that I don't see what the account would be of which fusions are propositions (presumably cat-fusions aren't but some fusion of Annie, liking and Carl is the proposition that Annie likes Carl) nor of why the fusions that are propositions have truth conditions (presumably cat-fusions don't). Further, I have serious doubts about the claim of ontological innocence, especially when uniqueness of fusion is denied. See also note 13, Chapter 2.

[7] Though claims about what the constituents are may constrain the answer to the question of what binds them together, and vice versa.

However, Gottlob Frege and Bertrand Russell both had views about what holds together the constituents of propositions, or, in Frege's case, thoughts.[8] Frege and Russell both defended accounts of propositions according to which they are individuated more finely than sets of possible worlds. Both Frege and Russell also had views of propositions according to which they had constituents that were bound together or arranged in a certain way. Thus, we would do well to consider what Frege and Russell had to say on these topics. Further, doing so will be good preparation for what is to come. And finally, giving the question we have raised some historical credentials by showing that Frege and Russell took it very seriously will perhaps incline contemporary philosophers to take it more seriously.

Frege famously held that all linguistic expressions are associated with senses and references.[9] Since we will be concerned with senses, because for Frege thoughts are senses, for the most part I won't consider the references of expressions. Proper names have senses that Frege called *complete* or *saturated*.[10] By contrast, *concept words* such as 'planet' have senses that Frege called *in need of completion* or *unsaturated*.[11] Further, expressions that stand for (2-place) relations, such as 'falls under' in the sentence 'The number 2 falls under the concept *prime number*', have senses that are "doubly unsaturated".[12]

As to (declarative) sentences, Frege appears to hold two significant theses about their senses (and presumably the senses of complex expressions generally). First, Frege held that the sense of a sentence, a thought, was "built out of" the senses of the parts of the sentence.[13] Call this *the building block claim* (henceforth *BBC*). Second, Frege held that (at least in many cases) the structure of words in a sentence was mirrored by the way their senses are structured in the thought the sentence expresses.[14] Call this the *mirror claim* (henceforth *MC*). Frege clearly makes both these claims in 'Logic in Mathematics' when he writes:

It is remarkable what language can achieve. With a few sounds and combinations of sounds it is capable of expressing a huge number of thoughts, and, in particular, thoughts

---

[8] Henceforth in talking about *both* Frege's and Russell's theories of thoughts and propositions (respectively) at the same time, I shall simply talk of their theories of propositions, ignoring Frege's use of the term 'thought'. When I discuss Frege's view of thoughts by itself, I shall use the term 'thoughts'.

[9] In fact, of course, some expressions lack references. Frege thought that names of fictional characters lack references. Frege in many places calls definite descriptions 'names' (e.g. in 'On Sinn and Bedeutung' he calls 'the negative square root of 4' a compound proper name p. 164—all page references to Frege are to Beaney (1997) unless otherwise indicated), and he considers the "name" 'the celestial body most distant from the Earth' to lack a reference (see 'On Sinn and Bedeutung' p. 153). As is well known, Frege was also eager to arbitrarily assign references to names that lack them.

[10] 'Introduction to Logic' p. 294; 'Notes for Ludwig Darmstaedter' p. 363.

[11] 'Comments on Sinn and Bedeutung' p. 174 note B.

[12] 'On Concept and Object' p. 193; 'Notes for Ludwig Darmstaedter' p. 363.

[13] Aside from the passage quoted below, Frege appears to say this in 'Letter to Jourdain, January 1914' p. 320; 'Notes for Ludwig Darmstaedter' pp. 364–5; 'Compound Thoughts' (Frege 1977: 55); and 'Logic in Mathematics' (Frege 1979: 243).

[14] Aside from the passage quoted below, Frege appears to say this in 'Notes for Ludwig Darmstaedter' pp. 364–65; and 'Compound Thoughts' (Frege 1977: 55).

which have not hitherto been grasped or expressed by any man. How can it achieve so much? By virtue of the fact that thoughts have parts out of which they are built up. And these parts, these building blocks, correspond to groups of sounds, out of which the sentence expressing the thought is built up, so that the construction of the sentence out of parts of a sentence corresponds to the construction of a thought out of parts of a thought. And as we take a thought to be the sense of a sentence, so we may call a part of a thought the sense of that part of the sentence which corresponds to it.[15]

Why does Frege endorse BBC and MC? In the above passage he mentions thoughts that no one has grasped before. Frege is even more explicit about this point in 'Compound Thoughts':

. . . even a thought grasped by a terrestrial being for the very first time can be put into a form of words which will be understood by someone to whom the thought is entirely new. This would be impossible, were we not able to distinguish parts in the thought corresponding to the parts of a sentence, so that the structure of the sentence serves as an image of the structure of the thought.[16]

Frege seems to say that the truth of BBC and MC make it possible for someone to grasp a thought that she has never grasped before by understanding a sentence. I think Frege's idea is this. If BBC and MC are true, a sentence basically tells us what the constituents of the thought it expresses are (the senses of the words in the sentence) and how they are combined or structured in the thought (the way the words of the sentence are structured in the sentence). Thus, even if I have never grasped the thought before, if I understand the sentence expressing it, in the sense of understanding its structure and the senses of the words in it, I am given the structure of the thought and its constituents, and thereby grasp it.[17] By contrast, suppose BBC and MC were false. Suppose instead that e.g. the syntax of a sentence determined a function that mapped the senses of the words in the sentence as they occur in the sentence to the thought expressed by the sentence, where the thought was in no way "built up" out of the senses of the parts of the sentence (BBC is false) and did not have a structure that mirrored the structure of the sentence (MC is false). If we now imagine that I encounter a sentence S

---

[15] 'Logic in Mathematics' (Frege 1979: 225). A very similar passage opens 'Compound Thoughts', part of which is quoted below. Though in the above passage Frege talks only about a sentence being built up out of "groups of sounds", it seems clear from this passage and what comes after it that he is thinking of words or phrases (and so a sentence being built up out of words or phrases). The similar passage in 'Compound Thoughts' talks of words instead of groups of sounds (part of which is quoted below), as does the passage in 'Letter to Jourdain, January 1914'. See previous two notes.

[16] Frege (1977: 55).

[17] I believe Frege assumes here that knowing what a thought's constituents are and how they are structured in the thought suffices for grasping it. In light of a comment by an anonymous referee, I should add that I don't think that Frege takes these considerations in favor of BBC and MC to be an argument in favor of positing thoughts. He gives independent arguments for this. Given that thoughts exist, he thinks that the truth of BBC and MC enable us to see how someone can grasp a thought for the first time by understanding a sentence (of course, presumably one might also grasp a thought for the first time without hearing a sentence that expresses it). Further, I don't mean to endorse Frege's thinking on these complex matters, which I have not yet thought through sufficiently.

expressing a thought T I have never grasped before, it is not at all clear how I could understand S and thereby grasp T. For if I have never grasped T, it isn't clear that I can grasp the function f from senses of words to thoughts that is determined by the syntax of S. After all, I couldn't know f maps some senses to T, since I have never grasped T. But if I don't know this about f, in what sense do I grasp f? And even if we do allow that in some sense I "partially grasp" f, this will be of no help in grasping T, since precisely what I don't know about f is that it maps some senses to T, since, again, I have never grasped T. But then under current assumptions it isn't clear that I can understand S and thereby grasp T. By contrast, as we have seen, if BBC and MC are true, we can give some account of how I could understand a sentence and thereby grasp a thought I have never grasped before.[18] Note that the problem here is not about understanding novel *sentences*. It may be that even if BBC and MC were false, I could understand a novel *sentence* S that expresses a thought T that I *have* grasped before.[19] What is not clear is whether, if BBC and MC were false, an account could be given of how I could understand a sentence that expresses a *thought* that I have never grasped before, and grasp the thought by understanding the sentence.

In any case, in holding BBC (and MC) it is clear that Frege confronts a version of the question we have raised: what holds the different senses of the parts of a sentence together in the thought expressed by the sentence? Frege's answer is that senses combine to form a thought by means of an unsaturated sense being completed or saturated by other senses. Frege writes:

For not all the parts of a thought can be complete; at least one must be unsaturated or predicative; otherwise they would not hold together.[20]

Frege apparently thought that unsaturated senses provided the glue that holds together the parts of a thought. In effect, he builds the element that holds the constituents of a thought together into some of the constituents: the unsaturated ones. To illustrate this point, let's consider the thoughts expressed by different kinds of sentences, the constituents of those thoughts and how they are held together.

As should be expected given what has been said to this point, a sentence like

2. Gödel is smart.

expresses a thought whose constituents are the complete sense expressed by the name 'Gödel' and the unsaturated sense expressed by the concept word 'smart'. As the above remarks indicate, the complete sense "completes" the unsaturated sense, with the result that they are bound together in a complex, complete sense:

[18] Dummett (1981) has a good discussion of essentially this point. See pp. 267–70 and pp. 276–7.

[19] Though remarks in 'Letter to Jourdain, January 1914' suggest that Frege also thought BBC and MC explain how we can understand novel *sentences* (p. 320).

[20] 'On Concept and Object' p. 193. See similar remarks in 'Notes for Ludwig Darmstaedter' p. 363.

the thought expressed by 2. It is easy to see how the structure of the thought mirrors the structure of the sentence, as MC claims. In 2, the name occupies the argument position of the predicate. In the thought 2 expresses, the sense of 'Gödel' saturates the unsaturated "position" in the sense of the predicate. In the case of sentences like

3. Carl loves Rebecca
4. Rebecca loves Carl

we have a doubly incomplete sense expressed by 'loves'. The two names express complete senses. The thoughts expressed by 3 and 4 differ in that in one case (i.e. 3) the sense expressed by 'Carl' saturates the "first position" in the unsaturated sense expressed by 'loves' and the sense expressed by 'Rebecca' saturates the second; in the other case (i.e. 4) the reverse is true.[21] So the unsaturated sense here both binds together the three constituents in virtue of the complete senses completing its unsaturated positions and it determines the structure of the resulting thought by having different positions that can be completed by the different complete senses. This is how the unsaturated sense both holds the thought together and allows two different thoughts to have the same constituents. Again, it should be clear how the structures of the thoughts expressed mirror the structures of the sentences. Next consider a sentence like:

5. Rebecca is strong and Lucy is shy.

Here the senses of the two conjuncts are like that expressed by 2 in terms of their structures and types of constituents. The sense of 'and' is doubly unsaturated, and is doubly completed by the complete senses of the two conjuncts, yielding a complete sense: the "conjunctive thought" expressed by the whole.[22] I assume it is easy to imagine how this account extends to other truth functional sentential connectives, including a one-place connective like 'not'.

Finally, consider a quantified sentence like:

6. Every woman is smart.

Here 'every' stands for (has as its referent) a "second level" relation: a relation between concepts.[23] So the sentence asserts that the ("first level") concepts that

---

[21] See 'Notes for Ludwig Darmstaedter' p. 363 where Frege talks about thoughts expressed by sentences like 3 and 4, where one part is doubly unsaturated and completed by two complete senses. Also, see 'Compound Thoughts' pp. 66–67 in Frege (1977) where Frege talks about 'positions in a thought', (the passage was garbled in the original text and a publishers erratum was added). These positions are what I am calling positions in unsaturated senses in the text.

[22] See 'Compound Thoughts' in Frege (1977: 59).

[23] Since Frege thought that first level concepts were functions of one argument from objects to truth values ('Function and Concept' pp. 139–41), and first level relations were functions with more than one argument from objects to truth values ('Function and Concept' p. 146), presumably the second level relation 'every' refers to is a function of two arguments from first level concepts to truth values ('Function and Concept' pp. 146–8). It maps the first level concepts A and B (in that order) to the True iff every object that falls under A (A maps to true) falls under B (B maps to true).

'woman' and 'smart' stand for stand in this relation (subordination: the concept *woman* is subordinated to the concept *smart*).[24] But this means that the sense of the relation word must be appropriate to a (two-place) relation: it must be a doubly unsaturated sense. So in the case of 6 we have *three* *un*saturated senses: that expressed by 'every' (doubly unsaturated), that expressed by 'woman' (singly unsaturated) and that expressed by 'smart' (singly unsaturated). The unsaturated senses expressed by 'woman' and 'smart' complete the doubly unsaturated sense of 'every', with the result being a complete sense: the thought expressed by 6. In this thought the sense of 'woman' saturates the first position in the sense of 'every', and that of 'smart' the second position.[25] So in this case, to repeat, we have three unsaturated senses combining to produce a complete sense. Here again, the sense of 'every' both binds together the constituents of the thought by the other constituents doubly completing it and imposes a structure on the constituents by allowing them to slot into different positions.

Frege says a variety of additional things that cohere nicely with the view I have been ascribing to him, including BBC and MC. In 'Negation', Frege says that the unsaturated sense of 'not' is part of the sense of the sentence 'not A', and that the thought expressed by the latter consists of the incomplete sense of 'not' combining with the complete sense of the sentence 'A'.[26] Given what has been said to this point, this is precisely what we should expect. This in turn would suggest that the sense of 'not[notA]' contains the sense of 'not' twice over, and consists of these combined with the sense of 'A'. If that were right, then the sense of 'not[notA]' would be different from the sense of 'A', since the former has the sense of 'not' as a part and the latter doesn't. And indeed, Frege appears to say this in 'Negation'.[27]

Unfortunately, Frege makes some remarks that are very much in tension with the view I have been attributing to him, including BBC and MC. In 'Compound Thoughts' Frege says a number of things that don't at all cohere with the view we have been describing. First, contrary to what he appears to say in 'Negation', Frege claims that 'A' and 'not[not A]' have the *same* sense.[28] But how could this be, given that Frege clearly claims that the sense of 'not' is a part of the sense of 'not A' and 'not[notA]', whereas one would think it is not in general part of the sense of 'A'? Second, Frege seems to claim that the sense of 'A or B' is the

---

[24] See 'Comments on Sinn and Bedeutung' p. 175 and 'On Concept and Object' pp. 187 and 189–90.

[25] This allows for the difference between the thoughts expressed by 'Every dog is a mammal' and 'Every mammal is a dog'.

[26] P. 355; p. 358.

[27] Pp. 360–1. After talking about the way in which the sense of 'not' combines twice over with a thought to form the sense of 'not[notA]', Frege writes: 'Thus of the *two thoughts*, A and the negation of the negation of A, either both are true or neither is.' (p. 361, my emphasis). So here Frege seems clearly to say that the thoughts are distinct.

[28] Frege (1977: 67).

same as the sense of 'not[notA and notB]'.[29] Again, how can that be, given that one would think that in general the sense of 'not' is part of the latter but not the former? Third, Frege clearly says that 'A', 'A or A' and 'A and A' all have the same sense.[30] But again, it is hard to see how that could be since the sense of 'A and A' must contain the sense of 'and' as a part, but the sense of 'A' does not, and so on. Thus, it is very hard to square these three claims with what appears to be Frege's view that the sense of a complex expression is built up out of the senses of its parts (BBC), where how those senses combine to yield the sense of the complex expression is mirrored by how the parts of the complex expression are combined in it (MC).

But the remark that is most seriously in tension with this latter view that I have been ascribing to Frege is made in 'Concept and Object'. There Frege writes:

In the sentence 'There is at least one square root of 4', we are saying something, not about (say) the definite number 2, nor about −2, but about a concept, *square root of 4*; viz. that it is not empty. But if I express the same thought thus: 'The concept *square root of 4* is realized', then the first six words form the proper name of an object. But notice carefully that what is being said here is not the same as was being said about the concept. This will be surprising only to somebody who fails to see that a thought can be split up in many ways, so that now one thing, now another appears as subject or predicate.[31]

Here Frege is making the point that you cannot say the same things about a concept that you can say about an object. But the striking claim is that the following two sentences express the same thought:

7. There is at least one square root of 4.
8. The concept *square root of 4* is realized.

This claim is striking, because the thought expressed by 7 should be the result of the unsaturated sense of the first level concept expression 'square root of 4' completing the incomplete sense of the second level concept expression 'There is at least one'.[32] By contrast, as Frege says, the first six words (counting '4' as a word) of 8 together form a proper name.[33] Hence their sense must be a complete sense. And 'is realized' must be a first level concept expression, whose sense is (singly) unsaturated.[34] But then the thought expressed by 8 must be the result of the complete sense of a name completing the unsaturated sense of a first level concept expression. Thus, it would appear that the *kinds* of senses that combine

---

[29] Frege (1977: 63–5).   [30] Frege (1977: 75).
[31] Pp. 187–8, my emphasis.   [32] See p. 188 and note O.
[33] Cf. Frege's infamous discussion of 'the concept *horse*' p. 184.
[34] Frege says '. . . that so-and-so is realized . . . is something that can be truly said only concerning a quite special kind of objects, viz. such as can be designated by proper names of the form "the concept *F*".' (p. 189) This strongly suggests that 'is realized' stands for a first order concept (that only maps a subset of these special objects to the True), and hence that its sense must be a singly unsaturated first order concept expression sense.

to form the thoughts expressed by 7 and 8 are quite different. Further, surely the structures of the sentences 7 and 8 are different as well. But BBC and MC claim that the thoughts expressed by 7 and 8 are the result of combining the senses of the words of the sentences in the way those words are combined in the sentences. How can such different *kinds* of senses combined in such different *ways* result in identical complex senses (thoughts)? It is in this way that Frege's claim that 7 and 8 express the same thought seems to violently conflict with BBC and MC.

Frege suggests in the above quotation that if we realize that thoughts can be split up in different ways, we won't be surprised that 7 and 8 express the same thought. But what he says about the possibility of thoughts being split up in different ways is of no help in resolving the tension between BBC and MC on the one hand and the claim that 7 and 8 express the same thought on the other. For when we turn to Frege's comments on thoughts being split up in different ways, it is clear that what Frege means is that one and the same thought can be "split up" into different saturated and unsaturated senses. As the following passage from 'Introduction to Logic' makes clear, a paradigm case of this is a thought expressed by a sentence containing several proper names:

If several proper names occur in a sentence, the corresponding thought can be analysed into a complete and unsaturated part in different ways. The sense of each of these proper names can be set up as the complete part over against the rest of the thought as the unsaturated part.[35]

I take it his idea is that a sentence like

9. Rebecca loves Carl.

expresses a thought consisting of the complete sense of 'Rebecca' saturating the first argument position of the doubly unsaturated sense expressed by 'loves', where the complete sense of 'Carl' occupies the second argument position. Thus, we can split up the thought into the complete sense of 'Rebecca' and the singly incomplete sense resulting from the sense of 'Carl' saturating the second argument position of the doubly unsaturated sense of 'loves', where nothing occupies the first argument position. Or we can split the thought up into the complete sense of 'Carl', and the singly incomplete sense resulting from the sense of 'Rebecca' occupying the first argument position in the doubly incomplete sense of 'loves', where nothing occupies the second argument position.[36]

---

[35] P. 295.

[36] I agree with Dummett (1981: 273–4) that one reason we must be able to view a thought as being split up in different ways for Frege is that only thereby can we make sense of different inferences it is involved in. In seeing 9 (or the thought it expresses) as following from 'Everyone loves Carl' (or maybe 'Everything loves Carl'—or the thought it expresses), we must see the thought expressed by 9 as split up in the first way mentioned above. In seeing 9 as following from 'Rebecca loves everyone', we must see the thought expressed by 9 as split up in the second way discussed above.

Frege discusses other examples of different kinds of thoughts being split up into complete and incomplete parts in different ways. For example, in 'Negation', Frege considers the thought expressed by 'the negation of the negation of A'.[37] He says that this thought can either be divided up into the sense of 'the negation of the negation of . . .' and the sense of 'A'; or the sense of 'the negation of' and the sense of 'the negation of A'. So Frege's claim is that thoughts, which must contain unsaturated senses as parts (after all, that is how they are held together),[38] can often be split up into complete and unsaturated parts in different ways, as illustrated above with sentences containing multiple names and double negation. Let's call this the *multiple analysis claim* (henceforth *MAC*).

Now MAC is at least in tension with the conjunction of BBC and MC. For according BBC and MC, the thought expressed by a sentence is a complex sense whose constituents are the senses of the words of the sentence, where these senses are combined in the complex sense in the way in which the words of the sentence expressing the complex sense are combined in the sentence. If we assume that a sentence has a unique syntactic analysis, that is, that the words of a sentence are combined syntactically in a unique way,[39] then BBC and MC seem to predict that a thought has unique constituents structured in a unique way. This would appear to mean that a thought can only be split up in one way, which is determined by its real structure.

The crucial point for our purposes is this. There is the tension just described between MAC on the one hand and the conjunction of MC and BBC on the other.[40] However, it is hard to see how any resolution of this tension will help with the tensions we have noted above. For all we have said, MAC only requires taking a thought with given constituents and splitting it up into those constituents in different ways. To repeat, the thought expressed by 9 has as constituents the senses of 'Rebecca', 'loves' and 'Carl'. That thought can be split up into the complete sense of 'Rebecca' and the singly incomplete sense resulting from the sense of 'Carl' saturating the second argument position of the doubly unsaturated sense of 'loves', where nothing occupies the first argument position. Or we can split the thought up into the complete sense of 'Carl', and the singly incomplete sense resulting from the sense of 'Rebecca' occupying the first argument position in the doubly incomplete sense of 'loves', where

---

[37] Pp. 360–1.

[38] 'On Concept and Object' p. 193; 'Notes for Ludwig Darmstaedter' p. 363; 'Compound Thoughts' Frege (1977: 55–6).

[39] Of course, there is syntactic ambiguity. But the sentences at issue (9 and a sentence that is a double negation) don't seem to be syntactically ambiguous. So they presumably do have unique syntactic analyses. It is true that Frege talks not only of thoughts being split up in different ways, but of the sentences expressing such thoughts being split up in different ways (see 'Negation' p. 360; 'Introduction to Logic' in Frege (1977: 195). How exactly to take these remarks (e.g. is Frege denying that sentences have a unique syntactic structure?) is part of the attempt to reconcile MAC with the conjunction of BBC and MC. As I say below, I won't attempt such a reconciliation.

[40] See Dummett (1981: 261–91) for an interesting attempt to resolve this tension.

nothing occupies the second argument position. But note that on either way of splitting up the thought, its ultimate constituents are the same: the senses of 'Rebecca', 'loves' and 'Carl'. The same holds for 'the negation of the negation of A'. So a resolution of the tension between MAC and the conjunction of BBC and MC will allow us to hold that though a thought has unique constituents structured in a unique way (BBC and MC), that thought may be split into those very constituents differently (MAC).[41] But it isn't at all clear how such a resolution would enable us to see how 'A' and 'not[not A]' could express the same sense, even though the sense of 'not[not A]' has the sense of 'not' as a constituent. And it isn't at all clear how such a resolution would allow us to see how 7 and 8, though they express thoughts with extremely different kinds of constituents combined extremely differently, could nonetheless express the same thought. So I conclude that even if we understood how to reconcile MAC with the conjunction of BBC and MC, this wouldn't help with the tensions we have found between the latter and the claim that 7 and 8 express the same thought, or the claim that 'A' and 'not[not A]' express the same thought.

In any case, putting these tensions in Frege's view aside, what can we say about his account of thoughts and how they are held together? First, an internal criticism. The account of what holds thoughts together and provides them with their structure seems rather unsatisfying. It is the unsaturatedness of some parts of a thought and their being completed by other parts that does all the work. The problem is that Frege himself seems to regard talk of unsaturatedness, and completing something unsaturated as metaphors.[42] It is not at all clear what these metaphors mean ultimately. But then it isn't clear what the account *is*. Further, even waiving the worry about metaphors, one feels as though no real account has been given. Appealing to the unsaturatedness of certain parts of thoughts as an account of what holds them together seems to essentially amount to saying that the parts hold together because some of them are "sticky". Unless we are given a substantial theory of *stickiness*, it doesn't seem that any real account has been given at all.

Finally, thoughts are supposed to be composed of the senses of names, predicates and so on. And the main motivation for thinking these expressions have senses, given in 'On Sinn and Bedeutung', is that names need to be

---

[41] Dummett's (1981: 261–91) resolution is of this sort for the most part. In the case of what Dummett calls "degenerate decomposition", we can split a thought up into parts of different sorts. Thus, Dummett (pp. 288–90) claims that the thought expressed by '6 is even' can be split up (decomposed) into the complete sense of '6' and the sense of the first level concept expression 'is even'; or it can be split into the sense of the first level concept expression 'is even' and the sense of a second level concept that maps a first level concept to True iff 6 falls under it (i.e. the first level concept maps 6 to True). Though here Dummett claims that thoughts can be split up into parts of different kinds, I still don't see how this rather special case sheds any light on how 7 and 8 can express the same thought, or how 'A' and 'not[not A]' can.

[42] 'On Concept and Object' p. 193; 'Negation' p. 361.

assigned senses to account for certain features of identity sentences.[43] Of course, Donnellan, Kripke, and their followers have given strong reasons for thinking that names don't have senses. But then such arguments undercut the motivation for senses generally. Hence we have been given good reason to think that the alleged component parts of thoughts don't exist. Of course some current philosophers continue to push various neo-Fregean accounts, and I am not pretending to have shown such accounts to be mistaken. Perhaps it is best at this point simply to express my own skepticism about accounts according to which the constituents of propositions aren't individuals, properties, relations and etc., but something like modes of presentation of such things. That said, let's turn to an account that does claim that the former sorts of things are constituents of propositions: the account of Bertrand Russell (1903).

In *The Principles of Mathematics* (1903), Bertrand Russell articulates a theory of propositions according to which propositions have constituents that are bound together in the proposition. And Russell gives an account of what those constituents are and what it is that holds them together. The main features of Russell's account are given in Chapter IV. Proper Names, Adjectives and Verbs. Russell introduces the notion of a *term* as follows:

Whatever may be an object of thought, or may occur in any true or false proposition, or can be counted as *one*, I call a *term*.[44]

Three sentences later, Russell writes:

A man, a moment, a number, a class, a relation, a chimaera, or anything else that can be mentioned, is sure to be a term; and to deny that such-and-such a thing is a term must always be false.[45]

Two points seem clear from these passages: all constituents of propositions are terms, and some terms are nonexistent.[46] Appropriately enough given the title of the chapter, early on Russell distinguishes between proper names, adjectives and verbs. Among terms, there are at least two kinds: *things*, which are "indicated" by proper names and *concepts*, which are indicated by other words.[47] There are in turn, two kinds of concepts: *predicates/class concepts*, indicated by adjectives; and *relations*, indicated by verbs.[48]

---

[43] Specifically, the possible informativeness of identity sentences of the form 'a=b'. As many have noted, the issues don't really seem to have anything to do specifically with identity sentences.

[44] P. 43.   [45] P. 43.

[46] I take the assertion that a chimera is a term to show that some terms do not exist. But if this is thought to be controversial, note that Russell explicitly talks of terms that do not exist at the end of section 48 Chapter IV p. 45.

[47] 'Indicate' is the word Russell uses for the semantic relation between an expression and what it contributes to propositions. It is important to distinguish indicating from denoting, which is a relation between a concept and an object, in Russell's technical sense of *object* (see p. 55 and first full footnote (*) on that page).

[48] In Chapter V, Russell actually distinguishes between predicates and class concepts (p. 54), but then says that class concepts 'differ little, if at all' (pp.54–5) from predicates. As a result, I'll ignore the distinction here.

To illustrate, consider the following sentences:

11. Socrates is human.
12. Socrates has humanity.

11 expresses a proposition containing the thing indicated by 'Socrates' and the predicate indicated by 'human'.[49] The predicate is predicated of the thing. 12 expresses a proposition containing the thing indicated by 'Socrates', the relation indicated by 'has' and the predicate indicated by 'humanity'.[50] The sentence asserts that Socrates bears the relation in question to the predicate in question.

Before turning to Russell's account of what holds together the constituents of propositions and imposes structure on them, let us briefly consider a problematic aspect of Russell's view. Russell claims that verbs express *relations*. In *Principles of Mathematics* Russell seems to be using the term 'relation' for what we would call *two-place relations*. For example, he says:

A primitive proposition in regard to relations is that every relation has a converse, i.e. that, if R be any relation, there is a relation R' such that xRy is equivalent to yR'x for all values of x and y.[51]

If this is Russell's view, it is hard to see why every verb should indicate a relation.[52] First, what about intransitive verbs? To his credit, Russell makes a brief remark about this immediately after saying that verbs indicate relations. He writes:

In intransitive verbs, the notion expressed by the verb is complex, and usually asserts a definite relation to an indefinite relatum, as in "Smith breathes".[53]

Considering Russell's sentence

13. Smith breathes.

the question is, in what sense does the intransitive verb here express a relation and what is meant by 'a definite relation to an indefinite relatum'? Two suggestions come to mind. On the first, there is a two-place relation that obtains between breathing things and what they breathe. Call it *breathes**. Consider the existential generalization of this relation on the what-is-breathed argument place. This will be a property (a one-place "relation"). It is expressed by 'breathes', so that 13 effectively asserts that Smith breathes* something. The problem with

---

[49] Russell also seems to think that 'is' in 11 contributes a relation to the proposition it expresses. See Chapter IV section 53. But getting into such details would take us too far afield.

[50] Russell thought that when you have a substantive (e.g. 'humanity') derived from an adjective ('human'), both indicate the same predicate. See Chapter IV section 49 and Chapter V section 57.

[51] P. 25. All of what Russell says in Chapter II sections 27–30 suggests that 'relation' means what we would mean by 'two-place relation'.

[52] Russell does say that verbs 'always or almost always' indicate relations (p. 44). But this hedge appears to concern whether 'is' expresses a relation in a sentence like 'Socrates is human'. In the end, Russell says it does, but wonders whether the point is verbal. See Chapter IV section 53. The hedge does not seem to have to do with worries about intransitive verbs.

[53] P. 44. I am not sure why Russell says 'usually' here.

this interpretation of Russell is that according to it, though 'breathes' expresses something complex (the existential generalization of breathes* on the what-is-breathed argument place), and we could construe it as asserting a definite relation (breathes*) to an indefinite relatum (in virtue of the existential quantification on the what-is-breathed argument place of breathes*), 'breathes' doesn't indicate a two-place relation. It indicates a one-place property that is the existential generalization of a two-place relation.

A second way to interpret Russell is as claiming that 'breathes' really does indicate a two-place relation and contribute it to what is expressed by 13. This leaves an argument place open, and that argument is supplied by context. On this view, 13 expresses different propositions in different contexts as a result of the different contexts providing different arguments for the second argument place of the relation indicated by 'breathes'. Though such a view seems implausible to me (it doesn't seem to me that in one context 13 asserts that Smith breathes normal air, in another, that he breathes pure oxygen etc.), it has the virtue of making it true that the verb indicates a relation, and so is consistent with Russell's claim that verbs express relations. On the other hand, on this interpretation of Russell, it isn't clear in what sense the verb expresses something complex as Russell claims intransitive verbs do.[54]

A final difficulty on this point of intransitive verbs indicating relations is this. If we could find an intransitive verb that expresses (indicates) an intrinsic property, it simply doesn't seem as though it could express a relation. By hypothesis, intrinsic properties cannot be relations (and presumably generally won't be relational properties).[55] And there do seem to be such verbs. Perhaps 'sleeps' is an example. In any case, we could certainly introduce such a verb. Just pick an intrinsic property P and introduce an intransitive verb 'to int' that is stipulated to express it. Thus 'Rebecca ints' attributes P to Rebecca. If there could be or are such intransitive verbs, then there could be or are verbs that don't indicate relations, contrary to what Russell seems to say.

In any case, let us turn away from these difficulties and consider Russell's account of what holds the constituents of propositions together and imposes structure on them. The following is the crucial passage in which Russell states his view:

Consider, for example, the proposition "A differs from B". The constituents of this proposition, if we analyse it, appear to be only A, difference, B. Yet these constituents, thus placed side by side, do not reconstitute the proposition. The difference which occurs

---

[54] An anonymous referee suggested a third interpretation of Russell here. Perhaps 'Smith breathes' expresses a proposition with three constituents: Smith, the two-place breathing relation and an indefinite object (the same one in every context). But as on the first interpretation of Russell discussed above, here too it seems that 'breathes' would express a one-place property (contrary to what Russell appears to say): the property of bearing the breathing relation to an indefinite object.

[55] Perhaps there are relational properties that are intrinsic. Presumably, however, many, many intrinsic properties aren't relational.

in the proposition actually relates A and B, whereas the difference after analysis is a notion which has no connection with A and B.[56]

A couple of sentences later, Russell adds

A proposition, in fact, is essentially a unity, and when analysis has destroyed the unity, no enumeration of constituents will restore the proposition. The verb, when used as a verb, embodies the unity of the proposition . . . [57]

Finally, three pages later Russell writes:

Owing to the way in which the verb actually relates the terms of a proposition, every proposition has a unity which renders it distinct from the sum of its constituents.[58]

Russell appears to be saying that in the proposition expressed by the following sentence

14. A differs from B.

the relation indicated by 'differs' holds together the proposition. Apparently it does so by actually relating A and B. If it is the relations expressed (indicated) by verbs that hold the constituents of propositions together, then clearly every proposition must contain such a relation. And Russell does say this.[59] Curiously, Russell says something stronger: he says that every proposition contains only one relation indicated by a verb (occurring as a relation).[60]

  Prima facie, the claims that relations indicated by verbs are what hold propositions together and that each proposition contains only one such relation (occurring as a relation) both seem false. It is hard to see how the proposition expressed by the following sentence

15. Socrates breathes and Scott hit Frank.

contains only one relation indicated by a verb, or is held together by a relation indicated by a verb.

  In any case, whether this is a problem for Russell or not, there does seem to be a an obvious great difficulty here. If in the proposition expressed by 14,

---

[56] P. 49.

[57] P. 50. Russell appears here to use the word 'verb' for the contribution a verb makes to a proposition (a relation). He appears to do this in other places as well. See p. 43 section 46 and p. 45 section 48. I'll come back to Russell's remarks about the unity of the proposition in Chapter 2.

[58] P. 52. Here again Russell appears to use 'verb' to mean propositional contribution of a verb. See previous note.

[59] P. 52. Though here again Russell uses 'verb' to mean relation. See previous two notes and next note.

[60] Here again Russell uses 'verb' to mean relation indicated by a verb. See previous three notes. Russell writes 'One verb, and one only, must occur as a verb in every proposition . . .' Immediately prior to this Russell says that 'The verb, we saw, is a concept . . .' (p. 52). Since relations indicated by verbs are a kind of concept, this makes pretty clear that Russell uses 'verb' here to mean a relation that the verb contributes to propositions.

the difference relation actually relates A and B, that sounds like it means that A stands in this relation to B. But A actually standing in the difference relation to B, one would think, would be a certain sort of fact. Indeed, if it is a fact, it would seem to be the fact that makes the proposition expressed by 14 true! So on Russell's account, we seem to get a collapse of true propositions into the facts that make them true. This, of course, also means that there are no false propositions. If A doesn't stand in the difference relation to B, then there is no proposition expressed by 14, since that proposition was to be A standing in the difference relation to B.

Is it really possible that Russell held a view with an obvious and very significant problem like this? I'm not sure. It just isn't clear to me how else to interpret Russell's remarks that relations indicated by verbs hold propositions together by actually relating their other constituents. In 'On the Nature of Truth and Falsehood' Russell explicitly rejects propositions (which he there calls *objectives*, following Meinong) as the objects of belief in favor of a view on which when I e.g. believe that Socrates was wise, this consists in a relation between me, Socrates, and being wise. There is no proposition, no single object of belief, on Russell's new view. When he raises the question of whether there *is* a single object of belief in that paper, he asks whether judging that Charles I died on the scaffold is a relation between me and a "fact" (or event), 'namely, Charles' death on the scaffold'.[61] Russell points out that when I believe or judge falsely this account would leave one without an object of belief or judgment. It is true that in this same work Russell does consider an account of objectives/propositions according to which they are distinct from facts that make true objectives true. But the fact that in 'On the Nature of Truth and Falsehood' when Russell first raises the question of whether there are single objects of belief, objectives or propositions, he simply *assumes* they would be the facts that make true objectives true and that he is fairly dismissive towards an account of objectives that distinguishes them from the facts that make true objectives true perhaps is some evidence for the claim that in *Principles of Mathematics*, Russell did hold a view that collapsed true propositions into facts and didn't allow for the existence of false propositions.

If this was Russell's account, looking back we can see one advantage of Frege's account of what holds the constituents of propositions together over Russell's. Both Frege and Russell held that certain sorts of constituents of propositions hold the others together (in Frege's case, unsaturated senses; in Russell's case, relations). Since Frege distinguished senses from the things in the physical world senses "determine", an unsaturated sense could hold together e.g. two complete senses, without the relation determined by the unsaturated sense actually relating the objects determined by the complete senses. Thus, for Frege, true thoughts

[61] Pp. 150–1.

don't collapse into facts in the physical world, and he has no problem with false thoughts.[62]

Having discussed the views of Frege and Russell on what imposes structure on and binds together the constituents of propositions, and having found the accounts to suffer various difficulties, we shall next attempt to provide a new account of the matter.

---

[62] Of course Frege used the term 'fact' to mean the same as 'true thought' ('Thought' p. 342). But the point is that Frege's thought that Annie likes Carl is distinct from Annie's actually liking Carl.)

2

A New Account of Structured Propositions

In Chapter 1, it was claimed that something must bind together the constituents of propositions and impose structure on them. In the present chapter, a detailed account of what it is that does this will be formulated.

I mentioned in Chapter 1 that I would assume that individuals, properties, and relations are constituents of propositions. Let me be a bit more specific about exactly what I am assuming. As I've already indicated, I will assume that names, demonstrative pronouns, and indexicals contribute the individuals they designate in contexts to the propositions expressed in those contexts by sentences in which they occur. I'll also assume that n-place predicates contribute n-place relations to propositions.[1] Further, I'll assume that truth functional sentential connectives (e.g. 'and') contribute truth functions to propositions. Finally, I'll assume that determiners ('every', 'some' etc.) contribute to propositions two-place relations between properties. Thus, for example, 'every' contributes to propositions the relation that obtains between properties A and B (in that order) iff every instance of A is an instance of B.

Prior to sketching an answer to the question of what holds the constituents of propositions together, let me state some constraints on any plausible answer to it, which I gestured at in the Introduction. I think there are at least two important constraints. First, any account of what holds together the constituents of propositions should leave no mystery about what propositions are and should give us confidence that propositions so construed really exist. For some reject propositions on the grounds that they are mysterious entities and that we have no reason to think they exist. An account of what holds together the constituents of propositions ought to be sensitive to these concerns and address them as directly as possible. It should say clearly and explicitly what propositions are; and it should give us reason to believe that there are things of this sort. Further, the reason in question should not be simply that it would be nice to have propositions around to perform certain philosophical chores. We should be given some sort of independent reason for thinking the things the account claims are propositions really do exist. Second, the account should shed light on the question of how it is that propositions are able to have truth conditions and so represent the world as

---

[1] More precisely, I'll assume that syntactically simple n-place predicates contribute n-place relations to propositions. I'll discuss this below.

being a certain way.[2] This feature of propositions is central to what they are. As a result, even if one managed to give an account of what holds the constituents of propositions together that results in it being unmysterious what propositions are and clear that they exist, so that the account satisfied the first constraint just mentioned, if the account shed no light on how or why propositions are able to represent the world as being a certain way, it would remain unclear whether the things it claims are propositions *really are* propositions. For we would have no reason to think that the alleged propositions are able to do the central thing that propositions do: represent the world as being a certain way. But then we would have no reason to think that the alleged propositions are propositions. It seems obvious that this would be a very serious drawback of the account. With these constraints in mind, we can now address the question of what it is that holds the constituents of propositions together and imposes structure on them.

It may be helpful at the outset to outline the *sort* of answer I intend to give to this question in very general terms and to provide some of the motivation for it prior to delving into the details of the view. Let's call an object possessing a property or n objects standing in an n-place relation, or n properties standing in an n-place relation or etc. a *fact*. We'll call the objects, properties and relations that are parts of a fact its *components*. So the fact of object o possessing property P has o and P as components. By definition, all facts obtain. For if an object o fails to possess a property P, then there is no fact of o possessing P. Thus, there are no facts that fail to obtain the way I am using the term.[3]

My claim is that propositions are just certain facts. Consider the proposition expressed by the following sentence:

1. Rebecca swims.

Given what I have said to this point, it should be clear that this proposition will have Rebecca and the property of swimming as constituents. I claim the *proposition* that Rebecca swims is a *fact* that has Rebecca and the property of swimming as components. But that proposition is *not* the fact consisting of Rebecca *possessing* the property of swimming. Rebecca does possess the property

---

[2] Of course in Chapter 1 I criticized the propositions-as-n-tuples account precisely for not being able to do this.

[3] When I say all facts obtain, I mean *in the actual world*. If o possesses P in the actual world, the fact of o possessing P obtains. If o fails to possess P in the actual world, there is no such fact. This leaves open the question of whether a fact could fail to exist. If a nonexistent object o could possess a property P in the actual world, then perhaps the fact of o possessing P fails to exist, though it obtains (in virtue of o possessing P). See note 29. I think that at least some facts are actually best construed as an object at a time possessing a property, or an object o at a time t standing in R to an object o' at time t', or etc. Issues such as this will be taken up in Chapter 3. Finally, if when o possesses P, it stands in the relation of instantiation to P (where instantiation is really a relation), then the instantiation relation is a component of the fact of o possessing P as well. I'll ignore this issue in what follows.

of swimming, so there is such a fact. But this fact makes the proposition that Rebecca swims true, where the proposition itself is a fact distinct from the fact consisting of Rebecca possessing the property of swimming. If Rebecca had failed to possess the property of swimming, that is, if there were no fact consisting of her possessing the property of swimming, the fact that is the proposition that Rebecca swims would still obtain, but sadly it would be false.[4] As we'll see, the fact that is the proposition that Rebecca swims has components other than Rebecca and the property of swimming, whereas the fact that is Rebecca possessing the property of swimming has only Rebecca and the property of swimming as components.

The motivation for this account is that it appears to be a good candidate to satisfy the constraints stated above on a plausible answer to the question of what binds together the constituents of a proposition. First, it will leave no mystery as to what propositions are and will render plausible the claim that propositions exist. Second, it will enable us to see how/why propositions are able to represent the world as being a certain way. I'll return to these issues after sketching my account. We will see that the account has other virtues in addition to satisfying these constraints.

Let me now turn to the task of actually sketching my answer to the question of what holds the constituents of propositions together. In attempting to answer this question, I begin with an unlikely topic: syntax. Obviously, any sort of semantics, whether for natural or artificial languages, must be defined over certain syntactic representations. In doing semantics, we assign meanings to syntactic representations. In the case of natural language, the question of the nature of the syntactic representations of sentences over which a semantics is to be defined is an empirical question. Though there is still considerable disagreement in contemporary syntax over the *precise* nature of the syntactic representations that are the inputs to semantics, there is some consensus as to certain features of these representations, at least among those working in a Chomskian minimalist style framework, which will be assumed here. It is customary for Chomskians to refer to the level of syntax that is the input to semantics as *LF*. I will adopt that usage here. I make the following assumptions about LF representations, which as far as I can see, are widely shared among current Chomskian syntacticians.[5] First, I assume that LF representations represent the syntactic structure of a sentence, including its internal structure and that of its complex constituents. Second, I assume that one main difference between the surface syntax of a sentence and its LF representation is that the relative scopes of quantifiers and other scope taking

---

[4] My idea that propositions are certain facts was inspired by remarks in Wittgenstein (1958). Given the difficulties of interpreting that work, I shall not attempt to further connect the present account of propositions to the one sketched therein.

[5] See for example Beghelli and Stowell (1997) and Szabolcsi (1997 and 2001).

elements are explicitly represented in LF representations. Thus, a sentence with a quantifier scope ambiguity such as:

2. Every surfer loves a surf spot.

will be assigned two LF representations, one of which gives the universal quantifier widest scope and the other of which gives the existential widest scope. In general, each reading of a sentence with scope ambiguities results from a distinct LF representation.[6,7] I will assume that LF representations are syntactically disambiguated generally. For convenience and simplicity, I'll picture these LF representations as follows, even though the picture makes no claim to actually accurately depicting real LF representations, which are without doubt much more complicated[8]:

2a. [[every surfer: x][some surf spot: y][x loves y]]]
2b. [[some surf spot: y][[every surfer: x][x loves y]]]

All that 2a and 2b are intended to capture are our two assumptions about LF: 1) that LF representations represent the internal syntactic structure of sentences and their complex constituents; and 2) that LF representations explicitly represent relative scopes of quantifiers and other scoped elements. In 2a and 2b the syntactic structure of the sentences are captured by the brackets. Often, the syntactic structure will be depicted in tree form instead.

If we look at syntactic representations such as 2a and 2b, we see that in them words stand in syntactic relations to each other. These relations are captured by the brackets in 2a and 2b. They bind together and impose structure on lexical items in a sentence. Consider the following sentence and its LF representation:[9]

---

[6] Beghelli and Stowell (1997) suggest that they hold that quantifier scope is explicitly represented in LF representations, so that a sentence like 2 is assigned two LF representations corresponding to the two possible relative scopes of the quantifiers, when they write 'We adopt two central assumptions of the standard theory of quantifier scope in generative grammar. First, quantifier scope is determined by c-command relations holding at the level of Logical Form (LF).' (p. 72). Further, their discussion of 'Every student read two books' (pp. 80–1) makes clear that the scope ambiguity it exhibits is the result of assigning the sentence two different LF representations in which the quantifiers have their c-command relations reversed. In addition, in personal communication, Stowell has said that on the view of Beghelli and Stowell (1997) each reading of a sentence with a quantifier scope ambiguity results from a distinct LF representation. Finally, Szabolcsi (1997) provides empirical evidence for, and endorses the account of, Beghelli and Stowell (1997).

[7] Quantifiers are said to "move" at LF with the result that they often occupy different positions at LF from those they occupy in surface structure. This movement results in explicit representation of quantifier scope. Open questions here include: what is the mechanism that produces the movement; and what are the sites where the quantifiers end up at LF. See papers in the previous note for discussion.

[8] Also, I don't claim that the real LFs associated with 2 have variables exactly where they occur in 2a and 2b. They are there to enhance readability.

[9] Since there are no quantifiers here, I assume the LF representation of 3 is very much like the surface string. I think the LF representation is more complex than 3a, but I believe the additional complexity, due to syntactic structure not captured by 3a, is irrelevant to present concerns. In

3. Rachel can help Nicole.
3a. [Rachel [can [help Nicole]]]   R.P. (h,ρ N)

The syntactic relation that binds together the lexical items in 3, represented again by brackets in 3a, is complex in the sense that for the words to stand in this relation is for 'help' and 'Nicole' to stand in a relation, and for the words standing in that relation to stand in a relation to 'can' and so on. I shall call the complex relations that bind together lexical items in LF representations *sentential relations*.[10]

A semantics that makes use of structured propositions will have two components. First, there are rules that map LF representations (relative to contexts) to structured propositions. Second, there is a definition of truth (relative to whatever parameters are required—e.g. a world) for structured propositions. Thus, the first component here maps one structured entity, an LF representation consisting of words standing in a sentential relation, to another structured entity, a structured proposition consisting of the semantic values of those words (relative to a context) held together by some relation that provides the structure to the proposition. Our question, of course, is what relation binds together the constituents of these structured propositions.

Because it is a bit hard to state the view I intend to endorse without some initiation, I'll begin with a very simple sentence and state a first approximation to the view I will eventually endorse. I will then motivate making two amendments to this first approximation, which will leave us with the view I endorse. So consider again the following sentence:

4. Rebecca swims.

Simplifying considerably, let's assume that its LF representation looks as follows, this time in "tree form":

4a.

Call the sentential relation relating the words in the LF 4a, which is represented by the branching lines, *R*. Now we want to know what relation holds together Rebecca and the property of swimming in the structured proposition to which

general, the details concerning the actual nature of LF representations are, I believe, irrelevant to the view I wish to defend.

10 These relations may have "unfilled" terminal nodes as well. Again, this is irrelevant to present concerns.

our semantics maps 4a. Simply in virtue of the sentence existing and the words 'Rebecca' and 'swims' having the semantic values they have, we know one relation that obtains between Rebecca and the property of swimming. Rebecca is related to the property of swimming in the following way: Rebecca is the semantic value of an expression of a language that occurs in subject position in the following sentential relation (which is R):

and an expression of the language occurs at the terminal node of the right branch of this sentential relation that has as its semantic value the property of swimming. This really is a relation that Rebecca and the property of swimming stand in. And I claim, to a first approximation anyway, it is the relation that binds together Rebecca and the property of swimming in the proposition that Rebecca swims. We can represent this relation, and the proposition that Rebecca swims, in tree form as follows:

4b.

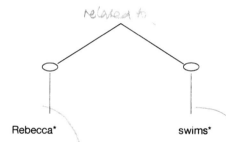

The branching structure at the top of 4b is the very relation R that is the sentential relation binding together the words in the LF 4a. Rebecca* is the person Rebecca and swims* is the property of swimming. The vertical lines above Rebecca* and swim* are the semantic relations 'Rebecca' bears to Rebecca* and 'swims' bears to swims*. Both of the small ovals between the vertical lines and R are the relation between properties of *joint instantiation*. The oval on the left in 4b represents the fact that the property (of words) of referring to Rebecca (Rebecca*), which is represented in 4b as follows:

4bi.

(where the top of the vertical line represents the "argument place" of the property—the word 'Rebecca' possesses this property and so occupies that argument place) and the property (of words) of occurring at the left terminal node in R and having at the right terminal node a word expressing the property of swimming, represented in 4b as:

4bii.

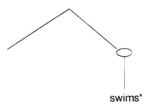

swims*

(where the tip of the line branching to the left represents the "argument place" of this property) are jointly instantiated. And those properties, 4bi and 4bii, *are* jointly instantiated by (the word) 'Rebecca': 'Rebecca' possesses both properties in question. It *both* refers to Rebecca (Rebecca*—i.e. possesses 4bi) *and* occurs at the left terminal node of R, where at the right terminal node is an expression whose semantic value is the property of swimming (i.e. possesses 4bii). The existence of the LF representation 4a insures that this is so, given that the semantic value of 'Rebecca' is Rebecca and that of 'swims' is the property of swimming. Similar remarks apply to the oval on the right of 4b, which once again represents the fact that two properties of words are jointly instantiated (this time by 'swims').

To repeat, the relation obtaining between Rebecca* (Rebecca) and the property of swimming that binds them together in the proposition 4b is the following: there are words x and y of some language occurring in the sentential relation R as follows:

x   y

such that x has its semantic value___ and y has as its semantic value . . . . . Rebecca stands in this relation (and occupies the spot___) to the property of swimming (which occupies the spot . . . .). Roughly, this relation, which I claim holds Rebecca and the property of swimming together in the proposition that Rebecca swims, results from composing the sentential relation R with the referring/expressing relations between 'Rebecca' and Rebecca and 'swims' and the property of swimming, while existentially generalizing away the words 'Rebecca' and 'swims'.[11]

---

[11] We also existentially generalize away the language, in this case English.

On this view, then, the sentential relation R that binds together the words in the LF representation 4a is a component, literally a part, of the relation that binds together Rebecca and the property of swimming in the proposition that Rebecca swims (4b). Let's call relations like that in 4b that bind together constituents of propositions *propositional relations*. The relata of propositional relations, in the case of 4b Rebecca and the property of swimming, are the *constituents* of the proposition. In general, not only are sentential relations parts of the propositional relations of the propositions expressed by the sentences with those sentential relations, but the sentential relations will provide all the significant structure to the propositional relations, and hence to propositions. For as can be seen in the simple case of 4a and 4b, the sentential relation of 4a provides all the significant structure to the propositional relation of 4b. The semantic relations between words and semantic values (represented by vertical lines in 4b) simply extend terminal nodes in the sentential relation straight down without adding additional structure. This will be true in the general case.[12]

Because the view I am articulating can be hard to grasp initially, let me try putting it another way. Recall our use of the term 'fact', on which an object possessing a property or n objects standing in an n-place relation, or n properties standing in an n-place relation or etc. is a *fact*. The proposition that Rebecca swims, 4b, is a fact. It is the fact of Rebecca standing in a certain relation to the property of swimming. This is a fact because Rebecca actually bears the relation in 4b to the property of swimming: Rebecca *is* the semantic value of an expression of a language that occupies the left terminal node of the sentential relation R and an expression of that language that has the property of swimming as its semantic value *does* occur at the right terminal node of R. Again, the existence of the sentence 4a and the fact that 'Rebecca' has as its semantic value Rebecca and 'swims' has as its semantic value the property of swimming make this so. So Rebecca actually standing in that relation to the property of swimming is a fact. As my comments have suggested, this *is* a fact partly in virtue of English existing and in virtue of a name being introduced with 'Rebecca' as its semantic value, etc. We will discuss these matters subsequently. I claim that this fact *is* the proposition that Rebecca swims.

Now as I indicated above, Rebecca does possess the property of swimming. That too is a fact. Indeed, it is the fact that makes the proposition 4b true. But as promised, Rebecca possessing the property of swimming is a quite different fact from the fact I am claiming is the proposition that Rebecca swims (i.e. 4b).[13] The

---

[12] There is one qualification to this made below, (see the discussion of 4b' and 4c).

[13] John Hawthorne (p.c.) suggested a quite different account of what the proposition that Rebecca swims is and how it differs from the fact of her swimming, (though he didn't endorse the view). One could have a mereology on which there is not a unique fusion of given parts. Thus, the proposition that Rebecca swims is a fusion of Rebecca and the property of swimming; and

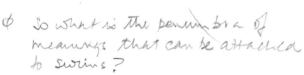

latter is the fact of Rebecca being the semantic value of an expression of a language occurring at the left terminal node of the sentential relation R (the sentential relation of 4a) and an expression of that language that has as its semantic value the property of swimming occurring at the right terminal node of R. Note that this fact, which I am claiming is the proposition that Rebecca swims, would have obtained even if the fact of Rebecca possessing the property of swimming hadn't obtained. In that case, of course, the proposition would have been false. Finally, note the fact that I claim is the proposition that Rebecca swims has components (e.g. the sentential relation R) not had by the fact that is Rebecca possessing the property of swimming. At present I am not concerned with whether the reader finds it plausible that the fact in question *is* the proposition that Rebecca swims. I am simply trying to make clear what fact I am claiming is that proposition and how it differs from the fact that makes the proposition true.

The view of propositions I have just sketched is the one I defended in King (1995). Before turning to a defense of the view, as I indicated above, I need to make two amendments or additions to it.

---

the fact that Rebecca swims is a distinct fusion of Rebecca and the property of swimming. Of course, if we now consider the proposition that Carl loves Lucy and the proposition that Lucy loves Carl, there must be two distinct fusions of Carl, Lucy and loving that are those two propositions. Then, if in fact Carl does love Lucy and Lucy does love Carl, there must be two more fusions of those same parts, in order that we have both the fact that Carl loves Lucy and the fact that Lucy loves Carl in addition to the propositions in question, giving us a total of four fusions of these same parts, though if neither loves the other, there are only two such fusions. Of course if only one loves the other, we must have only one additional fusion of Lucy, Carl and loving, giving us a total of three fusions of these parts. This all seems a bit strange, but my main concern with this view is that it doesn't seem so much an account of what propositions and facts are as much as something that provides the formal structure of an account. For it doesn't answer questions such as: why are the fusions that are propositions true and false but the fusions that are facts are not? Why does the fusion that is the proposition that Carl loves Lucy exist whether Carl loves her or not, whereas the fusion that is the fact that Carl loves Lucy only exists if Carl loves Lucy? The account of propositions I am sketching answers these questions. It may be that one could supplement the sort of account Hawthorne had in mind to answer such questions, but without doing so it seems to merely deliver distinct objects to be the various facts and propositions in question without giving any account of why they have the various properties they have. As a result, it provides us with no intuitive grasp of facts and propositions and how they differ. This is why I say it provides the formal structure of an account of the relevant facts and propositions without giving an account of what they really are. I believe Hawthorne would agree with all of this. His point was simply that one is not *forced* to find some component/part of the proposition that Rebecca swims that is not a part of the fact that Rebecca swims in order to hold they are distinct. Similarly, he pointed out, one could hold that a statue and the clay from which it is made are different fusions of the same parts. Again here, one is not forced to find a part that the statue has and the clay lacks in order to hold that they are distinct. I agree that one is not forced to do this, but I also believe: 1) that my account of the fact that is the proposition that Rebecca swims and how it is different from the fact of Rebecca swimming answers the questions mentioned above, which as I said are not answered simply by positing different fusions of the same elements; and 2) that my account has many other virtues as well. Thus, though I do not think that one is forced to a theory of the sort I am defending, I think the theory has many virtues and benefits. These will be discussed subsequently. Thanks to David Manley for helping to clarify my thinking about these matters.

The first amendment results from reflection on the semantic significance of syntax.[14] The sentence 4/4a is true iff Rebecca instantiates the property of swimming. What is it that tells us that the sentence is evaluated for truth and falsity by checking whether Rebecca *instantiates* the property of swimming? Well, it seems that syntactically concatenating a name with a one-place predicate in English in the manner of 4/4a has the result that we evaluate the sentence as true if the semantic value of the name instantiates the semantic value of the predicate. But then this means that this syntactic concatenation, this bit of syntax, provides instructions as to how to evaluate the sentence. In effect, we can think of this bit of syntax as giving the instruction to map an object o (the semantic value of the expression at its left terminal node) and a property P (the semantic value of the expression at its right terminal node) to true (at a world) iff o instantiates P (at that world). This instruction has two crucial features. First, it involves a specific function f: the function that maps an object and a property to true (at a world) iff the object *instantiates* the property (at the world).[15] Call this function f *the instantiation function*. Second, the instruction instructs that f *is to be applied* to the semantic values of the expressions at the left and right terminal nodes (and a world) to determine the truth value of the sentence (at the world). Let's put these two points by saying that the syntactic concatenation in 4/4a *encodes* the instantiation function. Talk of the syntactic concatenation in question *encoding* the instantiation function f, instead of talking of the concatenation having f as its *semantic value*, is intended to evoke the idea that the syntax actually provides an instruction as to how to evaluate the sentence for truth or falsity: it instructs that f is to be applied to the semantic values of the expressions at the left and right terminal nodes (and a world) to determine the truth value of the sentence (at the world).

Because some readers may find the idea of syntax "providing instructions" odd, let me pause to note that on any approach to compositional semantics for natural languages, even one that eschews propositions altogether, one will have to invoke this idea. For on any compositional semantics, the semantic values of expressions at terminal nodes need to compose to yield new semantic values for non-terminal nodes, which themselves must compose, until we get a sentence level semantic value. The syntax gives the instructions as to how the semantic values are composed, (this can sometimes be obscured by the fact that on certain approaches the instruction provided by the syntax is so simple—as on Montagovian approaches, where the syntax simply instructs that one semantic value (a function) is to be applied to another (its argument)). Semantic approaches differ only on what they claim *is* the instruction that a given bit of syntax provides. They are all stuck with the idea of syntax providing instructions.

---

[14] Mark Richard (p.c.) first raised issues related to those about to be discussed some years ago.
[15] So we should think of f as a function that maps an object, property and world to a truth value.

In any case, surely that the syntactic concatenation in 4/4a encodes the instantiation function is a contingent fact. There are actually two contingent facts here corresponding to the two crucial features of the instructions given by the syntactic concatenation in 4/4a mentioned above. These can be brought out by considering two languages that resemble but differ from English.

First, there could have been a language, which I will call *Nenglish*, in which 4 with the very LF 4a is grammatical and in which the semantic values of 'Rebecca' and 'swims' are just as they are in English.[16] Nenglish differs from English only regarding the semantic significance of syntactic concatenation. The sentence 4/4a is true in Nenglish iff Rebecca *fails* to instantiate the property of swimming. So in Nenglish, the syntactic concatenation in 4/4a encodes the *anti*-instantiation function (which maps an object and a property to true (at a world) iff the object fails to instantiate the property (at the world)). The Nenglish syntactic concatenation in 4/4a instructs that the anti-instantiation function be applied to the object that is the semantic value of the expression at the left terminal node and the property that is the semantic value of the expression at the right terminal node in evaluating the sentence for truth and falsity. What the possibility of Nenglish shows is that the fact that we have a language in which the syntactic concatenation in 4/4a instructs that the *instantiation function f* is to be applied to the semantic values of the expressions at the left and right terminal nodes (and a world) to determine the truth value of the sentence (at the world) is contingent. Nenglish shows that that very syntactic concatenation could have instructed us to so apply the *anti-instantiation function*, or some other function.[17]

But the possibility of Nenglish also raises a problem for my view. The problem is that had Nenglish existed, on the view of propositions described above, the proposition expressed by 4/4a in Nenglish would have been the same as the proposition actually expressed by 4/4a in English. The English and Nenglish sentences 4/4a would both express the proposition 4b. But this means that that proposition might have had different truth conditions: it might have had the truth conditions that it would have endowed the Nenglish sentence 4/4a with. Worse yet, it means that had English and Nenglish *both* existed, the *proposition* expressed by 4/4a—not just the *sentence* 4/4a—would have been ambiguous and had two sets of truth conditions. This latter result seems to me quite undesirable, if not just unacceptable. I return to this below.

---

[16] I do not claim that Nenglish is a possible human language. But there might have been creatures that spoke it. I introduced Nenglish to make an objection to a point of Zoltan Szabo's (2000). See his note 41.

[17] It is important to be clear about exactly what is contingent here. It is presumably not contingent that *in English* the sentential relation of 4/4a encodes the instantiation function. A language in which that syntactic relation didn't encode the instantiation function wouldn't be English. What is contingent is that there is a language in which the sentential relation of 4/4a encodes the instantiation function, instead of there being a language in which it encodes some other function.

The second contingent fact involved in the syntactic concatenation in 4/4a encoding the instantiation function can be brought out by considering another possible language.[18] There could have been a language, which I will call *Englist*, in which 4 with the very LF 4a is grammatical and in which the semantic values of 'Rebecca' and 'swims' are just as they are in English. Like Nenglish, Englist differs from English only in the semantic significance of syntactic concatenation. In Englist, 4/4a functions as a list of Rebecca, the instantiation function, and the property of swimming. So in Englist, 4/4a is neither true nor false any more than in English the list 'Rebecca, the instantiation function and the property of swimming' is true or false. Of course, in Englist, lists have constituent structure. Though in Englist 'John loves Sue' and 'Sue loves John' list the same things (and both are neither true nor false), Englist speakers intuit that in the former 'loves Sue' is a constituent (and 'John loves' is not) and in the latter 'loves John' is a constituent (and 'Sue loves' is not). What the possibility of Englist shows is that not only is it a contingent fact that the semantic significance of the syntactic concatenation in 4/4a involves the instantiation function f (which the possibility of Nenglish showed), but it is also a contingent fact that that syntactic concatenation *instructs* that f is to be *applied* to the semantic values of the expressions at the left and right terminal nodes (and a world) to determine the truth value of the sentence (at the world). The syntactic concatenation in 4/4a in Englist precisely fails to so instruct.

The content of 4/4a in English had better be different from the contents of that sentence in Nenglish and Englist. The proposition expressed by 4/4a in English is different from the proposition expressed by 4/4a in Nenglish, as shown by the difference in their truth conditions. And 4/4a doesn't even express a proposition, something capable of being true or false, in Englist. Somehow the fact that in English the relevant syntax encodes the instantiation function, whereas in Nenglish it encodes another function and in Englist it encodes no function,[19] must be reflected in the content of 4/4a in English to distinguish it from the contents of 4/4a in Nenglish and Englist.

The most straightforward way to do this is to build into the proposition expressed by 4/4a in English that the syntactic concatenation in 4/4a encodes the instantiation function and to build into the proposition expressed by 4/4a in Nenglish that the syntactic concatenation in 4/4a encodes the anti-instantiation function. Let *I* be the instantiation function and let *AI* be the anti-instantiation function. Then on my modified view, 4/4a expresses the following proposition in English:

[18] John Hawthorne suggested bringing out the relevant contingent fact in this way.

[19] Recall that for the syntax to *encode* a function f it must *instruct* that f is to be applied to the semantic values of the expressions at the left and right terminal nodes (and a world) to determine the truth value of the sentence (at the world). Englist syntax fails to do this and so encodes no function.

4b'.

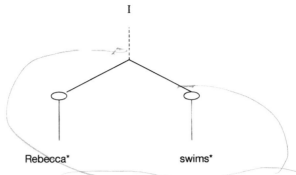

The dotted vertical line from the instantiation function I to the sentential relation R is the semantic relation R bears to I (encoding). I have used a dotted line to represent the relation of encoding, because it is so different from the sorts of semantic relations that obtain between words and things like Rebecca and the property of swimming, which semantic relations are represented in 4b' by the vertical lines from the small ovals to Rebecca* (Rebecca) and swims* (the property of swimming). The fact that I am claiming is the proposition expressed by 4/4a in English (i.e. 4b') can be characterized in words as follows: there are lexical items a and b of some language L occurring at the left and right terminal nodes (respectively) of the sentential relation R that in L encodes the instantiation function, where the semantic value of a is Rebecca and the semantic value of b is the property of swimming.

By contrast, in Nenglish, 4/4a expresses the following proposition:

4c.

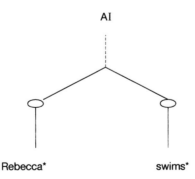

In this case, because in Nenglish the sentential relation R encodes the anti-instantiation function (AI), the latter function occurs in the proposition. Again, the dotted vertical line from AI to R is the semantic relation the latter bears to the former (encoding). If we wanted to say in English what fact the proposition 4c is, we could put it as follows: there are lexical items a and b of some language

L occurring at the left and right terminal nodes (respectively) of the sentential relation R that in L encodes the anti-instantiation function, where the semantic value of a is Rebecca and the semantic value of b is the property of swimming. It should be clear that we now have 4/4a expressing different propositions in English and Nenglish, as required.

What about the content of 4/4a in Englist? It can be represented as follows:

4d.

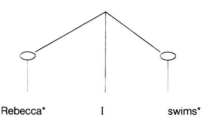

Rebecca*   I   swims*

Here the vertical line from R to the instantiation function I is represented as a solid line, as are the semantic relations between words and Rebecca* (Rebecca) and swims* (the property of swimming). This is because in Englist R doesn't encode anything but rather in effect serves as a name of the instantiation function. Englist syntax provides no *instruction* that a function be applied to anything, unlike English and Nenglish syntax. This is why the content of 4/4a in Englist (i.e. 4d) functions as a list of Rebecca, the instantiation function and the property of swimming and so is not a proposition at all. We could express the fact that is the content of 4/4a in Englist as follows: there are lexical items a and b of some language L occurring at the left and right terminal nodes (respectively) of the sentential relation R that in L has as its semantic value the instantiation function, where the semantic value of a is Rebecca and the semantic value of b is the property of swimming.

Above, I said that on the view I am defending, the structure of a proposition is identical to the structure of the sentence expressing it. Looking at 4b' and 4c, we can see that this is not quite true. In virtue of I and AI occurring in 4b' and 4c, respectively, these propositions have an extra bit of structure not had by the sentences expressing them. Still in virtue of the sentential relation being the primary component of the propositional relation, there is a sense in which the proposition has the same structure, or all of the structure, had by the sentence (plus a bit more). Thus, when nothing hangs on it, below I shall characterize this fact by talking of a proposition having the same structure as the sentence expressing it. The way in which this should be qualified in light of 4b' and 4c should be borne in mind.

The second amendment required involves the semantic values (relative to contexts) of contextually sensitive expressions and things that aren't the semantic value of any expression (i.e. things that aren't even the semantic values relative to contexts of demonstrative pronouns and indexicals speakers have actually employed in those contexts). Thus far, we have considered only semantic relations that obtain between a lexical item and its semantic value independently of context. Thus, Rebecca is the semantic value of 'Rebecca' and the property of swimming that of 'swims'. These relations are in part what bind Rebecca and the property of swimming together in the proposition 4b', (again, they are the vertical lines running from Rebecca* and swims* to the relation of joint instantiation (small ovals)). But that means that for all we've said thus far, propositions only have as constituents things that are the semantic values of words taken independently of any context. For the only semantic relations holding constituents in propositions discussed thus far are those that obtain independently of any context, such as that between 'Rebecca' and Rebecca. Thus, for all we've said there are no propositions whose constituents include things that no word bears a semantic relation to independently of any context. This would mean, of course, that there are no propositions whose constituents include things that have only been the semantic values of expressions taken in contexts (the semantic values in contexts of contextually sensitive expressions) or things that have never been the semantic value of any expression even taken relative to a context.[20] These points can be addressed in the following way.

First, we allow semantic relations between expressions and their semantic values that are relativized to contexts to bind constituents into propositions. This way, there will be propositions having as constituents things that have only been the semantic values of contextually sensitive expressions. Recall that in 4b' (unrelativized) semantic relations were represented by the vertical lines above Rebecca* and swims*. Now we don't want *particular* contexts occurring in our relations binding together the constituents of propositions. This would have as a consequence that no two sentences taken in different contexts could express the same proposition. Thus, we need to existentially generalize over contexts. So we shall now say that the proposition that Rebecca swims is the following fact: there is a context c and there are lexical items a and b of some language L such that a has as its semantic value in c Rebecca and occurs at the left terminal node of the sentential relation R that in L encodes the instantiation function and b occurs at R's right terminal node and has as its semantic value in c the property of swimming. I claim that this fact, finally, is the proposition that Rebecca swims, and so is true iff she swims.[21] Thus in describing the fact that is the proposition that Rebecca swims as I did (i.e. there is a context c and there are lexical items a and b of some language L such that a has as its semantic value in c Rebecca, etc.) I of course am not giving the *truth conditions* of the proposition that Rebecca swims. I am saying what fact *is* that proposition; and the proposition in question is true iff Rebecca swims.

---

[20] Correspondence with Matthew McGrath on this topic was a great aid to my thinking through it.
[21] This will be qualified slightly at the end of the present chapter.

Since a picture is sometimes worth lots of words, I'll provide the following rough representation of this proposition/ fact:

4b".

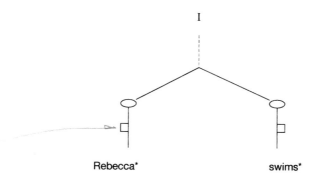

I

Rebecca*   swims*

The only additions are the small squares on the reference/expressing relations that are the vertical lines above Rebecca* and swims*. Both of these squares are the property of properties of *having an instance*. Call this property H. The properties that have this property in 4b" are properties of contexts of utterance. Very roughly, the left side of 4b" from the oval to Rebecca*:

4b"i.

Rebecca*

is the relational property (had by properties of words) of being coinstantiated with (oval) the property of being a word that has Rebecca as its semantic value in some context (box).[22] What H (box) does here is turn the three-place relation of x having y as its semantic value in context z into the two-place relation of x having y as its semantic value in some context. To put it another way, consider the following property of contexts: 'Rebecca' has Rebecca as its semantic value in context z. Since this property (of contexts) has instances, it possesses the property of having instances. But that is just the property H (box). Now consider the property of being a word that has Rebecca as its semantic value in some context. Call this property *P*. The property that is the left side of 4b" from the oval down (i.e. 4b"i) is the property (of properties of words) of being coinstantiated with P. Similar remarks apply to the right side of 4b" from the oval down.

To summarize, the relation holding Rebecca* and swims* together in 4b" is the following relation between a person (x) and a property (y): there is some

---

[22] For simplicity I suppress reference to a language here.

context c and some words a and b of some language L such that a has x as its semantic value relative to c and occurs at the left terminal node of the sentential relation R that in L encodes the instantiation function and b occurs at the right terminal node and has as its semantic value in c y. In virtue of the existence of the English sentence 4/4a, the words 'Rebecca' and 'swims' (among others) having the semantic values they do, and R encoding the instantiation function in English, Rebecca does stand in this relation to the property of swimming. Thus, Rebecca standing in this relation to the property of swimming is a fact. And I claim this fact is the proposition that Rebecca swims. This fact/proposition is made true by the quite different fact of Rebecca possessing the property of swimming. Finally, the English sentence 'I swim' taken in context c of which Rebecca is the agent expresses precisely the same proposition, as does any other sentence of a language L with the same LF as 4 (4a) taken in a context c', whose sentential relation R encodes in L the instantiation function, and whose lexical items a and b of L occurring at the left and right terminal nodes of R have as their semantic values in c' Rebecca and the property of swimming, respectively.

Given what I have said to this point, the attentive reader may legitimately wonder what sorts of propositions are expressed by quantified sentences. Recall our sentence 2:

2. Every surfer loves a surf spot.

whose scope ambiguity we claimed results from its having two LF representations

2a. [[every surfer: x][[some surf spot: y][x loves y]]]
2b. [[some surf spot: y][[every surfer: x][x loves y]]]

Looking at 2b, what sort of proposition does it express? Presumably, the lexical items contribute their semantic values to the proposition expressed by 2b. Since the structure of the proposition expressed by 2b is identical to that of 2b, those semantic values are structured in the proposition just as the lexical items are structured in 2b. But what about the variables? What do they contribute to the proposition expressed by 2b? In a sense the answer is nothing.[23] The two-place predicate 'loves' in 2b contributes a two-place relation to the proposition expressed by 2b. This relation, I assume, really has two argument positions, however that notion is ultimately understood. There will be other argument positions in the proposition expressed by 2b as well. The variables in 2b have the effect that certain empty argument positions in the proposition expressed by 2b are *linked* to each other. Intuitively, the idea is that empty argument positions in a proposition are linked in virtue of corresponding to argument positions in the sentence(s) expressing it that are occupied by the same variable.[24]

[23] In prior work I took variables to contribute themselves to propositions and so occur in them. Obviously, I no longer think that.

[24] As I discuss in the Appendix, I take *being linked* to be a real relation between argument positions in propositions.

So variables don't contribute anything to propositions in the sense that the argument positions in a proposition corresponding to the argument positions in a sentence expressing it occupied by variables are empty. However, variables in sentences result in these empty argument positions in propositions being linked. In the present case, letting e* be the semantic value of expression e and suppressing some structure, the proposition expressed by 2b looks as follows (using brackets instead of a tree):

2b'. [[some* surf* spot*__][[every* surfer*__][__loves__]]]

I've ignored the functions that are encoded by syntactic concatenation here. Linking is indicated in the obvious way and '__' is used to indicate empty argument positions. In the Appendix, I articulate this account of quantified propositions more formally and show how it works semantically.

The facts that I have identified with propositions are facts of there being a context and there being such-and-such words of a language L whose semantic values relative to the context are so-and-so, occurring in such-and-such way in so-and-so sentential relation that in L encodes such-and-such. What such facts there are, and so what propositions there are if I am right, depends on whether the facts are facts of there being *actual* contexts of utterance and etc. or facts of there being *possible* contexts of utterance and etc. If the former, then there are no propositions that have as constituents objects that have no names and *actually* have never been referred to by contextually sensitive expressions. For consider such an object o. There will be no facts of the following sort: there is a (actual) context c and there are such-and-such words of some language one of which has o as its semantic value in c and etc. But since these facts are propositions with o as a constituent on my view, there will be no propositions having o as a constituent.

On the other hand, if the facts that I claim are propositions are facts of there being a *possible* context etc., then there will be propositions having o as a constituent. For presumably there will be a *possible* context c and such-and-such words of some language such that one of them has o as its semantic value in c and etc. And this is just to say that the sorts of facts I claim are propositions include facts that have o as a component (in the proper way).

To summarize, if the facts that are propositions are facts of there being *actual* contexts and etc., there will be no propositions that have as constituents objects without names that have never actually been referred to using contextually sensitive expressions.[25] If, by contrast, the facts in question are facts of there

----

[25] Similar remarks apply to properties.

being *possible* contexts and etc., there will be propositions having such objects as constituents. I believe that the question of whether there are facts that have as components possible contexts of utterance hinges primarily on whether *there are* possible contexts of utterance. I think there are, and so I think that there are propositions that have as constituents objects that *actually* have never been referred to.

Before explaining what possible contexts of utterance are and why they exist, it is worth pointing out that the need for possible contexts of utterance is independent of present concerns. In semantics when we consider a sentence relative to a context of utterance, it seems clear that we are talking of possible contexts of utterance. We routinely talk of what proposition is expressed by 'I am here now.' when uttered by e.g. Ronald Reagan in Montana on June 12, 1987. In doing so, we don't concern ourselves with whether Reagan really was in Montana on that day.[26] Nonetheless, we think that that sentence taken relative to that context expresses a proposition that is true just in case Reagan was in Montana on June 12, 1987. But this means that we are considering possible contexts of utterance. Further, and more significantly, logical truths of the logic of demonstratives are sentences that are true in all contexts of utterance.[27] If the quantification over all contexts of utterance here were over all *actual* contexts of utterance, this would yield bizarre results.[28] For example, if no one ever actually wears a tie that has one million different colors, then 'I am not wearing a tie that has one million different colors.' would be a truth of the logic of demonstratives. Thus, to characterize logical truth for the logic of demonstratives, we need to quantify over possible contexts of utterance. For these reasons, possible contexts of utterance are needed by semanticists quite independently of the account of propositions I am defending.

Turning now to the question of why we should think there are possible contexts of utterance and so not be worried about being committed to them, let me first note that I am an actualist. That means that if I hold that possible contexts of utterance exist, they must exist in the actual world. And in any case, as I have already said, facts by definition actually obtain and I think propositions are certain sorts of facts. So any fact/proposition involving a possible context must actually obtain. But that presumably also requires possible contexts to

---

[26] He wasn't. He spent much of that day at the Berlin Wall.

[27] Kaplan (1989). Assuming that in the first instance we assign sentences truth values relative to both contexts (say a world, speaker, place and time) and circumstances of evaluation (say a world), truth in a context is truth relative to a context and the world of the context.

[28] How bizarre the results are depends on whether we require a sentence to be uttered in a context in order to be evaluated with respect to it. If we did require this, the consequences would be worse, so following David Kaplan (1989: 546) I'll assume this isn't required. This will be discussed below. An actual context of utterance, then, is a person who is (timelessly) actually at a certain place at a certain time. In evaluating a sentence in such a context, we take the person to be the speaker and the time and place to be the time and place of utterance (even if the speaker isn't saying anything). I discuss this further below.

actually exist.[29] I think possible contexts of utterance are possible worlds with a designated speaker, place and time.[30] Presumably what is worrisome about possible contexts is that many of them involve merely possible worlds. This means that to vindicate possible contexts of utterance we need to vindicate possible worlds. Like many other philosophers, I think possible worlds are large, uninstantiated properties: properties the concrete world might have had.[31] I think these uninstantiated properties actually exist. So I think possible worlds actually exist.

As indicated above, a possible context of utterance is just a possible world with a designated speaker, time and location.[32] However, most of those who employ possible contexts follow Kaplan (1989) in thinking that the "speaker" of a context need not be speaking in the world of the context at the time and location of the context, though he/she must be located there at that time.[33] Given this, how should we think of a person at a time and location in a possible world being *designated* as the speaker, time and location of the resulting context?[34] Since the person may not be speaking at that time and location in that world, being designated the speaker cannot involve the world of the context representing the person as speaking. Indeed, it doesn't seem as though being designated involves the world of the context representing the person in any particular way. In light of this, it seems to me that we should take a possible context to be any space-time location in a possible world at which a person is located. What makes each such location a context is our practice of allowing any such location to be used to fix the values of indexicals. The practice in question is explicit in formal semantics and implicit in our ordinary talk to the effect that if Lucy had uttered 'I am hungry' in a certain situation, she would have expressed the claim that such-and-such. On the sort of view I have in mind, then, a possible context of utterance is any space-time location in a possible world at which a person is located, where what makes the location a context is our practice of allowing the location and the person located there to fix the values of indexicals. If this is right, invoking

---

[29] There are some who seem to deny this. Recall that a fact is an object possessing a property, or n objects standing in an n-place relation, or n properties standing in an n-place relation or etc. Now some, e.g. Salmon (1998), claim that entities can possess properties (or stand in relations) even though those entities don't exist. I tend to shy away from this claim. The question of whether objects that don't exist can possess properties is taken up in Chapter 3.

[30] Perhaps other elements are required as well, but we won't worry about that. See note 27.

[31] Stalnaker (2003) and Soames (2005) both endorse this view. In King (2005), I discuss in more detail my conception of possible worlds qua properties.

[32] I would need to have demonstratives somehow take on semantic values relative to contexts. This might require contexts to be more complex if one didn't employ the approach of Kaplan (1989) and instead added demonstrata or speaker intentions or what have you to contexts in order to fix the semantic values of demonstratives relative to contexts. Because these matters are complex and would require a very detailed discussion, I suppress them here.

[33] One reason is we don't want 'I am speaking' to be a truth of the logic of demonstratives and we want 'I am here now' to be.

[34] Thanks to Scott Soames for raising this concern.

possible contexts of utterance doesn't add anything to our ontology above and beyond space-time locations in possible worlds.[35]

As I've indicated, on my account the facts that are propositions are facts of there being a context and there being *some words* in *some language L* whose semantic values relative to the context are so-and-so occurring in such-and-such way in so-and-so sentential relation that in L encodes such-and-such. I have just argued that the contexts being quantified over here are possible contexts of utterance, and hence that there are more propositions (facts of the above sort) than there may initially appear to be on my account. But what propositions/facts there are will also depend on whether these are facts of there being possible contexts of utterance and there being *actual* words in some *actual* language etc., etc.; or facts of their being possible contexts of utterance and there being *possible* words in some *actual* language etc., etc.; or facts of there being possible contexts of utterance and there being *possible* words in some *possible* language, etc., etc.[36] That is, if the facts that are propositions are facts of either of the latter two sorts, involving merely *possible* words in an *actual* language or merely *possible* words in a *possible* language in addition to actual words in an actual language, there may well be more propositions than there would be if propositions are facts of the former sort, involving only actual words in an actual language. Even if there are propositions that are facts of there being possible contexts of utterance and there being possible words in a (merely) *possible* language, etc., etc., it is hard for me to see how such propositions could be objects of *our* attitudes, or designated by *our* that-clauses. For I would think that for such propositions to be designated by our that-clauses and to be the objects of our attitudes, we would have to have a fairly robust epistemic connection to such languages that we do not in fact have. Hence

---

[35] There are different notions of context in the literature and those who think of contexts in some other way are welcome to plug their accounts in here. Further, there is another way to do the job I am doing with possible contexts here, as Scott Soames pointed out to me. One could dispense with possible contexts of utterance, and instead of relativizing the semantic relation between words and their semantic values to possible contexts, relativize it to speech situations in other possible worlds. That is, we consider the semantic value of a contextually sensitive expression e of English (with the meaning it has in English) as used by person s at time t and location l in world w. In such a case, s really is uttering e at t and l in w. It would then be this relation, *v is the semantic value of e as uttered by s in w at t and l,* that would help bind constituents in propositions rather than the relation *v is the semantic value of e in (possible) context c.* I shall continue to talk as though it is the latter relation that helps bind constituents in propositions, but the former is also an option. An anonymous referee worried that taking this route would make 'I'm speaking' a logical truth. But by itself it wouldn't! I am not suggesting using speech situations in other possible worlds (instead of possible contexts) to construct a *logic* for demonstratives and indexicals. I am imagining using them to secure relations between words and their semantic values that will hold the semantic values in propositions. On the other hand, I am only considering this strategy because some (not me!) might balk at possible contexts of utterance. And as I've indicated, those who reject possible contexts for my use here must reject them in constructing a logic for demonstratives and indexicals too. Such a person would have to face tough decisions about such a logic.

[36] I assume that propositions cannot be facts of there being possible contexts of utterance and there being *actual* words in some (merely) *possible* language etc., etc., because it seems to me that there cannot be actual words in a merely possible language.

I'll ignore this possibility here. This leaves open the question of whether there might be propositions that are facts of there being possible contexts of utterance and there being *possible* words in some actual language etc., etc., in addition to there being the propositions that are facts of there being possible contexts of utterance and there being actual words in an actual language, etc., etc.

As should be clear from my discussion of possible contexts of utterance, for there to be facts of there being a possible context c and (merely) *possible* words a,b,c in some actual language etc., etc., given my commitment to actualism, (merely) possible words of actual languages must exist in the actual world. So do they? The problem is that it isn't clear exactly what a (merely) possible word of an actual language is.[37] It may be that word types are properties had by all word tokens of that type. Perhaps then for a word to be actual is in part for the word type to have instances (of the proper sort). This account would be clearly incorrect for linguistic expressions generally, since presumably some sentence types of English have no instances and yet these sentences presumably are actual, and not merely possible, sentences of English. But it seems plausible to suppose that for a *word* to be actual is in part for the word type to have instances. How could a *word* be an actual word of English without instances?[38] If this is right, then perhaps a (merely) possible word of an actual language is a word type with no instances, or no instances of the proper sort.[39] And it may be that such types/properties exist (uninstantiated) in the actual world. If all this is correct, then possible words of actual languages *do* exist in the actual world and there may well be facts/propositions of there being a possible context c and (merely) *possible*

[37] Nor is it clear exactly what it is for a possible word of an actual language to have o as its semantic value relative to context c. I'll ignore the unclarity of this issue, since the unclarity of the issue discussed in the body is enough to make the point I wish to make.

[38] Having instances doesn't seem to be enough to make a word actual. 'Scron' is a (possible) word type of English that now has an instance. But that doesn't seem to make it an actual word of English or any language. An anonymous referee claimed that something could be a word without having instances if it were "built up in the right way from the right parts". He/she supposed that you can always add 'able' to a verb to get an adjective and that you can add 'un' to any adjective to form another adjective, and gave 'undematerializeable' as an example of something that was an actual word prior to its having instances. In response, let me first say that these assumptions seem wrong. Many adjectives don't seem to have 'un' counterparts: e.g. * 'unfat' (I was just reading a syntax book that blithely asserted that 'unfat' is not a word). Similarly, many verbs have no 'able' adjective counterparts: e.g. * 'sleepable'. My own inclination is to think that when there are 'un' and 'able' counterparts to adjectives and verbs, there are so partly in virtue of these counterparts having (the right sorts of) instances. Thus, it seems to me 'undematerializable' is not an actual word (this is consistent, of course, with our knowing what it would mean were it a word). Second, even if the referee were right for things like 'undematerializable', it seems to me that its being a word is parasitic on some "root word" (e.g. 'material') being a word, where for the root word to be a word requires it to have instances of the right sort. But that means that for anything to be an actual word, some root word of it must have the right sort of instances. That would be enough for the point I am trying to make.

[39] As indicated, 'scron' is a merely possible word of English but it has instances. Further, presumably for a word (type) to be a possible word of a given language, it would have to satisfy certain morphological and phonological constraints.

words a,b,c in some actual language etc.[40] However, this is highly speculative, depending as it does on what it is to be a possible word of an actual language and what it is for (merely) possible words to exist in the actual world.[41] Thus I shall not assume that there are facts/propositions of there being a possible context c and (merely) possible words a,b,c in some actual language etc., etc. But I note there *may* be propositions/facts of this sort on the present account.

I have claimed that the propositional relations that bind together constituents in propositions are in part built out of sentential relations binding together lexical items in sentences. However, some may feel that this doesn't fully answer the question as to what propositional relations, and so propositions, ultimately are unless we say something about what sentential relations are.[42] We have represented sentential relations by means of trees. Often, linguists and philosophers identify trees with set theoretical or mathematical objects of some sort.[43] But if that view is adopted and if propositional relations are partly built out of sentential relations, the worry arises that we ourselves will face a Benacerraf argument. It seems likely that a number of set theoretic or mathematical entities would be equally well suited for being a given syntactic tree. But then there may be no principled reason for identifying the tree with one rather than the other. This suggests that neither really *is* the tree, and leaves us without an account of what sentential relations are, and so without an account of what propositional relations are. For these reasons, we should say something about what sentential relations are and we had better not identify them with set theoretic or mathematical objects.

Consider a simple sentence, such as:

5.

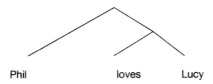

Phil   loves   Lucy

On current thinking within the Chomskian tradition in syntax, 5 was "built up" by means of an operation called *Merge*.[44] Thus, the right side of 5 depicts the result of Merge combining 'loves' and 'Lucy', forming the VP 'loves Lucy'.

---

[40] I say there *may* be such facts/propositions if there are possible words, because we would also need the possible words to have the relevant things as their semantic values relative to the possible contexts in question. See note 37.

[41] As well as on what it is for a possible word of an actual language to have a semantic value relative to a possible context. See previous note.

[42] Thanks to an anonymous referee for the proposal for the present book for raising this question.

[43] See Lewis (1970: 201–2) and Chomsky (1995: 243).

[44] See Chomsky (1995: 241–9). 5's structure is likely considerably more complex than I have represented it as being. But as before, I don't think this affects issues that concern me.

In turn, Merge combines 'Phil' and the VP 'loves Lucy' to form the sentence 5. Roughly, given two "syntactic objects" α and β, Merge combines them to form the more complex object $\alpha\beta$ of category γ, where the category is determined by either α or β. But then this means that given every node in a syntactic tree, the subtree of the tree rooted in that node is the output of Merge operating on the sisters immediately dominated by the node in question. If we assume, as certainly seems plausible, that any two objects that are combined by Merge stand in the same syntactic relation R, this means that in a given tree all we ever have are pairs of expressions standing in R. In 5, 'loves' stand in R to 'Lucy', and 'Phil' stands in R to 'loves Lucy'.[45] But this means that to give an account of what sentential relations are, all we need to do is to say what R is. What, then, is this relation? What relation do 'loves' and 'Lucy' stand in in 5, for example?[46]

One might think that reflection on Merge would shed light on this question. Given α and β as input, $\alpha R\beta$ is the output of Merge. So one might think that reflection on questions about how Merge combines α and β would shed light on what R is. But, of course, this is confused. Merge can't *literally* combine expressions. If it did, the combination would occur at some particular time. But it doesn't. Merge merely maps a pair of expressions to a new expression of which they are parts. So reflection on Merge is not likely to help much here.[47]

[45] There is some debate as to whether the outputs of Merge have a linear order. Trees depict them as having linear order: in the VP 'loves Lucy', 'loves' comes before 'Lucy' in the linear order. However, it is common for linguists to claim that applied to two objects α, β Merge yields $\{\gamma, \{\alpha, \beta\}\}$, where γ is the category of the new more complex syntactic object. (See Chomsky (1995: 243)—of course here syntactic relations are being identified with set theoretic constructions, contrary to what I claim needs to be done). Here α and β have no linear order in the new syntactic object (represented by !) $\{\gamma\{\alpha, \beta\}\}$. If this is correct, then trees really misrepresent phrase structure by making it appear that syntactic objects are linearly ordered. Others, however, think that phrase structure relations impose linear order. See Fukui (2001) for discussion. Because the issue has yet to be resolved, I'll try to remain neutral on the question of whether phrase structure involves linear order here. Also, I am ignoring here trees that result from one or more applications of the movement rule Move. I am hoping, as Epstein (1999) argues, that the output of Move is something of a sort identical to the output of Merge (see pp. 324 and 329–30). If this is right, then the output of Move would just be a complex syntactic object consisting of a bunch of syntactic objects bearing R to each other. Hence again, R is the only relation occurring in a tree. Even if this weren't so, it appears that there would only be two relations occurring in a tree: those introduced by Merge and those introduced by Move. This would only slightly complicate the issues being discussed. We would have to give an account of these two relations instead of just R.

[46] Of course I am ultimately interested in the relations words stand in at LF—the level of syntactic representation that provides the syntactic inputs to semantics. But presumably at LF expressions stand in the same kinds of relations they stand in in surface grammar. Thus, R is the only relation expressions stand in at LF too, (though see previous note).

[47] But I think it does clarify one point. Given α and β as input, the output of Merge is something like the following: α concatenated with β forms C, where C is the category of the result, which is itself either α or β, and is usually called the *head* of the resulting phrase. So really, R is a three place relation. That is, each branch of our syntactic trees represents the expressions α and β and a head α or β standing in the following relation: the concatenation of α and β forms a ("is a") α/β (one or the other). So our question as to what relation R is really is the question as to what the following relation is: the concatenation of___ and___is a___. I'll ignore this in what follows since it doesn't affect the issues I am concerned with so far as I can see.

In fact, I don't think it will be possible to say what R is by reference to other syntactic relations. R appears to be the basic syntactic relation by means of which others (c-command; head/complement, etc) are defined.[48] So from the standpoint of syntax itself, R is primitive: one can't say what relation R is in terms of other syntactic relations, because it is more basic than they are. I think this means one of two things: either 1) R must be taken as completely primitive; or 2) some further account of R must be given in non-syntactic terms. I do think that some properties and relations probably are completely primitive in that there simply is no further philosophical account of them.[49] Perhaps R is of this sort. Let's call this view the *primitive R view*. On the other hand, sometimes properties and relations that are primitive from the standpoint of one area of inquiry are such that philosophical accounts can be given of them in terms of properties and relations from another area. For example, perhaps *referring* is a relation that is primitive from the standpoint of semantics in that no account of reference can be given using other semantic notions (rather, reference is used in giving accounts of other semantic relations and properties). But in the end, perhaps some "naturalized account" in terms of causation and other non-semantic notions can be given of the reference relation. Let's call the view that something like this is so for R, the (non-syntactically) *analysed R view*. On this view, there is an account of R in terms of non-syntactic properties and relations.

What are the prospects for the analysed R view? I think it is hard to say. But before we even begin to think about that, we need to ask ourselves the following question. If the analysed R view is correct, what sorts of properties and relations will be appealed to in giving an account of R? We already know they won't be syntactic. I don't think the answer to this question is at all obvious. But it seems to me that the most likely answer is that the properties and relations will be mental or neurological. If we think that ultimately the structure of human language has its basis in the human mind or brain, in the sense that there is a Universal Grammar that governs all human languages and whose properties and features reflect features of the human mind or brain, then if there is to be any account of the must fundamental syntactic relation that occurs in human language, it seems to me likely to be in terms of human mental or neurological properties and relations. Perhaps such an account of R can be given some day. If so, I think that day is still a very long way off. But if such an account can be given and if the present view is correct, it will bring with it a complete account of propositional relations. Further, it would dispel any worries of the sort

---

[48] See Epstein (1999).

[49] Since I take some properties and relations to be complex, and have other properties and relations as components, I tend to think that the completely primitive properties and relations are those that are not complex in this way. Because they don't have other properties and relations as components, there is no philosophical account of them. On this view, philosophical accounts of particular properties and relations amount to specifying (at least some of) their components. Some of the issues here are taken up in Chapter 7.

raised above that Benacerraf problems might arise on the present account. For those worries were generated by identifying sentential relations with certain set theoretic or mathematical objects. But on the present view, sentential relations can all be understood in terms of R, and in the situation we are imagining R itself can in turn be understood in human mental or neurological terms.

On the other hand, suppose the primitive R view prevails. Then no account can be given of the most basic syntactic relation. This seems unlikely to me, but I don't see how it can be completely ruled out. Some will worry that on the primitive R view, we have no real account of propositional relations. For we claim that they are built out of sentential relations, which in turn are understood in terms of R, where R is primitive. Indeed, some will wonder why we shouldn't simply take propositional relations themselves as primitive in this case. But I think the worry and the wonder are both misplaced.

The worry is just incorrect: we do have an account of propositional relations (partly) in terms of sentential relations. It is true that sentential relations are then understood in terms of the primitive relation R. But it seems likely that *some* properties and relations are primitive. As I say, it would be surprising if R were. But if it turns out that way, giving an account of propositional relations partly in terms of primitive R is still giving an account of them!

The wonder can be easily answered as well. Many doubt that there are propositions and propositional relations at all. Indeed, part of the point of the present account is to address such skeptics. However, taking propositional relations as primitive would do nothing to address such skepticism. Skeptics about propositions are bound to be skeptics about propositional relations. By contrast, virtually everyone who takes seriously the serious study of language has to believe that there is a level of syntax over which semantics is defined. In the situation we are imaging, it turns out that the most basic syntactic relation in terms of which representations at that level are characterized has to be taken as primitive. But then everyone is stuck with this primitive! Hence, if we use this primitive *that everyone is stuck with* to give a plausible account of propositional relations on which it is hard to deny propositions exist (see below), this is importantly different from taking propositional relations themselves, which not everyone antecedently believes in, as primitive and so just assuming that propositions exist. Finally, we still are immune from Benacerraf worries, since even here we have not identified syntactic relations with set theoretic or mathematical objects.

Before turning to virtues of the account of propositions I have now sketched, let me raise a worry concerning giving *any* sort of account or analysis of what propositions are, including of course the present one, that *seems* to trace back to Russell (1903).[50] Russell writes:

Consider, for example, the proposition "A differs from B". The constituents of this proposition, if we analyse it, appear to be only A, difference, B. Yet these constituents,

---

[50] Thanks to Scott Soames for raising the issues I am about to address.

thus placed side by side, do not reconstitute the proposition . . . . A proposition, in fact, is essentially a unity, and when analysis has destroyed the unity, no enumeration of constituents will restore the proposition.[51]

A couple things appear to be going on in this passage. First, as other remarks Russell makes suggest, he is puzzled by the fact that when one "analyzes" a proposition by listing its constituents, one cannot by looking at the list tell what proposition is analyzed since two propositions may have the same constituents.[52] Hence, a (mere) list-of-constituents analysis will give the same analysis for distinct propositions. This concern can be addressed by including in the analysis *how* the constituents are configured in the proposition instead of simply listing them. Thus, one could say that in the proposition that A is greater than B, A occurs in a certain position in the proposition and B occurs in a different one, whereas the reverse is true in the proposition that B is greater than A. Of course, this would require one to say something about positions of propositions. But the point is simply that an analysis of a proposition might include more than a list of the constituents. It might tell us how they are combined. Obviously, my account or "analysis" of propositions does just this.

But Russell has what appears to be another concern as well. He puts it as follows:

A proposition has a certain indefinable unity, in virtue of which it is an assertion. And this is so completely lost by analysis that no enumeration of constituents will restore it . . . [53]

It is not clear to me exactly what Russell has in mind by talk of assertion here, but Russell's comments suggest to me the following worry, which may or may not be his. When I consider the proposition that Rebecca swims, I cannot help seeing that it has truth conditions, what those truth conditions are, at least some of its inferential relations to other propositions, and so on.[54] However, consider now my "analysis" of that proposition: that proposition is the fact of there being a context c and there being lexical items a and b in some language L such that a has as its semantic value in c Rebecca and occurs at the left terminal node of the sentential relation R that in L encodes the instantiation function and b occurs at R's right terminal node and has as its semantic value in c the property of swimming. In considering this fact, one could, it seems, easily fail to see what its truth conditions are or even that it has truth conditions. But how could that be, if this fact is indeed the proposition that Rebecca swims? If the fact and proposition are the same, when considering the fact in question it may seem that I *must* see

---

[51] Pp. 49–50. See similar remarks on pp. 52, 107, and 466–7.

[52] " . . . 'A is greater than B' and 'B is greater than A'. These two propositions, though different, have precisely the same constituents. This is characteristic of relations, and an instance of the loss resulting from analysis" p. 107.

[53] P. 107.

[54] My thought is that Russell's talk of a proposition making an assertion is at least intimately tied to its being capable of being true or false.

it as having truth conditions and etc., since this is the case with the proposition that Rebecca swims. But it doesn't seem that in considering the fact in question, I must see that it has truth conditions and etc. Sometimes Russell's comments suggest that as a result of this kind of concern (and perhaps the previous one as well), he held that the analysis of a proposition, considered as the "sum" of its constituents, is distinct from the proposition itself. Thus he writes:

Owing to the way in which the verb actually relates the terms of a proposition, every proposition has a unity which renders it distinct from the sum of its parts.[55]

Whether that is what Russell was getting at or not, I think that the explanation of why we must see the proposition that Rebecca swims as having truth conditions and inferential relations but not so for the fact I am claiming *is* that proposition is not that the fact and proposition are distinct. Rather, it seems to me that there is this fact that we can be acquainted with in two different ways. On the one hand, I can be acquainted with it as the proposition that Rebecca swims. When I am so acquainted with it, I cannot help but see it as having truth conditions and so on. But I can also be acquainted with it as the fact of there being a context c and there being lexical items a and b in some language L such that a has as its semantic value in c Rebecca and occurs at the left terminal node of the sentential relation R that in L encodes the instantiation function and b occurs at R's right terminal node and has as its semantic value in c the property of swimming. When I am acquainted with the fact/proposition in this way, I need only see it as another fact in the world, and so need not see it as representing anything or having truth conditions. There are other differences as well. When I am acquainted with the proposition that Rebecca swims qua proposition, I need not know about the nature of the complex relation (the propositional relation) binding together Rebecca and swimming in the proposition, nor what the components of that relation are (e.g. the sentential relation).[56] However, when I am acquainted with this proposition qua fact of there being a context c and there being lexical items a and b of some language L such that a has as its semantic value in c Rebecca etc., I certainly must know the nature of the relation binding together Rebecca and swimming in the fact/proposition. Thus, I believe that one can be presented with a single fact in these two different ways and that this explains why we must see it as having truth conditions and so on when presented in one way, but not when presented in the other. If that is so, that we can do this does not at all tend to show that the fact in question is not the proposition that Rebecca swims.[57]

---

[55] P. 52.

[56] To be acquainted with, and so entertain, the proposition, I must presumably have some sort of cognitive connection to Rebecca and the property of swimming.

[57] John Hawthorne and David Manley raised a question that I believe is related to this point. They wondered why, if I am right about the fact in question being the proposition that Rebecca swims, the following two sentences seem as though they could diverge in truth value:

1. John thinks about/grasps the proposition that Rebecca swims.

Let's finally turn to virtues of the view of propositions I have been sketching. As we'll see, these virtues include satisfying the constraints on a plausible answer to the question of what holds the constituents of propositions together that I stated early on in the chapter. But we begin with other virtues. The first three virtues of the present view of propositions all flow from a consequence the view has for the nature of propositions expressed by sentences containing syntactically complex predicates.[58] Consider a simple example of this sort:

2. John thinks about/grasps the fact of there being a context c and lexical items a and b of some language L such that a has as its semantic value in c Rebecca and occurs at the left terminal node of the sentential relation R that in L encodes the instantiation function and b occurs at R's right terminal node and has as its semantic value in c the property of swimming.

given that on my view the proposition that Rebecca swims is the fact of there being a context c and lexical items a and b of some language L such that a has as its semantic value in c Rebecca and occurs at the left terminal node of the sentential relation R that in L encodes the instantiation function and b occurs at R's right terminal node and has as its semantic value in c the property of swimming. (Of course 1 and 2 express different propositions on my view, but there still is the question as to why they may diverge in truth value.)

One might also ask why, if I am right, the following two sentences seems as though they could diverge in truth value:

3. John believes that Rebecca swims.

4. John believes the fact of there being a context c and lexical items a and b of some language L such that a has as its semantic value in c Rebecca and occurs at the left terminal node of the sentential relation R that in L encodes the instantiation function and b occurs at R's right terminal node and has as its semantic value in c the property of swimming.

To respond to this concern, one must either hold that the sentences cannot in fact diverge in truth value even though it initially seems that they can or explain how they can diverge in truth value despite the fact that the proposition that Rebecca swims is the fact of there being a context c and lexical items a and b of some language L such that a has as its semantic value in c Rebecca and occurs at the left terminal node of the sentential relation R that in L encodes the instantiation function and b occurs at R's right terminal node and has as its semantic value in c the property of swimming. However, I don't think there is much pressure to respond to the concern here. For *any* theory of propositions that says anything about what they are is subject to the problem. For example, consider the view that propositions are sets of possible worlds, the view that propositions are n-tuples of objects, properties and relations and even Bealer's (1993, 1998) "algebraic view" of propositions according to which they are "sui generis" entities. Then corresponding to 2 (similarly for 4) above, we will have

5. John thinks about/grasps the set of possible worlds in which Rebecca swims.

6. John thinks about/grasps the ordered pair whose first element is Rebecca and whose second element is the property of swimming.

7. John thinks about/grasps the result of applying pred$_s$ to swimming and Rebecca.

To the extent that one thinks 1 and 2 can diverge in truth value, one will think 1 and 5, 6 and 7 can as well. Since the alleged problem is not specific to the present proposal, there is not much pressure to address it here. That said, I cannot help but think that at some level part of the explanation of the phenomena discussed here has to do with the fact that the proposition that Rebecca swims can be presented to me in (at least) two different ways: qua proposition and qua fact.

[58] This is discussed in King (1995), where, as I indicated above, I defend a slightly different view of propositions from the one defended here.

6.

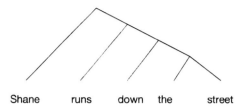

Shane   runs   down   the   street

As we have seen, on the present view of propositions, the proposition 6 expresses will have the same structure as 6, with the semantic values of the lexical items in 6 at the terminal nodes of its propositional relation.[59] One might have expected 6 to express a proposition whose constituents are Shane and the property of running down the street. But on the present view it doesn't. Instead of contributing the property of running down the street to the proposition expressed by 6, the verb phrase in 6 contributes (something like) the following:

6.'

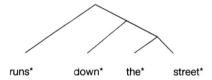

runs*   down*   the*   street*

where runs* is the semantic value of 'runs' (presumably the property of running), and so on, (I've suppressed various features of 6'). The verb phrase must contribute something like 6' to the proposition expressed by 6, if, as I have claimed, the structure of the proposition is identical to the syntactic structure of the sentence expressing it. It should be clear that 6' is not the property of running down the street. It is a certain fact. It is the fact that there is a context c such that relative to c runs* is the semantic value of a word that occurs in a such-and-such sentential relation in such-and-such a way, etc. This fact, which is part of the fact that is the proposition expressed by 6, is clearly not the property of running down the street. In my view at least, the property of running down the street is clearly not the fact that runs* is the semantic value relative to some context of a word that occurs in a sentential relation etc. Properties like the property of running down the street do not have as components syntactic relations, whereas the fact 6' does. On the other hand, for the proposition expressed by 6 to be true, it would seem that Shane must possess the property of running down the street. So somehow, that property, though not what the verb phrase contributes to the proposition expressed by 6, is involved in the truth conditions of that proposition. How could that be? I claim that this is because 6', the part of the

---

[59] Recall the slight qualification to this made in discussing 4b' and 4c. I'll suppress that here, because it is not relevant to present concerns.

proposition expressed by 6 contributed by 'runs down the street', is a complex "sub-propositional constituent" that *represents* the property of running down the street. Thus, as part of the definition of truth for propositions we will need a definition of a complex sub-propositional constituent representing a property. This definition will associate properties with the contributions to propositions made by complex predicates (such as 6'). The definition of truth for proposition will presuppose this association.[60]

The point to be emphasized here is that on the present view, syntactically complex predicates contribute to propositions not properties, but structured sub-propositional constituents that represent properties and whose structures are identical to the syntactic structures of the predicates contributing them. As I mentioned above, from this feature of the present account of propositions three salutary consequences follow. First, it allows that there may be distinct syntactically complex predicates that as a consequence make different contributions to propositions, but nonetheless those contributions represent the *same* property. This allows us to distinguish between propositions that could not be distinguished on a view according to which syntactically complex predicates contribute properties to propositions. So consider the following two sentence pairs:

7a. Shane ran 10 kilometers.
7b. Shane ran 6.2137 miles.
8a. Tracy was gone for one fortnight.
8b. Tracy was gone for fourteen days.

On the present view the sentences in these pairs express distinct propositions, since the predicates in them make different contributions to the propositions they express. But it *may* be that e.g. 7a and 7b are nonetheless both true iff there is some one property P possessed by Shane (the property of running a certain distance). This, if true, would be because the *distinct* contributions made by 'ran 10 kilometers' and 'ran 6.2137 miles' to the propositions expressed by 7a and 7b respectively represent the *same* property. This in turn would allow us to say that the following belief ascriptions might differ in truth value:

9a. Annie believes Shane ran 10 kilometers.
9b. Annie believes Shane ran 6.2137 miles.

even though 7a and 7b ascribe the same property to Shane. This is all to the good. For it seems to me very likely that there *are* distinct syntactically complex predicates that *are* used to ascribe the same property to individuals, where belief ascriptions that differ only in that one contains an occurrence of one of the predicates exactly where the other contains an occurrence of the other may differ in truth value.

---

[60] The notion of a sub-propositional complex entity of the sort being discussed *representing* a property is discussed briefly in the Appendix. These issues are also discussed in Chapter 7.

A second desirable feature of the consequence of our view under discussion is that it allows sentences containing complex predicates to express propositions, even if the complex predicates don't stand for any property.[61] To illustrate, suppose for reductio that there is a property of *being a property that doesn't instantiate itself.* Call it *I.* Suppose I instantiates itself. Then it possesses the property of not instantiating itself. So it doesn't instantiate itself. Suppose I doesn't instantiate itself. Then I possesses the property of not instantiating itself. So I instantiates itself. Since I must either instantiate itself or not, it must be that there is no property I. Now I realize that there are various points in this argument that one might challenge. But suppose that you accept it. Still, it seems that sentences such as:

10. Happiness is a property that doesn't instantiate itself.

express propositions. After all, the following, it would seem, might be true:[62]

11. Rebecca believes that happiness is a property that doesn't instantiate itself.

But doesn't 11 assert that Rebecca stands in a relation to a proposition? On the present view, 10 does express a proposition, since 'is a property that doesn't instantiate itself' contributes a complex sub-propositional constituent to 10. It just turns out this constituent represents no property. As indicated, one might not accept that there is no property of *being a property that doesn't instantiate itself.* But still, it seems likely that *some* syntactically complex predicates don't "pick out" properties. And on the present view, we can hold that sentences containing them nonetheless express propositions, and so belief ascriptions that embed such sentences can be true or false. This seems a desirable feature of the view.

The third virtue of the present account of propositions that follows from the fact that on this view syntactically complex predicates contribute to propositions complex sub-propositional constituents whose structures are identical to the syntactic structures of the predicates contributing them, concerns the paradox of analysis. This aspect of our view provides us with the materials to dissolve the paradox and address related worries. Again, this is a highly desirable feature of the present view. It will be discussed in detail in Chapter 7.

Turning now to virtues of the present view of propositions due to other features of it, the first is that it yields a view of structured propositions on which they have sufficient structure to do what they are supposed to do. As I indicated in the Introduction and Chapter 1, what inclines one to think that propositions *are* structured are considerations involving propositional attitudes. In particular,

---

[61] A complex predicate stands for a property iff it contributes to propositions a complex sub-propositional constituent that represents that property.

[62] Of course, 10 seems true too. But if there is no property of *being a property that doesn't instantiate itself,* it seems doubtful that 10 is true. If there is no such property, it seems that 10 expresses a proposition that is neither true nor false.

assuming that propositions are the objects of belief, doubt and so on, it seems as though one can e.g. believe a proposition while failing to believe another necessarily equivalent to it. If propositions have structure and constituents, we can see how that could be. For necessarily equivalent propositions might nonetheless be distinct in virtue of having different constituents or structures. The present account comprises a theory of structured propositions on which propositions are individuated very finely. Since on the present view, the sentential relation in a sentence provides all the significant structure to the propositional relation binding together the constituents of the proposition it expresses, the structure of a proposition will be identical to the syntactic structure of the sentence expressing it. And of course, this means that propositions will be individuated very finely. Indeed, in Chapter 3 we will consider the objection that the present view individuates propositions *too* finely. But for now, I wish to note that the present view assigns structure to propositions that allows for very fine distinctions between them. And since allowing for fine distinctions between propositions is the reason for adopting the view that propositions are structured, at least the present view yields an account of structured propositions on which propositions that need to be distinguished are.

A further virtue of the present view of structured propositions is that on this view, it is no mystery what propositions are and the account gives us good independent reason to think that they exist. At the beginning of this chapter, I said that having these features is a constraint on any plausible answer to the question of what it is that binds together the constituents of propositions. I hope to already have made clear precisely what propositions are. They are facts of a certain sort. Specifically, they are facts of there being a context of utterance and there being lexical items of some language L that stand in a certain syntactic relation that itself in L encodes a certain function, where the lexical items have such-and-such semantic values relative to the context. It seems to me quite easy to understand what sorts of facts these are, and hence quite easy to understand what propositions are.

As to their existing, given very minimal assumptions, it follows that propositions exist on the present account. First, one must assume that the constituents of propositions exist: objects, properties and relations. Some might think that if you admit that properties and relations exist, there is no reason to deny that propositions exist. But I don't think this is correct. Propositions represent the world as being a certain way: propositions have truth conditions. Properties and relations do not. Hence, it would be perfectly reasonable to hold that properties and relations exist, but propositions don't. For one might think there is no reasonable explanation of, or account of, the fact that propositions *represent* and that this cannot be taken to be a primitive fact.[63] Or one might accept properties

63 Michael Jubien (2001) rejects propositions while accepting that there are properties and relations for more or less this sort of reason.

and relations, but think that if propositions exist, they must be structured. And one might then hold that there is no reasonable answer to the question of what structures propositions and holds their constituent together.[64] Thus, one would be led to deny that propositions exist even while allowing that properties and relations do. So I think there are various reasons that one might accept the existence of properties and relations but deny the existence of propositions. Thus, assuming that properties and relations exist does not by itself guarantee that propositions exist. In any case, it seems to me that many philosophers are inclined to admit that properties and relations, however understood, exist and so endorse our first assumption. Second, one must assume that words bear semantic relations to objects, properties and relations (relative to contexts) and so have these things as their semantic values. One must accept as well that syntactic concatenation has semantic significance (i.e. encodes certain functions). It seems to me that the vast majority of philosophers of language do accept these things. At any rate, they seem to me very hard to deny. Third, one must assume that words stand in sentential relations to each other at a level of syntax at which quantifier scope relations (and other scope relations) are explicitly represented. I have already claimed that this is the far and away dominant view among syntacticians in the broadly Chomskian tradition.[65] Once one makes these assumptions, which many philosophers are willing to make, it is virtually certain that propositions as I understand them exist. Consider again the proposition that Rebecca swims. I claim this proposition is the following fact: there is a context c and there are lexical items a and b of some language L such that a has as its semantic value in c Rebecca and occurs at the left terminal node of the sentential relation R that in L encodes the instantiation function and b occurs at R's right terminal node and has as its semantic value in c the property of swimming. Now if you accept that words have objects, properties and relations as semantic values (relative to contexts) and that they stand in sentential relations (which themselves have semantic significance) at the appropriate level of syntax, I don't see how you can deny the existence of facts of the sort I just mentioned. For the fact just amounts to certain words having certain objects and properties as semantic values relative to a context and standing in a certain syntactical relation with a certain semantic significance. Thus, given the assumptions I mentioned, which are accepted by many philosophers, propositions as I understand them exist.

[64] This *might* have been Russell's reason for abandoning propositions. As mentioned in Chapter 1, Russell (1903) seems to have identified the proposition that A differs from B with A standing in the *differs from* relation to B. This would identify a true proposition with the fact that makes it true, and hence make the existence of false propositions problematic. It may be that Russell could think of no other way for the constituents of the proposition that A differs from B to be held together except that A and B stand in the *differs from* relation. But since this view couldn't account for false propositions, perhaps Russell gave up on propositions.

[65] A fourth assumption required for the existence of certain propositions is that there are possible contexts of utterance. See discussion above.

A final virtue of the present view of propositions is that it makes it possible to begin to understand how propositions represent the world as being a certain way, that is, how propositions have truth conditions. For the sake of simplicity, let's consider again our simple proposition that Rebecca swims:

4b".

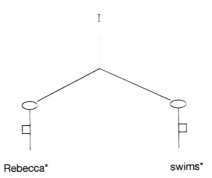

Rebecca*   swims*

Now in this proposition, Rebecca (Rebecca*) and the property of swimming (swims*) are configured in a certain way, and the sentential relation that provides all of the structure to the propositional relation encodes the instantiation function. Somehow, that this is so results in the proposition representing Rebecca instantiating swimming and so the proposition is true iff she does so. That is, somehow that 4b" configures Rebecca and the property of swimming in the way it does and that the sentential relation encodes the instantiation function results in 4b" being true iff Rebecca instantiates the property of swimming. Our question is: what makes the fact/proposition 4b" represent Rebecca instantiating swimming, so that it is true iff she does? If we assume that the propositional relation of 4b" inherits its semantic significance from the sentential relation in it that provides all of its structure, then since the sentential relation in question encodes the instantiation function, so does the propositional relation of 4b". But then this would mean that the proposition is true iff Rebecca swims. For the propositional relation would then provide the instruction to apply the instantiation function to Rebecca, swimming and a world, yielding the truth value of the proposition at the world.[66] Hence the proposition would represent the world as one in which Rebecca instantiates swimming.

So if we assume that the propositional relation inherits its significance from the sentential relation that is part of it and provides it with all of its structure,

---

[66] There is a subtlety here. I've said that the sentential relation in 4/4a instructs that the instantiation function be applied to the semantic values of the expressions at its terminal nodes (and a world), whereas the propositional relation in 4b" instructs that the instantiation function be applied to Rebecca and the property of swimming (and a world). But since Rebecca and the property of swimming *are* the semantic values of the expressions at the terminal nodes of the sentential relation, I think these can be understood as the same instruction.

we can explain how/why the proposition has truth conditions and how/why it has the specific truth conditions it has. If we make this assumption, we should qualify our view as to what fact is the proposition that Rebecca swims. The fact should also include that the propositional relation possesses the property of encoding the instantiation function (it already included the sentential relation doing so).

But what is the basis for this assumption? What is the explanation for *why* the propositional relation inherits its significance from the sentential relation that is part of it and so itself encodes the instantiation function?[67] From the standpoint of the current view, certainly it must be something that we and our linguistic ancestors did. I think we can "rationally reconstruct" how and why the propositional relation inherited the semantic significance of the sentential relation that is part of it and so came to encode the instantiation function as follows. Consider the time when English, and hence sentences like 'Rebecca swims', first came into existence (and suppose 'Rebecca' named Rebecca back then). As should by now be clear, the existence of sentences such as 'Rebecca swims' brings into existence facts such as 4b":

4b".

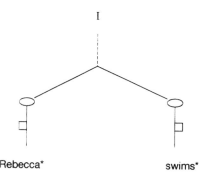

Rebecca*   swims*

where, let us suppose, the propositional relation doesn't yet encode the instantiation function, but the sentential relation of 'Rebecca swims' does. Since we now claim that the propositional relation encoding the instantiation function is part of the fact that is the proposition that Rebecca swims, 4b"is not yet that proposition. Indeed, neither the proposition that Rebecca swims, nor, we may suppose, any other proposition exists yet. Thus, it must be that the language does not yet contain verbs of attitude, modal operators, or that-clauses. However, sentences have truth conditions, in part in virtue of sentential relations encoding functions. As verbs of attitude, that-clauses and so on enter the language speakers begin to attempt to talk about structured contents. Naturally, their use of the

[67] Thanks to Dominic Gregory and an anonymous referee for pressing me on this important point.

structured content of 'Rebecca swims' (i.e. the way they begin to talk about it, etc.) is such as to implicitly take it to have the same truth conditions as the sentence 'Rebecca swims'. To do otherwise would border on being incoherent. This means that the constituents of this content, Rebecca and swimming, must compose in the same way as do the semantic values of the words in the sentence. Of course the way they compose in the sentence is by having the instantiation function applied to them (at a world). And it is the fact that the syntax was made to encode the instantiation function that comprised the specification as to how the semantic values are to be composed in the sentence. Since to have the same truth conditions as the sentence 'Rebecca swims', the structured content of the sentence must instruct that the instantiation function be applied to Rebecca, the property of swimming and a world to yield its truth value at that world, that speakers implicitly take the structured content to have the same truth conditions as the sentence results in it so instructing. That in turn means that the propositional relation of the structured content of 'Rebecca swims' inherits the semantic significance of the sentential relation of 'Rebecca swims', and so encodes the instantiation function. Since the fact 4b" is the most eligible of the facts eligible to be the structured content of 'Rebecca swims', as I'll argue subsequently, it comes to be the proposition that Rebecca swims and its propositional relation encodes the instantiation function.

In short, when English came into existence and prior to it having the resources to talk about propositions, it brought into existence facts like 4b" and closely related facts. As speakers began to attempt to talk about structured contents by means of that-clauses, they implicitly took these contents to have the same truth conditions as the sentences with those contents. The sentences in question had the truth conditions they did in part in virtue of sentential relations encoding functions. Perhaps it was indeterminate at first which eligible facts are the structured contents of sentences. But the facts that in the end are most eligible to be structured contents, propositions, must share the truth conditions of the sentences whose contents they are eligible to be, and so their propositional relations must inherit the semantic significance of sentential relations of the sentences whose contents they are eligible to be. 4b" is the most eligible fact to be the proposition that Rebecca swims; hence it is so, and its propositional relation inherits the semantic significance of the sentential relation of 'Rebecca swims'. We thus have the outline of an account of how/why propositions represent. I know of no other account of propositions that can claim this.

We now claim that the fact that is the proposition that Rebecca swims includes the propositional relation possessing the property of encoding the instantiation function. This being so, having truth conditions, and having the particular truth conditions it has, is an intrinsic and essential property of the proposition that Rebecca swims. It is intrinsic, because the proposition has it simply in virtue of the way it is in itself. That is, this fact, just in virtue of the way it is, has the truth conditions it has. Any duplicate of it has the same truth conditions. And having the truth conditions it has is essential, because in any world in which the proposition/fact is brought into existence by endowing the words with the semantic values they actually have, having the sentential relation encode the instantiation function as it actually does, and having the propositional relation inherit the semantic significance of the sentential relation and so itself encode the instantiation function, the fact/proposition has these truth conditions.

In the present chapter, I have claimed that propositions are certain sorts of facts. No doubt the reader could by now repeat in her sleep that the proposition that Rebecca swims is the fact consisting of Rebecca standing in the following relation to the property of swimming (in that order), where this very relation encodes the instantiation function: there is a context c and there are lexical items a and b of some language L such that a has as its semantic value in c x and occurs at the left terminal node of the sentential relation R that in L encodes the instantiation function and b occurs at R's right terminal node and has as its semantic value in c y. Rebecca and the property of swimming are *constituents* of the proposition that is this fact, in virtue of being the right sorts of *components* of the fact. I say 'the right sorts of components' because the facts that are propositions have components that are not constituents of those propositions. For example, the sentential relation of 4/4a is a component of the fact that is the proposition that Rebecca swims, but it is not a constituent of that proposition. If we picture a proposition in "tree form", as in 4b" above, the *constituents* of the proposition that is the fact are the *components* of the fact occurring at the terminal nodes of the propositional relation.

Above, I mentioned that there are facts that are very closely related to the facts that I have identified with propositions. This raises the question of the grounds on which I have identified propositions with the latter facts instead of the former facts. The concern here is closely related to the Benacerraf style worry I raised for the view that propositions are ordered n-tuples. If many similar facts each has equal claim to being the proposition that Rebecca swims and if no principled reason can be given as to why one is the proposition, this suggests that none of them is the proposition.

In order to answer this concern, we need to think about which facts, similar to the facts that I have identified with propositions, might be claimed to be equally good candidates for being propositions. Continuing to focus on the proposition that Rebecca swims, let's use the term *candidate facts* for facts for which a case can be made that they are equally good candidates for being this proposition as the fact that I claim is the proposition.[68] Presumably any candidate fact must have only Rebecca and the property of swimming at the terminal nodes of (what is claimed to be) the propositional relation. For this amounts to saying that the

---

[68] I'll sometimes use the term 'candidate facts' more generally to refer to facts for which a case can be made that they are equally good candidates for being propositions as the facts that I claim are propositions. Note that the fact I claim is the proposition that Rebecca swims is a candidate fact.

(alleged) proposition that is the fact has as constituents only Rebecca and the property of swimming. In addition, for a fact to be a candidate fact Rebecca and the property of swimming must be bound together in it by (what is claimed to be) a propositional relation that has as a component the sentential relation of 4/4a. For the explanation as to why propositions have truth conditions leaned heavily on the claim that the sentential relation is a component of the propositional relation. And I have claimed that any account of propositional relations must shed light on the question of how propositions manage to have truth conditions. This strongly suggests that any candidate fact must have a (alleged) propositional relation that has the sentential relation of 4/4a as a component. Further, we must have good reason to think that Rebecca and the property of swimming actually stand in the relation in question. For only if they do, does the alleged proposition exist. And I have claimed that any account of propositional relations had better give us good reason to think propositions exist. So any candidate fact will be a fact consisting of Rebecca standing in a relation to the property of swimming, where the relation relates no additional things (so that the alleged proposition will have no other constituents), there is good evidence she really does stand in that relation to the property of swimming and the relation has as a component the sentential relation.

As suggested above, we can now see that there will be some candidate facts that are very closely related to but distinct from the fact that I claim is the proposition that Rebecca swims. For example, there is the following fact (I have emphasized in the description of this fact that portion that characterizes the respect in which this fact differs from the fact I claim is the proposition that Rebecca swims—I'll do this below in the description of another candidate fact that is distinct from the fact I claim is the proposition that Rebecca swims): there is a context c and there are lexical items a and b *that are both fewer than one million symbols long* of some language L such that a has as its semantic value in c Rebecca and occurs at the left terminal node of the sentential relation R that in L encodes the instantiation function and b occurs at R's right terminal node and has as its semantic value in c the property of swimming. And here is another candidate fact distinct from the fact that I am claiming is the proposition that Rebecca swims: there is a context c and there are lexical items a and b of some language L *that contains no word that is over one million symbols long* such that a has as its semantic value in c Rebecca and occurs at the left terminal node of the sentential relation R that in L encodes the instantiation function and b occurs at R's right terminal node and has as its semantic value in c the property of swimming.[69] I feel sure the reader could

---

[69] The two candidate facts just described differ from the fact I claim is the proposition that Rebecca swims in that one includes the instantiation of the property of being a lexical item fewer than one million symbols long (the fact that is the proposition that Rebecca swims does not) and the other includes the instantiation of the property of being a language that contains no word over one million symbols long (the fact that is the proposition that Rebecca swims does not). I should add that the mere fact that two descriptions are different does not mean that they describe different

describe many other candidate facts of this general sort. So why is the fact that I claim is the proposition that Rebecca swims that proposition rather than one of these other candidate facts? I think the answer is given by considerations adduced in Merrill (1980) and Lewis (1983). Our talk about propositions, both by using the term 'propositions' and by using that-clauses to talk about them, together with the various jobs propositions are expected to perform (bearers of truth and falsity, objects of the attitudes, bearers of modal properties) and the constraints I have suggested (we must have reason to think they exist; we must be able to see how/why they have truth conditions) characterize what we might call *the proposition role*. If, as we have assumed, all candidate facts satisfy the constraints I have suggested, then, as I suggested above, I think all candidate facts are to some extent eligible to play the proposition role and so be propositions. However, I don't think all the candidate facts are equally eligible. I think that the fact I identify with the proposition that Rebecca swims is intrinsically more eligible to play that role than the other candidates. In the case of the candidate facts I have considered here, perhaps this will be intuitively clear. The other candidate facts have additional components not had by the fact I claim is the proposition that Rebecca swims and these components play no role in the candidate fact's suitability to play the proposition role. So the facts I identify with propositions are "the smallest" facts (i.e. those with the fewest components) that are eligible for the proposition role. This makes them more eligible than the other candidates to be propositions and that is why they are the propositions and the others aren't.[70]

facts. For example, 'the fact of a possessing the relational property of *bearing R to b*' and 'the fact of a bearing R to b' are different descriptions. But the fact they both describe has the same components: a, R and b. And it is the fact of a bearing R to b. By contrast the candidate facts described above have components not had by the fact that is the proposition that Rebecca swims (e.g. the property of containing no word that is over one million symbols long). Thus the candidate facts are different facts from the fact that is the proposition that Rebecca swims.

[70] I am often attracted to the idea that there are certain facts closely related to the facts I claim are propositions and that our talk about propositions is sometimes talk about the facts I claim are propositions and sometimes talk about these closely related facts. Or perhaps it is even vague which such facts are propositions. But I am unable to pursue this line of thinking here.

3

Objections to the New Account

I have now sketched an account of the relations that bind together the constituents of structured propositions. The purpose of the present chapter is to investigate some consequences of the resulting account of propositions, especially those that initially seem problematic or undesirable.

FIRST OBJECTION: ORIGINS

Let's begin by addressing a worry regarding how propositions came to be.[1] On the present view, the facts that are propositions came into existence in part as a result of lexical items acquiring semantic values and syntactic relations coming to encode certain functions. It would seem that when we attempt to explain how our proto-linguistic ancestors brought it about that words had semantic values and sentential relations encoded certain functions, we will appeal to beliefs and intentions they had: they believed that a certain sort of thing (say a dog) was in the area and they intended to communicate information about it, and so on. But on the present view, prior to the existence of language there were no propositions, which are the objects of attitudes like intending and believing. So it seems we have a problem here. Propositions, which are the objects of attitudes, must exist in order for creatures to have propositional attitudes (attitudes with propositional content). But the account of how propositions came into existence on the present view will have to presuppose that creatures had propositional attitudes prior to propositions existing.[2]

---

[1] Thanks to Scott Soames for raising this worry.

[2] The worry here is that the view I am defending is subject to a sort of regress. If one claims that propositions came into existence at a certain past time, one will have to suppose that creatures had propositional attitudes, and hence that propositions existed, prior to that time. Talk of propositions "coming into existence" will be understood differently by presentists and eternalists, who are discussed below. For eternalists, the claim that propositions came into existence at a certain time amounts to the claim that propositions are temporally located at a certain time (and not before). But the present worry is that when she attempts to explain why/how propositions are temporally located there, she will be forced to admit they are temporally located prior to that time. For presentists, the claim that propositions came into existence at a certain time amounts to the claim that they existed when that time was present and didn't exist in the past of that time. But the present worry is that when she attempts to explain how/why propositions existed at that time, she will be forced to claim they existed in the past of that time. So both presentists and eternalists face the same sort of regress

Before directly addressing this concern, it will help to clarify one feature of the present view of propositions.[3] The fundamental thought behind the present view of structured propositions is that the *vehicles* by means of which propositions are expressed (e.g. English LF representations) consist of entities (e.g. lexical items) standing in relations and that these very relations provide all of the significant structure to the propositions expressed by those vehicles. The vehicles we have considered thus far are LF representations underlying natural language sentences. But, for example, if there are "mental sentences", these too are vehicles for the expression of propositions. And the "mental sentential" relation obtaining between the "mental lexical items" in the mental sentence provides the significant structure to the proposition it expresses in just the way the sentential relation obtaining between the lexical items of the LF representation did. As in the natural language case, the propositional relation will consist of the composition of the relation between the lexical items in the mental sentence and the semantic relations (perhaps relative to contexts) the mental lexical items bear to their semantic values (again, existentially quantifying over the lexical items).

Thus on the present view, there may be propositions even in the absence of any public natural languages. However, in any circumstance in which there is no public language or language of thought, propositions fail to exist.[4]

This of course means that *if* there is a language of thought, and *if* our proto- linguistic ancestors thought in it, propositions could have existed, and our ancestors could have had attitudes towards them, prior to the existence of public language. Such attitudes could then be appealed to in the account of how lexical items acquired semantic values and so on.

However, I am not happy resting my response here on the claim that there is a language of thought and our proto-linguistic ancestors thought in it. So let us suppose this claim is false. Then I think we must say that strictly speaking our proto-linguistic ancestors did not have propositional attitudes, because propositions didn't exist then. Hence they did not have the sorts of beliefs and intentions we enjoy today. However we can say that they had some sorts of "proto-intentional states": proto-beliefs and proto-intentions. I'm not sure exactly how to describe such states that play a role in "proto-intentional" action and that don't have propositional content. But it seems to me likely that many animals currently have only states of this sort and so it wouldn't be surprising that in our pre- and proto-linguistic stages we were rather like them in this respect.

---

here, though the details of the nature of the regress differ. I discuss the present worry in intuitive terms independently of the debate between presentists and eternalists because it seems to me that they will both have to avoid the regress in a similar way.

[3] This paragraph and the next two are drawn from King (1995). Thanks to *Noûs* and Blackwell Publishing for their kind permission to use this material.

[4] Below I will discuss the possibility that language existed prior to life existing, and hence that propositions existed then. Here I assume that language, and hence propositions, came into existence after conscious creatures existed.

The idea would be that these proto-intentional states were enough to begin to attach lexical items to semantic values and more generally to do what had to be done to bring propositions into existence. The view, then, is that propositions and real intentional states with propositional content came into existence together. Hence we need not suppose that our proto-linguistic ancestors literally had propositional attitudes prior to the existence of language and propositions. It is enough to suppose that they had proto-intentional states not too different in kind from those had by many animals today.

It is important to see that even those who think propositions are eternal face a version of the problem I am now addressing.[5] For even if propositions exist eternally, there was a time at which no creatures had mental states with propositional content. Hence, some account must be given of how creatures came to have propositional attitudes. If we consider creatures immediately prior to the time when creatures had propositional attitudes and creatures who first had them, some explanation will have to be given of how the latter managed to get in cognitive contact with propositions. But in sketching such an account one is faced with the challenge of describing the minds of our ancestors without using verbs of propositional attitude. Here again it seems one would have to invoke proto-intentional states and proto-intentional action as part of the explanation, just as I did above. Hence, on this score my account is not in any worse shape than an account on which propositions are eternal.

SECOND OBJECTION: TRUTHS IN THE REMOTE PAST

There is another worry arising from the fact that the view of propositions I've been defending apparently entails that propositions came into existence at a certain time in the past. On the present view, for propositions to exist, there must exist sentences with parts that have semantic values (relative to contexts), and the sentential relations holding these parts together must have semantic significance. Now consider a time in the remote past, say two minutes after the Big Bang. I have to this point assumed that languages and hence sentences didn't exist at such times, nor did lexical items have semantic values (relative to contexts) nor did sentential relations have semantic significance.[6] Hence, propositions didn't exist in the remote past. Given that propositions are the primary bearers of truth and falsity, this, in turn, would mean that nothing was true in the remote past.[7] But surely, one might think, something has gone wrong. Two minutes after the Big Bang certain things *were* true: it was true that particles bore certain spatial

---

[5] Thanks to David Manley for pointing this out.

[6] One might also think that the lexical items didn't exist, nor did sentential relations. This will be discussed subsequently.

[7] I assume that to be true in the remote past propositions had to exist then. I discuss this assumption in due course.

relations to each other, that the universe was a certain average temperature and so on. If the present view is committed to there being no propositions, and hence no truths, in the remote past, it is just wrong, an objector might say.[8]

How we address this objection depends on which theory of time we accept. Though I am more sympathetic to one of these theories than I am to the other, I would like my theory of propositions to be available to advocates of each view. Thus, I shall consider how to respond to the objection given each theory of time.

Presentism is the view that the present time is the only time that exists and objects that are temporally present are the only objects that exist.[9] Thus, there are no past or future things (such as dinosaurs or colonies on the moon). *Eternalism* is the view that all past, present and future times equally exist, as do all past, present and future objects.[10] On this view, future objects and past objects exist as much as do objects that are temporally present. It's just that such objects are located else*when* in just the way in which some objects are located else*where*. According to the eternalist, being located at a time other than this time doesn't impugn a thing's existence any more than being located at a place other than this place does. Let's consider what to say about the objection raised above taking each of these theories of time in turn and conjoining it with the present theory of propositions.

Taking presentism first, consider again a time in the remote past. According to the presentist, at that time it was the only time that existed.[11] Further, at that

---

[8] These issues are discussed in King (1994), though I there thought of expressions such as 'Sometimes' and 'One million years ago' as index shifting tense operators and so thought that truth was defined relative to a world and a time. As I will indicate, I no longer think such expressions are index shifting operators (see King (2003), which will be discussed in Chapter 6) and so don't think truth must be defined relative to a world and time. Further, my discussion here makes much more contact with current work in metaphysics.

[9] See Zimmerman (1998), Sider (2001) and Crisp (2003) for discussion. 'Exist' is used tenselessly in my characterization of presentism in the body of the text. Often presentism is characterized as the view that always everything is temporally present (some presentists add that this is necessary). The requirement of being always true is intended to distinguish presentism from what is often called the "growing block" view. On this view, which objects and times exist changes as time passes. At a given time, what exists is everything at that time and in the past of that time, so that the universe is a "growing" four dimensional spacetime. If this view were correct and there were a first moment of time, it is thought that the claim that everything is temporally present would be true at that one moment of time (and false at all other times). Thus, it is claimed that presentism cannot just be the view that everything is temporally present, on pain of being true at the first moment of time if the growing block view is correct, (presentism is supposed to be incompatible with the growing block theory). Hence, it is held that presentism is the view that always everything is temporally present (waiving the worry about necessity). I suspect that this particular line of reasoning assumes that propositions can change truth value over time (when it is said that the claim that everything is temporally present would be true at the first moment of time and false at all other times on the growing block view), and I reject that view. This is discussed in Chapter 6. Nevertheless, I think that presentism should be understood as the view that always everything is temporally present (or perhaps the view that the latter is necessary as well). I don't consider the growing block view in the text, because I don't think it raises any new issues.

[10] See Sider (2001) for discussion.

[11] Some presentists think that just as the actualist can hold that there are other ersatz (non-concrete) possible worlds that exist in the actual world, so they can hold that there are other ersatz

time only objects then present existed. Taking a *fact*, as we did in the previous chapter, to be an object possessing a property or n objects standing in an n-place relation, or n properties standing in an n-place relation or etc., presumably the only facts that existed at that time were facts that were temporally present. And presumably, for a fact to be temporally present, its component objects, properties and relations must be temporally present as well. Now assuming presentism, did the facts that I am claiming are propositions exist two minutes after the Big Bang? This amounts to asking whether *at that time* languages and words existed, words had semantic values (relative to contexts) and stood in sentential relations (thus forming sentences of a language), which themselves had semantic significance then. It seems to me doubtful that all these things were so, and hence doubtful that propositions did exist at that time if presentism is correct.

To see this, let me first note that if presentism is true, there is at least good reason to doubt that English words and sentences (or those of any other language, for that matter) existed two minutes after the Big Bang. For we are strongly inclined to deny that worlds with no sentient life at all are worlds according to which English (or any other language) exists. After all, at such worlds there are no language users, and hence no facts about language users; and it would seem that English could not exist independently of such facts. But according to presentism, our own world at two minutes after the Big Bang likewise contained no facts at all about language users. So it would seem that it did not contain any words or sentences of English or any other language. And on the present account of propositions, if there were no words and sentences of any language, there were no propositions either.

There is a second reason to doubt that propositions existed two minutes after the Big Bang, which is independent of the question whether words and sentences existed then. For on the present view, the existence of propositions requires that sentential relations have semantic significance. Thus, as indicated in the previous chapter, the sentential relation in the following sentence

1. Rebecca swims.

which looks as follows in "tree form"

---

times that exist at the present time. See Crisp (2003) for discussion. At any rate, the presentist holds that at a given time, that time is the only "concrete" time that exists. Ersatz times will be discussed later.

must encode the instantiation function in order for the proposition (now) expressed by this sentence to exist. But then if presentism is true, for that proposition to have existed two minutes after the Big Bang, that sentential relation must have encoded the instantiation function then.[12] Can it be claimed that it did? Further, for propositions like this to exist in the remote past given the truth of presentism, words must have had semantic values (relative to contexts) then. Can it be claimed that words had semantic values in the remote past?[13] Well, even if presentism is true, one is free to hold that properties and relations existed in the remote past. So the sentential relation of 1/1a, the instantiation function and the semantic relation that currently obtains between the former and the latter all existed in the remote past. Similarly, (we are supposing that) the word (type) 'charge' existed in the remote past, as did the property of having charge and the semantic relation that obtains between a predicate and a property when the latter is the semantic value of the former. The only remaining questions, then, are whether a sentential relation like R (of 1/1a) actually could have stood in a semantic relation to the instantiation function in the remote past; and whether a word could have had a semantic value (relative to a context) in the remote past.

If R did bear a semantic relation to the instantiation function two minutes after the Big Bang, one tends to want to ask why. What made it the case then that R bore this relation to the instantiation function? Similarly, what made it the case then that a word had a particular semantic value (relative to a context)? I can think of no account of why these things would have been so then. Of course one could hold that these facts obtained then and that there is no explanation as to how or why. They are primitive facts that have no further explanation. But the fact that one thing represents or stands in some other semantic relation to another thing seems to be precisely the kind of thing that requires further explanation! Moreover, to take it as primitive that things stand in the particular semantic relations that they do would undermine a virtue claimed for the present view of propositions: that it can in broad outline explain why/how propositions represent the world. The explanation in part was that they do so because we and our linguistic predecessors did things that resulted in sentential relations having semantic significance and words having semantic values. But if instead it is a primitive fact that sentential relations have the semantic significance they do and similarly for words having semantic values, we end up "explaining" how propositions represent by appealing to primitive facts about what sentential

---

[12] I am ignoring tense here. Were we to think about tense seriously, I think it would be more likely that the proposition now expressed by 1/1a didn't exist in the remote past if presentism is true, even putting aside the non-existence of Rebecca then. That is because it is likely that the proposition now expressed by 1/1a contains the present time as a constituent and if presentism is true that time did not exist in the remote past. See Chapter 6.

[13] To avoid complications, here I consider a word ('charge') whose semantic value (having charge) presumably existed in the remote past.

relations and words represent. This doesn't seem much better than taking as primitive the fact that propositions represent.[14]

To summarize the discussion to this point, the present view of propositions taken together with presentism leads us to the conclusion that propositions did not exist in the remote past. For, first, there is reason to doubt that words and sentences existed in the remote past. And if they didn't, neither did propositions on the present view. Second, even if words and sentences did exist in the remote past assuming presentism, for propositions to exist in the remote past on the account being defended, sentential relations would have had to have semantic significance then and words would have had to have semantic values then. But there appears to be no explanation of how/why words or sentential relations stood in semantic relations to other things in the remote past. Further, if propositions did not exist in the remote past, nothing was true or false then. So the conjunction of presentism and the theory of propositions I have been defending is to this point without a response to the objection under consideration: namely, that in the remote past many things *were* true.[15]

But I think there is a good response to the objection. The objection can seem much stronger than it is because of a failure to distinguish between the following two claims: 1) nothing was true in the remote past;[16] 2) things weren't a determinate way in the remote past. When we are told a theory entails 1, we tend to think it entails 2 as well. And 2 seems, and probably is, absurd! But 1 doesn't require the truth of 2. If the present theory of propositions is correct and presentism is correct, it seems that 1 is correct. Nothing was true in the remote past because the things that are the bearers of truth, propositions, didn't exist then. But that doesn't at all commit us to 2. Of course things *were a certain way* in the remote past. Particles stood in relations to one another, things were a certain temperature and so on. It's just that since propositions didn't exist then, there was nothing then to *represent* things as being the way they in fact were. But they were still that way. In other words, certain facts obtained in the remote past. Particles possessed charge properties, stood in spatial relations to each other,

[14] In Chapter 2, I claimed that taking the basic syntactic relation as primitive was preferable to taking propositional relations as primitive. Here I claim that taking it to be a primitive fact that sentential relations and words represent is not really preferable to taking it as primitive that propositions represent. Some might feel a tension between these two claims. But I don't think there is. The former roughly amounts to the claim that from the standpoint of addressing skepticism about propositions, it is preferable to take syntactic relations as primitive than to take propositional relations as primitive. The latter amounts to the claim that if in attempting to explain how/why propositions represent one appeals to primitive facts about sentential relations and words representing, one has not made any real progress in explaining representation.

[15] Again here I assume that presentists will hold that to be true in the past, a proposition must exist then. This assumption will be discussed subsequently.

[16] Here and later when I talk about whether a proposition was true in the remote past (or later whether a proposition at a time t was true), I am talking about whether the proposition at the time in question possessed the property of being true. I am not talking about a relational property of *being true at t*, where t is a time (and possibly an ersatz time). This will be made clear later.

and so on. But the facts that are propositions didn't exist in the remote past, and so the facts that did exist then made nothing true. For example, a particle's possessing a certain charge property did not make any proposition true back then; but the particle's possessing the charge property was nevertheless a fact back then. This takes a lot of sting out of the claim that nothing was true in the remote past. As long as there were particles standing in relations, and, later, planets orbiting stars, that nothing was true despite this seems rather harmless.

Further, the idea I am employing here to defend the conjunction of my account of propositions and presentism, that things could be a certain way in the remote past even though there wasn't at that time a true proposition describing things being that way, is one that most presentists are going to need anyway.[17] It seems that because George Bush didn't exist in the remote past, no propositions with George Bush as a constituent existed then either. But then though the remote past was a way that included lacking Bush, there was no true proposition then to the effect that Bush doesn't exist describing that way the world was.[18] So in this case it seems that my account of propositions aside, the presentist must hold that things were a certain way in the remote past even though there was not then a true proposition describing that way things were. Hence, to invoke this idea in defending the conjunction of my account of propositions with presentism involves no additional cost to the presentist.

Though the conjunction of my account of propositions and presentism leads to the conclusion that nothing was true in the remote past, we can now say true and false things about the remote past. Since things were a certain way in the remote past and since we now have propositions that are about the past, there are now true and false things to be said about the past. So, for example, the proposition that there were dinosaurs millions of years ago is true, as is the proposition that the average temperature in the universe was above one million degrees Kelvin two minutes after the Big Bang.[19]

In summary, while the present view of propositions coupled with presentism denies that there were truths in the remote past, it maintains that things were a certain way then. Moreover, it allows that propositions about the remote past, now that they exist, are true and false (even though they didn't exist then). Given this, it's hard to see what's unacceptable—rather than just surprising—about the conclusion that propositions didn't exist and so weren't true in the remote past.

---

[17] As David Manley pointed out to me.

[18] I again assume here that presentists will hold that for a proposition to possess the property of being true at a given time, it must exist then. I am about to discuss presentists who deny this.

[19] Of course, it may be that presentists are constrained in how they can think of the propositions expressed by tensed sentences. For example, they may have to think of tenses as operators and so think of the propositions expressed by tensed sentences accordingly. I think such a view is implausible. See Chapter 6. Further, presentists may have trouble saying what *grounds* many truths about the past. See Sider (2001) and Crisp (2003). But the general point here is that now that propositions exist, even if presentism is true nothing in principle prevents the defender of the current view of propositions from claiming that there are true propositions about the past.

Before turning to the question of how to respond to the objection we have been considering from the standpoint of the conjunction of the current theory of propositions and eternalism, two points need to be briefly addressed. First, in arguing, as I just did, that the conjunction of the present view of propositions and presentism entails that nothing was true in the remote past, I assumed that if propositions didn't exist in the remote past they weren't true then. I take this to be a particular instance of a more general claim to the effect that for anything to possess a property or stand in a relation at a given time, it must exist at that time. In fact, some philosophers deny this claim.[20] I will subsequently argue that presentists shouldn't deny this claim. Before arguing this, let me emphasize that the presentist who *does* deny this claim and accepts my account of propositions has an easy response to the objection we have been considering. If we assume that nonexistents *can* possess properties at times when they don't exist, then from the fact that propositions didn't exist in the remote past, it doesn't follow that nothing was true or false then. Thus, if we assume that nonexistents can possess properties at times when they don't exist, the objection we have been considering to the conjunction of presentism and the present view of propositions can be easily defused: though this conjunction entails that propositions didn't exist in the remote past, it doesn't entail that nothing was true or false then. Hence, by *not* assuming *here* that nonexistents can possess properties at times when they don't exist I have made the objection raised against the conjunction of presentism and the present view of propositions harder to meet. But as we have seen, it still can be met.

In any case, I think there are reasons to hold that for anything to possess a property or stand in a relation at a given time, it must exist at that time. What are these reasons? Well, there appear to be lots of clear cases of properties one can possess and relations one can stand in at a time only if one exists at that time. Consider the properties: having mass, sitting on a beach, and skiing down a mountain. Consider the relations: being five feet from, kissing and hitting. The crucial point, I think, is that these are clear cases of properties and relations that one can possess and stand in at a time only if one exists at that time *independently of our having made any other controversial philosophical assumptions.* That is, their being clear cases does not require us to make controversial assumptions in metaphysics or philosophy of language. For example, an eternalist would hold that to possess the above properties and stand in the above relations, a thing

[20] Salmon (1998) does, as does Hinchliff (1996). The former is quite explicit about holding that things can possess properties and stand in relations at times when they don't exist. Putting aside the case of what he calls *tensed properties* (such as having been straight; see pp. 125, 127–8 and note 17), the latter seems to endorse the view that objects can stand in relations at times they don't exist when he claims that we can refer to Cicero, who doesn't (any more) exist, (p. 125). This suggests that on the views of Salmon and Hinchliff, a fact (as I understand facts) could fail to exist at a time because some of its component objects, properties and relations don't exist then. For if e.g. an object o can possess a property P at a time when o doesn't exist, it would seem that the fact of o possessing P doesn't exist at that time either (though it obtains in virtue of o possessing P).

must exist (timelessly—as all past present and future objects do) and be (at least partly) temporally located at the time of possessing the property and standing in the relation. A presentist would hold that to possess or stand in the above properties and relations at a given time, a thing must exist at that time. I know of no plausible view according to which a thing can fail to exist and yet possess or stand in the above properties and relations.

By contrast, it is hard to think of clear cases of nonexistent things possessing properties and standing in relations at times when they don't exist that are clear cases *independently of making controversial philosophical assumptions.* Perhaps you think that my referring to Socrates is a clear case of the currently nonexistent Socrates standing in a relation to me now. But this is only so given the controversial metaphysical assumption that Socrates doesn't exist, which the eternalist denies.[21] Or perhaps you think that John seeking Sherlock Holmes is a clear case of John now bearing a relation to the currently (and, presumably, always) nonexistent Holmes. But no account that I am familiar with of the semantics of intensional transitive verbs like 'seeks' have the result that the truth of 'John seeks Sherlock Holmes' uttered now requires John to stand in some relation to a non-existent thing now.[22] So John seeking Holmes now (and so the sentence 'John seeks Holmes' uttered now being true) is not at all a clear case of John bearing a relation to a current nonexistent. There just don't seem to be clear cases of a thing not existing at a time and possessing a property or standing in a relation at that time that are clear cases independently of making controversial assumptions in metaphysics or philosophy of language.

Further, when one tries to make sense of the idea that a thing could possess a property or stand in a relation at a time and yet fail to exist at that time, one is bound to find the idea puzzling. What is it about *some* properties and relations that allows something to fail to exist at a time and yet possess them or stand in them at that time? Is there really a difference between only currently non-existent things possessing a property now and the property being uninstantiated now? Why should we say that I stand in a *relation* at a time to a thing that doesn't exist then rather than saying instead that I possess some suitably related *property* at that time?[23] How can certain truths fail to be true on the basis of what exists?

These two facts, (1) that independently of any controversial philosophical assumptions there are *many* clear cases of properties and relations that require things to exist at a time to possess or stand in them then, whereas there are no

---

[21] Of course, the eternalist will agree that the English sentence 'Socrates doesn't exist' (uttered now) has a reading on which it is true. But she will claim that on this reading, the sentence merely asserts that Socrates is not temporally located in the present. On this reading, then, the verb 'exists' expresses (at time t) the property of being temporally located at t. But then on this reading, the sentence makes no claim about existence in the intended sense. These issues are further discussed below.

[22] See Montague (1974); Richard (1998); and Forbes (2000).

[23] Remarks in Bigelow (1996) suggest this question.

such clear cases of nonexistents possessing properties or standing in relations at times when they don't exist and (2) that the very idea that a thing could fail to exist at a time and possess a property or stand in a relation at that time is puzzling, suggest to me that the burden of proof here is squarely on those who claim that things can fail to exist at a time and yet possess properties and stand in relations at that time. Those who endorse this claim should provide some argument for it.

Moreover, and crucially, a presentist defense of this claim should not presuppose presentism. Once the presentist commits herself to the current non-existence of Socrates, she confronts the objection that we can now say true things about Socrates (e.g. 'Socrates' refers to Socrates). If Socrates doesn't exist now, the objection goes, how could that be? One response for the presentist is to claim that a current nonexistent can possess properties now and so some sentences truly attribute properties now to current nonexistents. So here the presentist invokes the principle that a thing can fail to exist at a time and yet possess properties then in defending presentism. As we have seen, the presentist owes us an argument for this principle. But that argument had better not *presuppose* presentism. For, as we have seen, we are invoking the principle to *defend* presentism! To then presuppose presentism in defending the principle would be obviously circular. And yet presentists often do seem to defend the principle by presupposing presentism. For example, having already committed himself to presentism and so to the current nonexistence of Socrates, Nathan Salmon claims that the principle that an object must exist in every circumstance in which it has properties 'has very clear counterexamples'.[24] One, he claims, is that Socrates had at the time of Salmon's writing the property of being discussed by Salmon.[25] But this counterexample to the principle that an object must exist at a time to have a property then clearly just assumes the truth of presentism by assuming that Socrates doesn't currently exist; and therefore, so does this argument for the principle that an object *can* possess properties at times it doesn't exist.[26] For the reasons given, this is simply illegitimate.

Thus, until presentists provide an argument for the claim that a thing can fail to exist at a time and still at that time possess properties and stand in relations that doesn't itself presuppose presentism, given the burden of proof discussed above, it seems to me that they should assume the denial of this claim.

---

[24] Salmon (1998) p. 290.

[25] Of course, this is a clear case of a thing failing to exist at a time and possessing a property then only given controversial philosophical assumptions (that Socrates doesn't exist), as were the cases discussed above.

[26] Similarly, Hinchliff (1996), who as a presentist commits himself to the current nonexistence of Cicero, then points out that we can currently refer to him. He seems to think that he has thereby shown that a thing can fail to exist at a time and yet possess properties then (even properties that aren't what he calls *tensed*—see pp. 125, 127-8 and note 17). See p. 125. Again, this argument for the claim that a thing can fail to exist at a time and possess properties then presupposes presentism and so is illegitimate for the reasons given in the text.

In responding to the objection I have been considering to the conjunction of presentism and my account of propositions, I have assumed the denial of this claim for two reasons. First, as I've just argued, the presentist isn't entitled to assume the claim without giving an independent argument for it. And second, as noted earlier, the presentist who endorses the claim has an easy response to the objection under consideration. But the crucial point, as again we saw earlier, is that even if the claim is denied, the presentist who holds my view of propositions has a good response to the objection.

The second point we need to address before turning to eternalism concerns (alleged) singular propositions "involving" past objects. Consider an utterance of the following sentence at the present time

2. Socrates had a beard.

On the present view of propositions, 2 uttered now, if it expresses any proposition, expresses a singular proposition with Socrates as a constituent. If presentism is correct, Socrates doesn't exist now. But then the singular proposition that one would have thought 2 expresses uttered now doesn't exist.[27] Doesn't this seem implausible? I agree that this is a problem presentists need to address.[28] But it is a problem for *any* theory of propositions according to which if 2 (uttered now) expresses a proposition, it expresses a proposition with Socrates as a constituent. I am concerned here to address alleged problems that are specific to the theory of propositions I am defending. Problems that it shares with all other accounts of structured, singular propositions (in this case, when combined with presentism) will have to be addressed another time.

Let's now consider the conjunction of eternalism and the present theory of propositions and ask how it fares with respect to the objection raised above. Recall that the objection was that on the current theory of propositions, they didn't exist in the remote past and so on the present account nothing was true or false then. But, the objector claims, surely some things were true and false in the remote past.

Introducing some terminology at this point will help us to both state and fully appreciate the eternalist's response to this objection.[29] First, according to the eternalist past things like Socrates and future things like Colin's children exist. Still, the eternalist is well aware that English speakers take sentences like 'Socrates doesn't exist now' when uttered at the present moment to be true. The eternalist will claim that in English, occurrences of 'exists' with tense or other temporal

---

[27] If Socrates doesn't exist, then I assume that the fact that I would identify with the proposition expressed by 2 uttered now doesn't exist either. For Socrates would have to be a component of that fact, and a fact can't exist if its components don't.

[28] This problem is discussed in Fitch (1994), Sider (1999), Crisp (2003), Markosian (2004) and elsewhere. Recall that I earlier claimed that most presentists will hold that singular propositions about Bush didn't exist in the remote past.

[29] Thanks to John Hawthorne for helpful suggestions as to how to state things in this section.

modifiers ('in 1950'; 'now') are used to talk about temporal location.[30] Thus, when I truly say that Socrates doesn't exist now, according to the eternalist I am truly saying that he is not at the present temporal location. The eternalist needs a way of talking about existence atemporally. For her, there is a notion of existence on which what exists doesn't vary over time, since her view is precisely that all past, present and future objects and times are equally real. In the following discussion of eternalism, I shall use the phrases 'exists at t' and 'is temporally located at t' as synonymous. I shall use 'exists' not temporally modified in any way to talk of atemporal existence. Thus, on this usage, the eternalist holds that though Socrates doesn't exist now (isn't temporally located now), he exists (is real).

Second, since according to the eternalist all past, present and future things exist, there is nothing in principle to prevent objects that are temporally distant from each other from standing in relations. To facilitate expressing such cross temporal relations between objects, where a and b are objects and t and t' are times, I'll use the locution *a at t bears R to b at t'*. To be consistent, in the case of a property P, I'll talk of *a at t possessing P*, (where in ordinary English, I might have said that a possesses P at t). I should say that my talk of facts in the present book is also best cashed out in this way. So a fact is an object at a time possessing a property, or an object o at time t bearing R to an object o' at time t', or etc. However, some eternalists may want to hold that a thing o simpliciter (i.e. not at any time) may possess property P or stand in a relation to something else, and I do not wish to rule this out.[31] Thus facts as I understand them often have times as components, though there may be facts without times as components as well.

Returning to the objection, the objector claims that on the present view of propositions, propositions didn't exist two minutes after the Big Bang. The

[30] For this reason, my previous discussion of the principle that a thing must exist at a time to possess a property or stand in a relation at that time was delicate. Since as stated, the principle talks of "existing at a time", the eternalist will understand this to be talk of temporal location and not existence in the intended sense, (i.e. the sense in which we are talking about what is real and not temporal location). My point was that the eternalist will agree that to possess or stand in the properties and relations discussed above (having mass, being five feet from, etc.) one must timelessly exist (and be (at least partly) temporally located at the time of possessing or standing in the property or relation). So the eternalist agrees that a thing must exist to possess and stand in these properties and relations, where 'exist' is not here used to talk of temporal location. And of course the presentist will agree that a thing must exist at a time to possess or stand in the properties and relations in question at a time, where she will take her use of 'exist' (at a time) to be talk of what is real (at that time). It is in this sense that the eternalist and presentist agree that for a thing to possess or stand in the properties and relations in question, it must exist.

[31] David Manley suggested that an eternalist might hold that when x is an ancestor of y, there may be no times t,t' such that x at t is an ancestor of y at t'. On the other hand, an eternalist may think that there are such times t, t' and they are the time intervals that are the temporal extents of x and y. Still, Manley pointed out that if abstract objects that aren't in time possess properties and stand in relations, for such an abstract object o there may be no time t such that o at t possesses P, though o (simpliciter) possesses P. Further, eternalists who endorse temporal parts might hold that they (simpliciter) possess properties. I should add that I also do not want to rule out the possibility of o (simpliciter—not at any time) bearing R to o' at t, and similar such things.

eternalist will agree, but point out that this means only that the facts that according to the present view are propositions are not located at that time.[32] From the claim that propositions didn't exist two minutes after the Big Bang, the objector infers that propositions at that time were neither true nor false (i.e. they at that time didn't possess the property of being true or the property of being false). By the eternalist's lights, this amounts to inferring from the claim that the facts that are propositions aren't temporally located at the time two minutes after the Big Bang, that propositions at that time didn't possess the properties of being true and false.[33] The eternalist will surely balk at this inference. She will point out that in general, a thing o may not be temporally located at t, and yet o at t might possess property P. For example, Socrates now possesses the property of being referred to by 'Socrates', even though Socrates is not located at the present time. Thus, the eternalist will claim, from the fact that a thing is not located at a time t, it just doesn't follow that the thing at t doesn't possess property P.

At first it seems that the eternalist's point is sufficient to dismiss the objection. But a doubt lingers. Though it is true that in general, from the fact that object o is not located at t, assuming eternalism it does not follow that o at t can't possess a property, there are properties P such that for an object o at t to possess P it must be temporally located at t. For example, for Lucy now to possess the property of being in France, Lucy must be temporally located in the present.[34] But then how do we know that truth is not such a property? That is, how do we know that for a proposition at t to be true, it needn't be temporally located at t? If for a proposition at t to be true, it must be temporally located at t, then the objector will be correct in claiming that nothing in the remote past was true, given eternalism.

---

[32] I assume that the eternalist holds that the fact that is o at t possessing P is located at t (of course some facts are located at (even quite large and possibly discontinuous) temporal intervals). So for example, the facts that I claim are propositions are temporally located over a large region, whose boundary in the past is sometime near when language using creatures appeared and whose future boundary is unknown. I also assume that the eternalist holds that all past, present and future facts exist.

[33] On the other hand, if the eternalist holds that a given proposition P (simpliciter) posseses the property of being true or false (i.e. holds that it isn't the case that P at t possesses the property of being true, but rather that P (simpliciter) possesses the property of being true), he will dismiss the objection as confused. For it assumes that a proposition at a time possesses the property of being true.

[34] My way of talking here suggests that I am thinking of the instantiation relation as being temporally indexed (Lucy instantiates-at-t the property of being in France) instead of thinking of properties themselves as temporally indexed (Lucy possesses the property of being-in-France-at-t). But I intend my terminology to be neutral on this and I think the issue I am concerned with is independent of which of the two ways (or other ways) we should think of things. The point is that the eternalist is going to distinguish between properties that one can possess at times when one is not located and those that one cannot. If you talk in terms of instantiating properties at times, this amounts to distinguishing between properties one can instantiate at t without being located (or having parts) at t and properties one can instantiate at t only if one is located at t. If you talk in terms of properties being indexed to times, this amounts to distinguishing between the properties F-at-t, such that one can have F-at-t without being located at t and properties F-at-t that one can have only if one is located at t. In either case, the relevant properties need to be distinguished by the eternalist. Thanks to David Manley for discussion.

I think there is a strong reason for thinking that truth *is* a property that a proposition at a time can possess even while not being temporally located at that time.[35] For what convinces us that a property P is such that an object o at t can possess P even though o is not temporally located at t? Well, presumably it is the fact that it seems true to say that Socrates now is referred to by 'Socrates' that convinces us that being referred to by 'Socrates' is a property that Socrates now can have, even though Socrates is not temporally located now. But now consider the following:

3. Two minutes after the Big Bang, the temperature of the universe was less than two billion degrees Kelvin.

Let's call the proposition 3 expresses *TBB*.[36] It seems true to say that TBB in the remote past was true. But if it seems true to say that TBB in the remote past was true, that should convince us that being true is a property TBB in the remote past can possess even though it is not temporally located in the remote past. The evidence here is exactly the same as it was in the case of Socrates now possessing the property of being referred to by 'Socrates', even though he is not temporally located in the present. In both cases, the claim that a thing at a time can possess a property while not being temporally located at that time is supported by the same sort of intuitive data: it seems true to say that the thing at a time possesses a property, even though the thing isn't located at the time. This response embarrasses the objector from the rear flank, so to speak, since the objector herself insists that *intuitively* things in the remote past were true and false. And surely the sorts of things she had in mind include TBB.

Thus, it does appear that if eternalism is true, propositions like TBB in the remote past were true. Hence, the eternalist's response to the objection is in the end to say that the objector incorrectly inferred that on the present view propositions in the remote past were not true from the fact that on the present view they are not temporally located in the remote past.[37]

In conclusion, then, whether she adopts presentism or eternalism, the advocate of the account of propositions I have been defending has a response to the objection that her view entails the incorrect conclusion that nothing was true in the remote past.

---

[35] I am indebted here to suggestions made by John Hawthorne.

[36] TBB is the proposition expressed by 3 now. What one takes that proposition to be depends in part on one's views about the semantics of tense. I suppress matters about tense here since they are mostly irrelevant to present concerns. These matters are discussed in Chapter 6.

[37] Though I won't address them here, there are two interesting questions about standing in relations and temporal location, one of which is the analogue for relations of the question as to whether an object at a time can possess a property, even though it isn't temporally located at that time, (to which we have given an affirmative answer). First, can it be that a at t bears R to b at t', when a isn't located at t (and perhaps neither is b located at t')? Second, can a at t bear R to b at t', when a is located at t but not t' and and b is located at t' but not t, and t and t' are very far apart temporally? The first is the analogue for relations of the question we addressed for properties. It seems to me the answer to both question is yes. Thanks again to John Hawthorne for discussion.

THIRD OBJECTION: TRUTHS AT DEPRIVED WORLDS

Since on the present view in any circumstance in which there is no public language or language of thought, propositions fail to exist, propositions won't exist according to many possible worlds. And this might be thought to create problems. Consider the possible worlds in which there is no life at all, and so no linguistic expressions with semantic values. Propositions won't exist according to such worlds if what I have just said is correct. And yet surely the proposition that there is no life should be true at these worlds. For the following sentence is true:

4. It is possible that there should have been no life.

It isn't a necessary truth that there is life. And presumably 4 is true in the actual world because the embedded sentence in 4 expresses a proposition that is true at some world w possible relative to the actual world. But on the present view of propositions, the proposition expressed by the embedded sentence in 4 doesn't exist according to w. So how could it be true there?

In discussing presentism, we claimed that a proposition can't be true at a time when it doesn't exist, because generally things can't possess properties at times when they don't exist.[38] We now confront the question of whether a proposition can be true at a *world* according to which it doesn't exist. At first it might seem that given that we have held that things can't possess properties, and so propositions can't be true, at times when they don't exist, to be consistent we ought to hold that propositions can't be true at worlds according to which they don't exist. However, I believe that the cases are importantly different. I think that the proposition expressed by the embedded sentence in 4 *can* be true at worlds according to which it doesn't exist, and that this is true of propositions generally. The intuitive idea is that propositions as I understand them actually exist, exist in this world, and have truth conditions. Further, since I am an actualist as I've already indicated, I hold that possible worlds according to which propositions don't exist also exist in the actual world.[39] Thus, since propositions and such possible worlds exist in the actual world, propositions can stand in the *true at* relation to such worlds in the actual world. This is why propositions "can be true at worlds according to which they don't exist" in one sense of this phrase. On the other hand, if presentism is true and so on my view propositions didn't exist in the remote past *in the actual world*, they couldn't have possessed the

---

[38] Strictly, we said that we should assume that things can't possess properties and stand in relations at times at which they don't exist until we are given a good argument for the denial of this claim that doesn't presuppose presentism. I discuss this further below.

[39] By 'the actual world', one might mean the one concrete world that exists or one might mean the maximal property that the one concrete world has in virtue of which it is in the state it is in. Merely possible worlds exist in the one concrete world and exist according to the maximal property that the concrete world instantiates.

properties of being true or false then in the actual world.[40] Thus the cases of times at which (according to the presentist) propositions didn't exist in the actual world and merely possible worlds, which exist in the actual world, according to which propositions don't exist are importantly different. I'll return to this point below.

The idea I am invoking here, that a proposition can be true at a world according to which it doesn't exist, or at any rate a closely related idea, has been invoked by others, most notably Adams (1981) and Fine (1985). Both Adams and Fine introduced the idea to explain how a proposition, such as the proposition that Socrates doesn't exist, can be true at a world according to which one of its constituents doesn't exist (Socrates) and so the proposition itself doesn't exist.[41] Of course on my view of propositions, the question of how a proposition can be true at a world according to which it doesn't exist is more pressing, since according to lifeless worlds *no* propositions exist. Yet surely 4 above is true.

Now some philosophers, including Williamson (2002) and Crisp (2003), claim not to understand the idea of a proposition being true at a world, where this doesn't require the proposition to exist according to the world. Crisp claims to have no idea of what it means to say that a proposition may be true at a world according to which it doesn't exist. Williamson considers a number of ways of understanding the notion of truth at a world (which he calls *true of a world*), rejects them and concludes that the thought that there is such a notion is an illusion.[42] Because the idea is significant for me given my view of propositions (e.g. in order that 4 can be true), the fact that some claim not to understand the idea or to think it is illusory makes it important for me to explain it.

I'll explain the idea of a proposition being true at a world by sketching how to define it. The definition will have the consequence that the proposition expressed by

5. There is no life.

is true at a world w just in case there is no life in w. The fact that this proposition doesn't exist according to w will prove irrelevant. Further, I'll assume that the semantics of modal operators makes use of the notion of truth at a world that I define. So 4 is true at w iff the proposition expressed by 5 is true at some w' (accessible from w). This will allow the proposition expressed by 4 to be true at the actual world in virtue of the proposition expressed by 5 being true at a lifeless

---

[40] When I talk about propositions being true or false at times here, I am not talking about ersatz times. I thinking of a "real" time being present and considering whether propositions possessed the property of being true when that time was present even though they didn't exist then. I'll talk about truth at ersatz times below.

[41] Adams invokes the idea to explain how the proposition that he doesn't exist, which appears metaphysically possible and so true at some possible world w, can be true at the world w though it doesn't exist there (since Adams doesn't exist there). Similarly, Fine invokes the idea to respond to an argument of Plantinga's that concludes that it is possible that Socrates doesn't exist and the proposition that Socrates doesn't exist exists. I'll consider Plantinga's argument subsequently.

[42] P. 11.

world according to propositions don't exist. In this way, we will both explain 4's truth in the actual world and explain the idea of truth at a world to those who are skeptical about it.

As will be seen, the crucial idea behind the definition of truth at a world is very simple. On any reasonable version of actualism, indeed on any reasonable view of possible worlds, one can read off from a world the extensions of properties at those worlds. This will allow us to define truth at a world for propositions. Since one can read off the extensions of properties even at worlds according to which propositions don't exist, our definition will have the result that propositions are true or false at such worlds. Because actualist views can differ in many ways, some of which will be discussed below, and because the details of the definition of truth at a world will depend on the details of the actualist view one adopts, my discussion here of necessity will be rather general and programmatic. But I believe that my sketch of how to define truth at a world will allow one to see how the details would go given different versions of actualism. It is important to emphasize too that I am *not* here trying to address all problems with actualism. Indeed, the *only* problem I am addressing is that of defining truth at a world in a way acceptable to actualists.

According to actualists who invoke them, possible worlds must be things in the actual world. I think that the two most promising accounts of possible worlds that are acceptable to actualists are: 1) the view that worlds are maximal properties that the world might have had and that exist in the actual word uninstantiated;[43] and 2) the view that worlds are maximally consistent sets of actually existing propositions.[44] As I suggested in Chapter 2, I hold the former view; but, as indicated above, I don't want advocates of the latter to feel left out. So I want to show that whichever of these views of worlds you adopt, truth at a world can be defined.

Whether worlds are sets of propositions or maximal properties, they somehow represent objects as possessing properties and standing in relations. If a world w represents the object o as possessing the property P, we'll say *o is in the extension of P at w*, (otherwise it fails to be in the extension). Obviously, we could similarly characterize an n-tuple of objects being in the extension of an n-place relation at w. It should be clear that my characterizations of something being in the extension of a property or relation at a world do not require propositions to exist according to that world. But given these materials we can define truth at a world so that, as required, for a proposition to be true at a world doesn't require it to exist according to the world. Because our primary concern is with propositions and not the sentences that express them, let's just suppose that we have some language that expresses propositions of the sorts we are about to consider. We shall use ordered n-tuples to represent our propositions, since details about the

---

[43] Robert Stalnaker (2003) and Scott Soames (2005) hold (different) versions of this view, as do I (King 2005).

[44] Robert Adams (1981) holds a version of this view.

real metaphysics and structure of propositions are not relevant here. For what follows, let $o, o_1, \ldots$ be objects; let P and Q be properties; let NOT be the truth function that maps T to F and F to T; let S be a proposition; let POSSIBLY be an operation that takes a proposition and a world to a truth value, where POSSIBLY(S,w)= T iff for some w' accessible to w, S is true at w'; and let SOME be the relation between properties that holds between properties A and B (in that order) just in case some entity that has A has B. If at least one thing is in the extension of both A and B at w, then we'll say that $<A, B>$ *is in the extension of SOME at w* (otherwise it fails to be in the extension).

Then the definition of truth at a world for propositions includes the following clauses:

1. A proposition $<o, P>$ is true at w iff o is in the extension of P at w; otherwise it is false at w.[45]

2. A proposition $<$NOT, $<S>>$ is true at w iff NOT($V_{S,w}$)=T, where $V_{S,w}$ is the truth value of S at w; otherwise it is false at w.

3. A proposition $<<$SOME,P$>$,Q$>$ is true at w iff $<P,Q>$ is in the extension of SOME at w; otherwise it is false at w.[46]

4. A proposition $<$POSSIBLY,$<S>>$ is true at w iff POSSIBLY(S,w)=T.

As promised, nothing in these clauses requires that propositions exist according to a world in order to be true at it. To see this, consider the proposition that no living thing exists (Q is the property of being a living thing and E is the property of existing): $<$NOT, $<<$SOME, Q$>$, E$>>$. Now consider a world w according to which there are no living things. On the present view of propositions, no propositions exist according to w. Whether the world w is a set of propositions or a maximal property, w does not represent any entity as being in the extension of both Q and E. So then $<Q,E>$ is not in the extension of SOME at w. But then by clause 3, $<<$SOME, Q$>$, E$>$ is false at w. Thus, by clause 2, $<$NOT, $<<$SOME, Q$>$, E$>>$ is true at w. Similarly, consider the proposition that Socrates doesn't exist: $<$NOT,$<o$, E$>>$, where o is Socrates, and E is the property of existing. Let's suppose that this proposition fails to exist according to any world according to which Socrates himself fails to exist. Now consider a world w according to which he doesn't exist. Then Socrates is not in the extension of the property of existing at w.[47] Hence by clause 1 above, $<o,E>$ is

---

[45] Propositions like $<o,P>$ are singular propositions. P here could be the property of existing or any other property. I omit a clause for singular propositions containing an n-place relation and n objects, but no difficulties emerge here.

[46] Clauses for quantifiers would have to be more complicated in various ways that are presently irrelevant.

[47] There are at least two ways a world might represent Socrates as not existing. It might do so by not representing him as being in the extension of *any* properties, including the property of existing. Or it might do so by representing him as being in the extension of other properties but not being in the extension of existing. I favor the former. But either way, he won't be in the extension of existing

false at w. So by clause 2 above, <NOT,<o, E>> is true at w. This is so, even though the proposition doesn't exist according to w.[48]

Above I mentioned that how the details of the definition of truth at a world and surrounding notions (i.e. being in the extension of a property at a world) are formulated would depend on the particular version of actualism one adopts. One dimension along which actualists may differ that would affect the details concerns how another world depicts a non-actual individual as existing. My father might have had a brother, though he doesn't have one. So some possible world must represent him as doing so. In principle, there are at least two ways it might do so. First, there might be some thing in the actual world that exists according to another possible world w and is some way there as a result of which w represents my father as having a brother. Perhaps, for example, an individual essence e exists unexemplified in the actual world, but also exists according to another possible world in which it is coexemplified with the property of *being Richard King's brother*.[49] Or perhaps there is a non-concrete object in the actual world (which is not of course my father's brother here) that is concrete in another possible world and is my father's brother there.[50] Let's call these accounts *particularist*, since particular actual things may be certain ways in other possible worlds as a result of which they represent particular things as existing that don't actually exist.[51] A particular actual essence may be unexemplified in the actual world but exemplified elsewhere; or a particular actual non-concrete object may be concrete in another possible world.

A second way a possible world might represent a nonactual individual like a brother of my father as existing is by representing the property of *being Richard King's brother* as being instantiated. On this view, there are no actual particular things that exist according to another possible world and by being some way there represent a non-actual individual as existing there. Further, since we are assuming actualism, there are no merely possible things. Thus, the only way to represent a non-actual individual as existing is to do so by representing certain properties as instantiated. Let's call these accounts *generalist*, since they do not represent non-actual individuals as existing according to other possible worlds by having particular actual things be certain ways there.

Clearly the details of how to define truth at a world will differ depending on whether one is a generalist or a particularist (as well as what kind of particularist

---

at such a world. I assume that if worlds are sets of propositions, a world according to which Socrates doesn't exist will not contain the proposition that Socrates doesn't exist.

[48] Given plausible assumptions, this definition of truth at a world (if filled out) would have the result that the proposition that Socrates doesn't exist could be true at a world, but the proposition that something doesn't exist would not be. In discussing his notion of truth at a world, Adams (1981) notes that his characterization has this consequence. There is nothing strange about this, since quantification is over objects that exist according to a world. I discuss this further below.

[49] Plantinga (1974 and 1976) defends a view of this sort.

[50] Linsky and Zalta (1994, 1996) defend a view of this sort, as does Williamson (2002).

[51] This term might be misleading, since essences are just properties on many views. But e.g. on an account like Plantinga's they are properties that only one thing can have. I'll ignore this possible misleadingness in what follows.

one is); but the above sketch provides an outline for a detailed definition given either view. Thus, we have shown how to characterize truth at a world in such a way that a proposition can be true at a world according to which it doesn't exist. Our having shown how to do this given a number of different versions of actualism ought to silence critics who claim not to understand the notion of truth at a world or who claim that the notion has never been or can't be explained. Further, we can maintain that the proposition that there is no life is true at lifeless worlds according to which it doesn't exist if the present account of propositions is correct. And so those who endorse the present view of propositions can hold that 4 above, repeated here, is true:

4. It is possible that there should have been no life.

in virtue of the fact that the proposition expressed by the embedded sentence is true at some worlds.

We can now make sense of the contrast mentioned earlier: propositions may be true at worlds according to which they don't exist, but cannot be true in the remote past when they didn't exist, assuming the truth of presentism. In saying that propositions were not true in the remote past if presentism is correct, I mean the following. There is the property of being true, which I will call *TRUE*, and propositions have this property at various worlds and times. For example, consider the time two minutes after the Big Bang. Propositions did not exist then if presentism is correct. But then, I claimed, we should hold that they did not possess any properties at that time (pending an argument that things can possess properties at times when they don't exist). Hence they did not possess TRUE then. By contrast, propositions, which exist now in the actual world, can stand in the *true at* relation in the actual world to possible worlds. Their doing so does not require them to possess properties or stand in relations at times or worlds according to which they don't exist. Thus, though propositions now may stand in the *true at* relation in the actual world to worlds according to which they don't exist (which also exist in the actual world), propositions cannot possess TRUE at times when they don't exist.

Of course, some presentists think that just as an actualist can make use of ersatz merely possible worlds (however construed) that exist in the actual world, so he can make use of ersatz past and future times that exist in the present (in the actual world). The idea then suggests itself of defining a *true at* relation for times on analogy with the *true at* relation to worlds, and holding that propositions in the present can be *true at* (ersatz) times according to which they don't exist. Since propositions and ersatz times both exist in the present, this doesn't require propositions to have properties or stand in relations at times when they don't exist. It will then turn out that TBB, the proposition expressed by 3:

3. Two minutes after the Big Bang, the temperature of the universe was less than two billion degrees Kelvin.

is true at the ersatz time two minutes after the Big Bang. I have no objection to defining such a *true at* relation to ersatz times, but it is important to see what it comes to. It would simply amount to saying that at the present time (the only "concrete" time that exists if presentism is true) TBB stands in the *true at* relation to the (ersatz) time two minutes after the Big Bang. It would still of course be true that when two minutes after the Big Bang was present, there were no propositions and nothing possessed the property TRUE on the present view of propositions if presentism is correct. So invoking ersatz times is not a way to avoid this consequence; luckily, as I have argued, the presentist has no need to avoid it.[52]

Further, as will be seen in Chapter 6, I don't think propositions change truth value over time. So any proposition true at one time is true at any other. Thus the notion is of much less interest than the relation of *true at* to worlds. But of course for presentists who think tenses and other temporal expressions should be treated as standard tense operators (I explain why I do not in Chapter 6) that shift ersatz times, the imagined definition of a *true at* relation to times would be more interesting. In the case of 3, for example, she would hold that 'Two minutes after the Big Bang' (together perhaps with the past tense on the sentence it embeds) is a tense operator in 3. Thus she would say that 3 is true at the present time iff the proposition that the temperature of the universe is less than two billion degrees Kelvin is true at the (ersatz) time two minutes after the Big Bang.

FURTHER ISSUES INVOLVING TRUE AND TRUE AT

As should now be clear, it is important to distinguish the claim that propositions may stand in the *true at* relation to worlds (or times) according to which they don't exist from the claim that propositions may possess TRUE at worlds (or times) according to which they don't exist.[53] We have shown that the former is unobjectionable by showing how to define truth at a world (or time) for propositions in such a way that they can be true at worlds (or times) according to which they don't exist. Our leading idea was that since propositions and possible worlds both exist in the actual world, a proposition and a world w according to which it doesn't exist may nonetheless stand in the *true at* relation *in the actual*

---

[52] I want to stress that I do not take the considerations just adduced to count *against* presentists who appeal to ersatz times. The crucial point is that, while the presentist who adopts my view of propositions cannot avoid the consequence that nothing possessed the property of being true (viz., TRUE) two minutes after the Big Bang, it would be a mistake to think that she has any need to. Indeed, as we'll see, I hold something analogous for worlds: viz. that while the proposition that there is no life stands in the *true at* relation to the (ersatz) world in which there is no life, it's still the case that in that world there are no propositions and nothing possesses the property TRUE.

[53] When I talk about possessing TRUE (or any other property) or existing *at* or *in* a world, I simply mean the thing possesses the property or exists according to the world. Though I generally try to speak of things possessing properties *according to worlds*, I use 'at' (and sometimes 'in') here and other places partly to avoid locutions such as 'propositions may possess TRUE according to worlds (or times) according to which they don't exist'. The distinction that one must be careful to observe is between a proposition being *true at a world* in the sense in which I have defined it above, and possessing *TRUE at, or according to, a world*. As we'll see, I claim a proposition can be true at a world and not possess TRUE there (if it fails to exist there).

world. In this case then, the proposition doesn't possess a property or stand in a relation at a world according to which it doesn't exist. On the other hand, the claim that propositions can possess TRUE at worlds according to which they don't exist obviously *does* require a proposition to possess a property at a world according to which it doesn't exist.[54] It therefore contradicts the claim that things don't possess any properties at worlds according to which they don't exist. This latter claim is often called *serious actualism*.

Should we accept the view that propositions cannot be in the extension of TRUE at worlds according to which they don't exist? Let's look at the question from the standpoint of the presentist and the eternalist in turn.

First, the presentist. We claim the presentist should deny that propositions can possess TRUE in the actual world at times when they don't exist, (recall that we have no problem with presentists holding that propositions are (now) *true at* past eratsz times according to which they didn't exist). Suppose we now say that propositions *can* possess TRUE at worlds according to which they don't exist. According to such worlds, propositions fail to exist at *all* times. But this means that according to lifeless worlds, propositions are in the extension of TRUE at times when they don't exist. I can see no reason for claiming that while in the actual world, propositions *can't* be in the extension of TRUE at times when they don't exist, according to lifeless worlds they *can* be in the extension of TRUE at times when they don't exist.

Further, the bizarreness of claiming that propositions can't be in the extension of TRUE in the actual world at times when they don't exist but that they can be in the extension of TRUE at lifeless worlds can be brought out by considering a lifeless world w according to which propositions never exist (say, because life never does) and a merely possible world w' exactly like @ (the actual world), except that a far off galaxy has one less electron in it than it does in @.[55] We assume that propositions are in the extension of TRUE in w but not in @ at times when they didn't exist. Were propositions in the extension of TRUE prior to the existence of life according to w'? If not, that really seems strange: that propositions failed to exist prior to life existing at w' keeps them out of the extension of TRUE at w' at those times, but that propositions *never* exist according to w doesn't keep them out of the extension of TRUE there. Too bad for w' that life sprang up there! But the claim that propositions *were* in the extension of TRUE according to w' prior to life existing there saddles us with problems as well. First, why should propositions be in the extension of TRUE according to w' prior to life existing there but fail to be in the extension of TRUE according to @ prior to life existing there? These worlds are exactly the same except for that one little electron! Second, w' is supposed to be a way things might have been. This suggests that a way things might have been is that propositions were in the extension of TRUE

---

[54] I've assumed here that TRUE really is a property, even if it is an unusual or special one.

[55] Or suppose that w' is as much like @ as it can be, given this difference.

before they existed. It just happens that the actual world isn't like that. It seems to me that if the actual world isn't like that, it couldn't have been otherwise. For these reasons, I think the presentist should accept the view that propositions cannot possess TRUE at worlds according to which they don't exist.

What now of the eternalist? I think it is less clear that she should accept the view that propositions cannot be in the extension of TRUE at worlds according to which they don't exist. Nonetheless, I think she should accept it. For it would be odd to hold without further explanation that propositions can be in the extension of TRUE at worlds according to which they don't exist, if there are not other cases of things possessing properties at worlds according to which they don't exist. But there don't seem to be philosophically uncontentious other cases of things possessing properties at worlds according to which they don't exist. If there aren't philosophically uncontentious clear other cases of things possessing properties at worlds according to which they don't exist, we are owed an explanation as to why propositions can be in the extension of the property TRUE at worlds according to which they don't exist. But I can't see what that explanation would be. Without such an explanation in hand, we should not endorse the latter claim. Further, it seems to me that the natural way for a world to represent something as not existing is to represent it as not having any properties, as opposed to merely representing it as not having the property of existing. This, of course, means that worlds according to which propositions don't exist shouldn't represent them as possessing TRUE there.

So it appears that both presentists and eternalists should reject the claim that propositions can be in the extension of TRUE at worlds according to which they don't exist.

Now that we have discussed the *true at* relation to worlds and the property TRUE, it is worth commenting on a number of other issues involving them.[56] First, I believe there are a number of arguments in the literature that seem persuasive because of a tendency to read 'true' in them as sometimes expressing the *true at* relation and sometimes expressing the property TRUE. If there really are two notions here not clearly distinguished in ordinary discourse, it wouldn't be surprising that even philosophers sometimes implicitly take 'true' as expressing the one notion and sometimes the other. Consider the following version of an argument offered by Plantinga against the view he calls *existentialism*: the view 'that singular propositions are ontologically dependent upon the objects they are about.'[57] The argument purports to show that it is possible for Socrates not to exist while the proposition that Socrates doesn't exist exists.[58]

---

[56] My thinking about *true at* and TRUE owes much to a correspondence with Matthew McGrath.

[57] Plantinga (1983: 6). Strictly, Plantinga calls this an existentialist thesis. Existentialism is the conjunction of this claim and the claim that properties like *being wiser than Nero* ("quidditative properties") are 'ontologically dependent on the individuals they involve' (p. 3).

[58] This version of the argument, slightly different from Plantinga's own, is formulated by Fine (1985).

1. Possibly Socrates does not exist.

2. Necessarily, if Socrates does not exist, then the proposition that Socrates does not exist is true.

3. Necessarily, if the proposition that Socrates does not exist is true, then the proposition that Socrates does not exist exists.

4. ∴ It is possible that Socrates does not exist and the proposition that Socrates does not exist exists.

2 and 3 are the crucial premises. I think they can be read in two different ways, depending on whether one takes 'true' in them to be talking about the *true at* relation or the property TRUE.[59] Read in the former way, 2 and 3 can be rendered as follows:

2TA. For any world w, if Socrates does not exist according to w, then the proposition that Socrates does not exist is true at w.

3TA. For any world w, if the proposition that Socrates does not exist is true at w, then the proposition that Socrates does not exist exists according to w.

2TA is perfectly true. So when premise 2 is understood in this way it is correct. However, given our characterization of *truth at*, 3TA fails. The proposition that Socrates does not exist is true at worlds according to which it fails to exist.[60] So when 3 is understood as 3TA, it is false.

[59] I am not saying the sentences are literally ambiguous. I am not sure if they are or not. I am claiming that people can take them in two different ways. This should be borne in mind in considering my discussion of 2TA, 3TA, 2T, 3T and my comments in notes 60–3. I am talking about ways people can interpret premises 2 and 3, not what they semantically express. Hence, my talk of "readings" of 2 and 3 should not be taken to be talk about interpretations they semantically express. I do think that the propositions they semantically express are probably among the possible interpretations I discuss. But I am agnostic as to which they do semantically express, except that I do think the modal operators (semantically) involve the notion of *truth at*. See next note and the discussion of sentence 4 above.

[60] It might be claimed that the relevant readings of 2 and 3 would be better represented as follows instead of as 2TA and 3TA:

2TA'. For any world w, the following proposition is true at w: the proposition that if Socrates does not exist, then the proposition that Socrates doesn't exist is true at w.

3TA'. For any world w, the following proposition is true at w: the proposition that if the proposition that Socrates doesn't exist is true at w, then the proposition that Socrates doesn't exist exists.

For recall that we are taking the modal operators to invoke *truth at*. Hence, 'Necessarily Q' is true at w iff the proposition expressed by 'Q' is *true at* every world w'. So the initial part of 2TA' and 3TA' ('For any world w, the following proposition is true at w') represents the significance of 'Necessarily' in 2 and 3. If we then interpret 'true' in 2 as expressing *truth at*, the proposition described in 2TA' seems to be what is expressed by the sentence embedded under 'Necessarily' in 2 (note that 2TA' tells us to consider different propositions for different choices of worlds in evaluating the quantifier over worlds). Similar remarks apply to 3 and 3TA'. Given what seem to me plausible assumptions, 3TA', like 3TA, is false. For consider a world w. Now consider the proposition 3TA' tells us is true at w. It is the proposition that if the proposition that Socrates doesn't exist is true at w, then the proposition that Socrates doesn't exist exists. We can represent this proposition as follows:

i. COND<<<NOT,<s,E>>,t_w >, <<NOT,<s,E>>,E>>

However, the premises could be taken differently. We could understand them as follows:

2T. For any world w, if Socrates does not exist according to w, then the proposition that Socrates does not exist is in the extension of the property TRUE according to w.

3T. For any world w, if the proposition that Socrates does not exist is in the extension of the property TRUE according to w, then the proposition that Socrates does not exist exists according to w.

3T is vacuously true, (though perhaps some would want to assign it a different status on the basis of the following considerations; but that status wouldn't be being true). For any world w, the proposition that Socrates doesn't exist fails to be in the extension of the property TRUE according to w. For if Socrates doesn't exist according to w, then the proposition that he doesn't exist itself doesn't exist according to w and so is not in the extension of TRUE there. And if Socrates does exist according to w, then the proposition that he does exist is in the extension of TRUE there, and so the proposition that he doesn't exist won't be. So if premise 3 is understood as 3T, it is (at most) vacuously true. However, if what we have said is correct, 2T is false. At worlds according to which Socrates does not exist, the proposition that Socrates does not exist also does not exist. But then it is not in the extension of TRUE at such worlds, and so 2T is false. Hence, so understood premise 2 is false.[61]

Thus, my diagnosis of what is wrong with the argument and why it can seem persuasive is that there is no way to consistently interpret 'true' in 2 and 3 so

---

This is the conditional proposition (COND is the truth function for the conditional) whose antecedent is the proposition that the proposition that Socrates doesn't exist is true at w, $<<\text{NOT},<s,E>>,t_w>$, and whose consequent is the proposition that the proposition that Socrates doesn't exist exists: $<<\text{NOT},<s,E>>,E>$. Suppose the antecedent of the conditional proposition is true at w. We haven't discussed the conditions under which a proposition to the effect that another proposition is true at w is itself true at w. But if we are going to evaluate such propositions at non-actual worlds (and if we don't, 2TA' and 3TA' are nonsense) at all it seems reasonable to say this (where P is a proposition and $<P,t_w>$ is the proposition that P is true at w):

ii. For any w, w': $<P,t_w>$ is true at w' iff P is true at w.

This basically tells us that to evaluate $<P,t_w>$ at a world w', we don't look at w' at all and instead check to see about P at w. This would allow, as it should, that $<P,t_w>$ could be true at w' (including the case where w=w') even though P doesn't exist there. After all, if P can be true at w without existing there, the proposition that P is true at w should also be capable of being true at worlds where P doesn't exist. So the supposition that the antecedent of i, $<<\text{NOT},<s,E>>,t_w>$, is true at w in conjunction with ii gives us that $<\text{NOT},<s,E>>$ is true at w. But then Socrates doesn't exist at w. So the proposition that Socrates doesn't exist itself doesn't exist at w. But then the proposition that the proposition that Socrates doesn't exist exists, $<<\text{NOT},<s,E>>,E>$, is not true at w. But that means the consequent of the proposition i is false at w. Hence 3TA' is false. So claiming that the relevant readings of 2 and 3 are better represented by 2TA' and 3TA' (instead of 2TA and 3TA) makes no difference. 3 is still false on the relevant reading. Thanks to David Manley for discussion.

[61] Again here, for the reasons given in the previous note, it might be claimed that the relevant readings of 2 and 3 should be represented as follows instead of as 2T and 3T:

that both premises are true. If we understand the premises as in 2TA and 3TA, premise 2 is true and premise 3 is false. If we understand the premises as in 2T and 3T, premise 2 is false and premise 3 is true. The argument can seem good, because we can read premise 2 as 2TA and premise 3 as 3T. But though this makes both premises true, the argument isn't valid with the premises so understood [62,63]

I would offer a similar criticism of the following argument from Williamson (2002):

1. Necessarily, if I do not exist then the proposition that I do not exist is true.

2. Necessarily, if the proposition that I do not exist is true then the proposition that I do not exist exists.

2T'. For any world w, the following proposition is true at w: the proposition that if Socrates does not exist, then the proposition that Socrates does not exist possesses the property TRUE.

3T'. For any world w, the following proposition is true at w: the proposition that if the proposition that Socrates doesn't exist possesses the property TRUE, then the proposition that Socrates doesn't exist exists.

However, again this doesn't help. 2T', like 2T, is false. Consider a world w in which Socrates doesn't exist. 2T' tells us that the following proposition is true at w (and all worlds): the proposition that if Socrates does not exist, then the proposition that Socrates does not exist possesses the property TRUE. We can represent this conditional proposition as follows:

i. COND<<NOT,<s,E>>, <<NOT,<s,E>>,TRUE>>

where <<NOT,<s,E>>,TRUE> is the proposition that the proposition that Socrates does not exist possesses the property TRUE. Now since Socrates doesn't exist in w, the antecedent of i is true at w. However, the proposition that Socrates doesn't exist itself doesn't exist at w. Hence in w, it can't possess the property TRUE. But then the consequent of i is false at w. Hence i is false at w and 2T' is false.

[62] Recall that I am understanding modal operators in English in such a way that they invoke *truth at* (see notes 59 and 60). This is to account for how sentence 4 above can be true. *If* one thought that the modal operators have another reading on which they invoke the property TRUE, so that 'Necessarily P' is in the extension of TRUE at w iff the proposition expressed by 'P' is in the extension of TRUE at w' for all (accessible) w', then 2 and 3 each would have two additional readings. For we would have a choice as to whether to read the modal operators as invoking the property TRUE or *truth at*, and we would have a choice as to whether to read 'true' in 2 and 3 as talking about the property TRUE or *truth at*. I ignore these additional "readings" because I don't think English modal operators have readings on which they invoke the property TRUE. But in any case, taking the modal operators to invoke the property TRUE would make premise 1 of Plantinga's argument false, because that premise would then require for its truth that the proposition that Socrates doesn't exist is in the extension of TRUE at some other world w. But as we've seen it can't be, because it doesn't exist at any world in which Socrates doesn't exist, and it isn't in the extension of TRUE at any world where he does exist. Moreover, any uniform interpretation of the argument (i.e. an interpretation on which the modal operators and 'true' in 2 and 3 are interpreted the same way) results in at least one of 2 and 3 (so read) being false. But I stick with 2TA and 3TA and 2T and 3T in the body of the text because I believe they are the interpretations that are actually responsible for the apparent validity of Plantinga's argument. Similar remarks to those in this note and notes 59–61 apply to 1TA and 2TA, and 1T and 2T discussed below in conjunction with Williamson's argument, except that Williamson himself makes clear that he interprets his premises (roughly) as my 1T and 2T below (see note 64). These remarks also apply to the discussion of NL, NLTA, and NLT below.

[63] Fine (1985) makes a similar objection to Plantinga's argument (pp. 163, and 170–1).

3. Necessarily, if the proposition that I do not exist exists then I exist.

4. ∴ Necessarily, if I do not exist then I exist.

5. ∴ Necessarily, I exist.

Here the crucial premises are 1 and 2, each of which again can be understood in two ways. First they can be understood as follows:

1TA. For any world w, if I do not exist according to w, then the proposition that I do not exist is true at w.

2TA. For any world w, if the proposition that I do not exist is true at w, then the proposition that I do not exist exists according to w.

As should be clear from the discussion of Plantinga's argument, though 1TA is true, 2TA is false. So when the premises are understood in this way, premise 2 is false. The second way the premises can be understood is as follows:

1T. For any world w, if I do not exist according to w then the proposition that I do not exist is in the extension of the property TRUE according to w.

2T. For any world w, if the proposition that I do not exist is in the extension of the property TRUE according to w, then the proposition that I do not exist exists according to w.

2T is again presumably vacuously true, since the proposition that I do not exist is not in the extension of the property TRUE according to any world. However, 1T is false. According to any world w where I don't exist, the proposition that I don't exist fails to exist in w and so is not in the extension of TRUE there. Thus, when the premises are understood in this way, premise 1 is false. Again, the claim is that there is no way of understanding 'true' in 1 and 2 on which both premises are true and the argument is valid. I should add that Williamson essentially stipulates that premise 2 is not to be understood as 2TA, but along the lines of 2T.[64] But then for the argument to be valid, 1 would have to be understood as the false 1T.[65]

---

[64] See p. 7. In my terminology, Williamson understands 2 to mean: for any world w, if the proposition that I do not exist would have possessed the property TRUE had w obtained, then the proposition that I do not exist would have existed had w obtained. But again, 1 read in the corresponding way would be: for any world w, if I would not have existed had w obtained, then the proposition that I do not exist would have possessed the property TRUE had w obtained. But this is false. Williamson considers the sort of objection to his argument I am raising. He imagines an opponent claiming that his premise 1 must be understood as 1TA, with the result that the argument would fail (since he stipulates 2 must be understood as 2T). His primary reason for dismissing such an opponent is his claim that the idea that there is a notion of (my) *true at* is an illusion (see p. 11—he uses the phrase 'true of' to mean what I mean by 'true at'). This is why it was important for me to sketch how to define a notion of *truth at worlds* for propositions on which they can be true at worlds where they don't exist. As a result we can see it is no illusion that there is such a notion. But then Williamson's response to the sort of objection I am making cannot be sustained.

[65] In doing the final revisions for the present book, I came across an unpublished manuscript online in which Robert Stalnaker makes essentially the same criticisms as I do of the above arguments of Plantinga and Williamson. Stalnaker (2006) is the most recent version of this paper.

A second point regarding TRUE and *true at*, very much related to the points just addressed, concerns claims of the form:

(NP) Necessarily, the proposition that p is true iff p.

One might think that every instance of NP is true. Now consider the following instance of NP:

(NL) Necessarily, the proposition that no living thing exists is true iff no living thing exists.

If, as I've suggested, 'true' can be sometimes used to talk about TRUE and sometimes used to talk about *true at*, NL (along with all instances of NP) has two different readings that can be represented as follows:[66]

(NLTA) For any world w, the proposition that no living thing exists is true at w iff according to w, no living thing exists.

(NLT) For any world w, the proposition that no living thing exists possesses TRUE according to w iff according to w, no living thing exists.

It should by now be clear that NLTA is true but NLT is false. Consider an arbitrary world w. Then NLTA entails that the following biconditional is true:

(NLTA') the proposition that no living thing exists is true at w iff according to w, no living thing exists.

If w contains life, both sides of NLTA' are false. If w is lifeless, both sides are true. Either way, NLTA' is true. So NLTA is true. By contrast, considering an arbitrary lifeless world w, NLT entails that the following is true:

(NLT') the proposition that no living thing exists possesses TRUE according to w iff according to w, no living thing exists.

The right side of NLT' is true, since w is lifeless. But that means no propositions exist according to w. But then no proposition possesses TRUE according to w. So the left side of NLT' is false. So NLT is false.[67] Thus, the present view predicts that NL has a reading on which it is true and a reading on which it is false. This seems to me exactly the right result. For there is some inclination to think that every instance of NP, including NL, is true. This inclination can be explained by the fact that all instances of NP, including NL, have true readings.

---

[66] Recall that I am understanding the modal operators as invoking *true at*. See also notes 59–62.

[67] Hoffmann (2003) notes the tension between the claim that every proposition that is singular with respect to an object o implies that o exists (EI) and the claim that some propositions are true with respect to worlds where they don't exist (TE). Suppose TE is true. If p is a proposition that is true with respect to a world w where it doesn't exist, then T(p), the singular proposition with respect to p that predicates truth of p, is true at w. But then the singular proposition T(p) that is singular with respect to p doesn't imply p exists. So EI is false. Hoffman resolves this tension by holding that p can be true at a world where T(p) is false. This is close to and in the spirit of the present view, on which a proposition can be true at a world w where it doesn't exist, and so is not in the extension of TRUE at w.

These correspond to things like NLTA. But then when one begins to reflect on NL in conjunction with the claim that propositions don't exist according to lifeless worlds, one can come to be convinced that some instances of NP, e.g. NL, must be false. For according to lifeless worlds, no living thing exists but no propositions exist either. So how could they be true there? In thinking this way, one is taking NL as NLT.

A third point on the relation between *true at* and TRUE can be illustrated by considering the view that propositions are maximal properties. Consider a possible world w, a maximal property the world might have had, according to which there is no life. Then the proposition that there is no life is true at w. Now had w been instantiated, would that proposition have been in the extension of TRUE? No, because had w been instantiated no propositions would exist, and hence nothing would have been in the extension of TRUE.[68]

A fourth issue involving TRUE and *true at* can be addressed by first considering a world according to which Socrates doesn't exist.[69] The proposition that Socrates doesn't exist will be true at that world, since Socrates will not be in the extension of the property of existing according to that world. But the proposition that something doesn't exist will not be true at that world, because there is nothing in the extension of the property of existing according to that world that fails to exist there.[70] So here we have a case where a proposition with an individual as a constituent is true at a world w (the proposition that Socrates doesn't exist), but the proposition that is a result of "existential generalizing" on that individual (the proposition that something is such that it doesn't exist) is not true at w.[71]

Another instance of this phenomenon is worth noting.[72] Consider a world w according to which there is no life and so propositions don't exist. Let S be the proposition that snow is white. Now consider the singular proposition that S is true. As should be clear, this proposition, <S, TRUE>, is not true at w, since propositions don't exist according to w and so can't be in the extension of TRUE there. Nonetheless the proposition that it is possible that S is true, namely <POSSIBLY,<S,TRUE>>, *will* be true at w, given our treatment of POSSIBLY above. For there is a world w' (accessible from w), such that <S, TRUE> is true at w'. And that makes <POSSIBLY,<S,TRUE>> true at w. Now if we suppose that our quantification ranges over individuals and propositions, and that individuals *and* propositions are in the extension of the property of existing

---

[68] See note 64.

[69] Of course, on the view of some, e.g. Williamson (2002) discussed above, there are no such worlds.

[70] I assume here that the quantifier 'something', or its propositional contribution, ranges over only individuals that exist at the world where it is being evaluated.

[71] More generally, a negated singular proposition such as it is not the case that o is P may be true at a world w, where the proposition that something is such that it is not the case that it is P is false at w. Similarly, as I am about to discuss, the proposition it is possible that o is P may be true at w, where the proposition that something is such that it is possible that it is P is false at w.

[72] Thanks to John Hawthorne for raising the issue I am about to discuss.

at worlds according to which they exist, we get the following result. While the proposition that it is possible that S is true is itself true at w, the proposition that there is *something* that is possibly true is not true at w. For there is nothing in the extension of the property of existing at w that is such that it is possible that it is true. So as in the above case, we have a "singular proposition" that is true at w (<POSSIBLY,<S,TRUE>>, which is singular with respect to S), where the proposition that is the result of existentially generalizing on the constituent with respect to which it is singular is not true at w (the proposition that something is such that it is possible that it is true). Again, this isn't really surprising or strange.

FOURTH OBJECTION: FINENESS OF GRAIN

On the present view, the structure of a proposition is identical to the structure of a sentence (at LF) expressing it.[73] This means that the present view will individuate propositions very finely. Sentences with different syntactic structures at LF ipso facto express different propositions. In the last chapter I noted that as a result, the present account gives all the fineness of grain a structured proposition theorist could want. But now the worry arises that the view individuates propositions *too* finely. I think there are actually two different objections here, and they need to be distinguished. The first is that the present view individuates the propositions expressed by sentences in a single language too finely. The second is that it individuates propositions expressed by sentences of different languages too finely. Let's consider each of these worries in turn.[74]

On the present view, the sentences 'Laura is happy and Scott is sad' and 'Scott is sad and Laura is happy' express different propositions; similarly for '1 = 2' and '2 = 1'. In both cases, the propositions expressed by the sentence pairs will have different constituents occurring at corresponding positions (terminal nodes) in the propositions. One might think that any account that has this consequence individuates propositions too finely.[75] But as discussed in the Introduction, there is good reason to think that propositions *should* be finely individuated. Why think the present view goes too far? I suspect that the idea behind the objection concerns the behavior of expressions that embed sentences, where the truth value of the resulting complex sentence is not a function of the truth value of the embedded sentence. Such expressions include 'John believes'; 'Laura deduced'; 'Necessarily'; 'It ought to be the case'; 'It is a truth of logic', etc.. It might be thought that for any such expression O, English sentence p and circumstance e,

---

[73] As we saw in Chapter 2 in discussing 4b' and 4c, this has to be slightly qualified. But the qualification is irrelevant here.

[74] The material in the next few pages is drawn from King (1996) and is used with kind permission of *The Journal of Philosophical Logic* and Springer Science and Business Media.

[75] Mark Richard (1990) considers this objection to the view he defends. My discussion owes much to Richard's.

whether Op is true or false in e depends only on e and the proposition p expresses, (and not on e.g. the character, in Kaplan's sense, of any expression in p).[76] Let us call any expression of this sort, whether simple or complex, a *propositional connective*. For any propositional connective O, if Op and Oq have different truth values in some circumstance, p and q must express different propositions. But one might go further and hold that two sentences p and q express distinct propositions if *and only if* for some propositional connective O, Op, and Oq differ in truth value in some circumstance. Let us call this principle *P*.[77] P, I believe, is the principle underlying the objection that the present theory cuts propositions too finely. For it might be claimed that the present view entails that for some sentences p and q and all propositional connectives O, Op, and Oq have the same truth value in all circumstances and yet p and q express distinct propositions. This claim runs afoul of P.

Before explaining why there is reason to doubt P, I want to note that the propositional connectives of English appear to cut quite finely, and so it is not clear that the present account of propositions is inconsistent with P. It is not easy to find two sentences that the present view claims express distinct propositions and are such that when embedded relative to any English propositional connective, the resulting complex sentences have the same truth values in all circumstances.[78] As Cresswell (1985) and Richard (1990) have noted, even 'A and B' and 'B and A' seem to result in sentences that can take different truth values in some circumstance when embedded relative to 'John deduced', which seems to be a propositional connective. So even if we accept P, it won't be a simple matter to show that the present view contradicts it.

In any case, as I suggested above, there are reasons for thinking that P is false. Suppose that it turns out that (e.g.) '1 = 2' and '2 = 1', when embedded relative to any propositional connective, result in sentences that have the same truth values in all circumstances. P says that they express the same proposition. But there are reasons for holding that they don't. Assume that '=' expresses a relation

---

[76] Actually, for the purposes of the present discussion, I am supposing that p (and later q) doesn't contain contextually sensitive expressions. Allowing p and q to contain e.g. indexicals would require a slight complication in various formulations, including the statement below of the principle I call P.

[77] P is to be used in determining when two sentences express the same proposition. Thus the quantifier on the right side of P must range over only a restricted set of propositional connectives. For example, it should not range over connectives like 'The proposition that___is identical to the proposition that 1 = 2.' For to decide whether sentences such as 'The proposition that 2 = 1 is identical to the proposition that 1 = 2' are true, one must decide whether two sentences express the same proposition. Thus one would have to determine whether two sentences express the same proposition prior to applying P and so P could play no role in that determination. We shall henceforth understand P as excluding connectives such as the one just discussed. Similarly, subsequent talk about all propositional connectives should be understood as excluding such connectives.

[78] One of the difficulties with testing this claim is that it requires one to isolate the class of propositional connectives and to know the syntactic representations at the level of LF of all sentences.

and that '1' and '2' are names of objects. Now we know that for other expressions that express relations and those very same names, switching the order of the names results in a different proposition expressed. '2 > 1' and '1 > 2' express different propositions. It is quite reasonable to suppose that the propositions expressed by '2>1' and '1>2' have the same constituents (e.g. two objects and a relation) and differ in the way in which these constituents are put together. Thus '2>1' and '1>2' suggest that in a sentence consisting of two names flanking a relation sign, the different possible orders of the names encodes some difference in the way in which the entities named and the relation expressed combine to form a proposition. And this gives us reason to think that '1 = 2' and '2 = 1' express different propositions in virtue of having *their* constituents differently combined. The "fact", if it is one, that '1 = 2' and '2 = 1' when combined with any propositional operator yield complex sentences that never diverge in truth value at any circumstance is due to special properties of the relation involved (e.g. symmetry).

Similar considerations suggest that 'A and B' and 'B and A' express different propositions. Clearly 'A if B' and 'B if A' express different propositions. But these two sentences express propositions that contain the same constituents (two propositions and a truth function). Hence it seems that they differ in the order in which the constituents occur. But then we have reason to believe that 'A and B' and 'B and A' express distinct propositions that differ in terms of the order in which their constituents occur.

Hence we ought to amend P as follows: two sentences p and q express different propositions if and only if for some propositional connective O, Op, and Oq differ in truth value in some circumstance or for some sentences r and t that are syntactically similar in the same way to p and q (respectively), Or and Ot differ in truth value in some circumstance, (I don't make the notion of *syntactic similarity in the same way* precise; the idea is that r and t result from performing the same substitutions in p and q (respectively)).

With P thus weakened, it is not at all clear that it conflicts with the present account of propositions. Recall that it isn't even clear whether P conflicts with our account. However, it seems to me that we ought not to believe even the weakened version of P. For consider the set of propositional connectives. We can think of the propositions expressed by sentences containing a connective in this set as consisting of a proposition (expressed by the embedded sentence) and a property of propositions (expressed by the connective). This "complex proposition" is true at a circumstance iff the constituent proposition possesses the property in question at the circumstance. From this perspective, the claim that two sentences express the same proposition if the results of embedding them with respect to all propositional connectives have the same truth values in all circumstances (and similarly for all syntactically similar pairs), essentially amounts to the claim that propositions that possess all properties of propositions expressed by English (or natural language) propositional connectives in common at all circumstances of evaluation (and similarly for all syntactically similar pairs) are identical, (recall the restriction mentioned in note 77—this means we are not including properties such as the property of *being identical with the proposition that r*). But why believe this? First, even if two propositions possessed *all* properties in common at all circumstances of evaluation, the claim that they therefore must be identical is controversial (again, excluding properties like *being identical to r*, and the like). But more importantly, there is no reason to believe that every property of propositions is expressed by some English (or natural language) propositional connective. Indeed, this is very likely to be false. So even if sentences (and all syntactically similar pairs) behave identically with regard to all propositional connectives of English, this shows only that they (and the similar pairs) express propositions that possess a lot of properties in common at circumstances of evaluation. And that is not enough to show that they are identical. To summarize, then, I find no convincing reason thus far for thinking that the present account of propositions individuates them too finely.

But now it might be objected that the present view individuates propositions too finely *across* languages. Consider the following three claims, in order of increasing logical strength, concerning the expressibility of propositions in different languages:

(A) At least some proposition(s) can be expressed in different natural languages.

(B) At least some proposition(s) expressed in one natural language can be expressed in any natural language.

(C) All propositions that can be expressed in one natural language can be expressed in any other.[79]

For it to be true on the present view that a proposition Q is expressible in different natural languages L and L', they must contain sentences S_L and $S_{L'}$ whose syntactic structures at the relevant level of syntax are identical; the semantic significance of these syntactic relations must be the same; and the semantic values of the lexical items occurring in the same places in the syntactic structures associated with S_L and $S_{L'}$ must be identical. Hence, for (A) to be true on the present view of propositions, the languages in question must contain sentences that are syntactically identical. Thus, it might be said, even the relatively modest (A) entails a substantial empirical claim about the syntactic structures of the languages in question. (B) would require all languages to have sentences that are syntactically identical; and (C) essentially requires languages to be structurally identical at the level of LF. Thus (B) and (C) entail successively stronger, and, it might be claimed, increasingly implausible empirical claims about the LFs of natural languages. Surely, one might claim, it is a strike against the present view

---

[79] Katz (1981) seems to endorse (C) when he says 'Each proposition [thought] is expressible by some sentence in every natural language.' (p. 226).

that the truth of (A), (B), and (C) require (increasingly) substantial empirical claims regarding the LF representations of sentences of natural languages.

In responding to this objection, we first need to recognize that (A) differs from both (B) and (C) in its pretheoretical plausibility. An important part of the philosophical motivation for propositions is the intuition that the same piece of information can be encoded by means of different sentences, whether in different languages or in the same language. Hence some might take (A) to be a sort of constraint on any theory of propositions. To take a clear case, it would be desirable for a theory of propositions to yield the result that '*Schnee ist weiss*' and 'Snow is white' express the same proposition. Any theory which doesn't yield this result will have a lot of explaining to do, (though I for one don't think this by itself should sink a theory). It is true that on the present view of propositions it is an empirical question whether these two sentences express the same proposition and, more generally, whether (A) is true.[80] However, it is likely that the pair do express the same proposition on the present view, and thus that (A) is true. For it is likely that the two sentences have the same syntactic structure. Assuming that the lexical items in the two sentences have the same semantic values and the syntactic structures have the same semantic significance, both of which again seem very likely, they express the same proposition. Indeed, the "clear cases" of two sentences of different languages expressing the same proposition, such as the above pair, that lend support to (A), also lend support to the present account of propositions. For it seems to me that *clear cases* of sentences of different languages expressing the same proposition are cases in which the sentences have the same surface structure and contain lexical items with the same semantic values. If the current account of propositions is correct, it explains why these seem to be such clear cases. For identity of surface structure at least suggests structural identity at the level of syntax that provides the syntactic representations that are the input to semantics. And this combined with sameness of semantic value for the lexical items and sameness of semantic significance of syntax suffices for the sentences to express the same proposition on the present view.

(B), and particularly (C), contrast strikingly with (A) in terms of their pretheoretical plausibility. Neither enjoys support from the intuition motivating the positing of propositions (i.e. that different sentences *sometimes* encode the same piece of information), as (A) did. The more one thinks about (B) and (C), the more one tends to think that the proper *pre*theoretical attitude to take toward (B) and (C) is agnosticism.

Some might disagree, holding that the following (alleged) facts about translation support (B) and (C) respectively:

(B') Some sentence of some language can be translated into any other language.

---

[80] In just the same way, if there is a language of thought it is an empirical question whether a given sentence in the language of thought and a given sentence of English express the same proposition.

(C') Any sentence of any language can be translated into any other language.

However, (B') and (C') support (B) and (C) only given the further premise that translation is a matter of pairing sentences of distinct languages that express the same proposition. This raises two questions: what is the evidence for (B') and (C')?; how plausible is the additional premise? Taking the latter first, translation may sometimes take the form of pairing sentences that express the same proposition, as in 'Schnee ist weiss'/'Snow is white'-type cases. However it does not always take this form. Think of the actual translations people perform—say a friend translating what a shopkeeper is saying in a market in Poland. It is obvious that the translation could be perfectly fine for the purposes at hand without the propositions in the translation matching those expressed by the original utterances. Of course the degree of precision required in some cases is much higher. But an extremely high degree of precision need not, and I suspect usually doesn't, take the form of pairing sentences that express the same proposition. In international political, legal and business negotiations, where a high degree of precision is required, an utterance of a single sentence will very often be translated by several sentences of the other language. Is it really credible to think that one among these (or all of them taken together?!) expresses the same proposition as the original utterance? One might insist that these are only translations in some loose sense and that in the strict sense of the term it is required that the paired sentences express the same proposition. Very well. I won't argue over a word, (though I would say that most of what we call 'translation' is only translation in this "loose" sense). However, with 'translation' understood in this strict sense, so that our additional premise is true by definition, let us return to the first of our questions: what pretheoretical evidence is there for (B') and (C')? Whatever pretheoretical plausibility (B') and (C') enjoyed was a result of homey observations such as that in going from one language to another people manage to "get across" what they need to for the purposes at hand. But of course this will often be translation in the loose sense. It just is not at all obvious, when 'translation' is understood in the strict sense proposed, whether (B') and (C') are true or not. In short, whatever pretheoretical plausibility (B') and (C') enjoy results from understanding 'translation' in such a way that the additional premise required for (B') and (C') to support (B) and (C) is very likely to be false; and when the additional premise is taken to be true, it is simply not at all clear whether (B') and (C') are true.

It is a virtue of the present account of propositions that it makes clear the conditions under which (B) and (C) would be true and suggests how to go about determining whether they are or not. This puts (B) and (C), or their negations, in what I suggested earlier is their proper place: as outcomes of theorizing about propositions and the empirical study of languages.

There is a final point to be made about the way the present account of propositions individuates propositions expressed by sentences in the same or different languages, and our intuitions about sameness of proposition expressed.[81] Perhaps what lies at the heart of the worry that the present view individuates propositions too finely is the idea that it individuates propositions in a way that is inconsistent with our pretheoretical intuitions about which sentences express the same proposition. It might be claimed, for example, that we have a pretheoretical intuition that 'A and B' and 'B and A' express the same proposition. And so it might be thought that the failure of the present account to honor that intuition constitutes a strike against it. But I think this idea and the objection it gives rise to are misguided. The notion of the proposition expressed by a sentence is a theoretical one.[82] But that means we just don't have pretheoretical intuitions about which sentences express the same propositions. At most, we have pretheoretical intuitions about which sentences "say the same thing", or "provide the same information", or some such thing. But then who is to say that these intuitions track when sentences express the same propositions? After all, on the present view, though the sentences 'Rachel is at the movies and Rebecca is swimming' and 'Rebecca is swimming and Rachel is at the movies' don't express the same proposition, the distinct propositions these sentences do express are very intimately related. Not only are these propositions true at all the same possible worlds, but they have the same constituents and are made true there by precisely the same facts. Let's put this by saying that the propositions in question *represent the same facts*. It may be that our pretheoretical intuitions about which sentences "say the same thing" or "contain the same information" track whether sentences express propositions that represent the same facts and not whether they express the same proposition. Or it may even be that these pretheoretical intuitions are not responsive to any single thing.[83]

[81] Thanks to John Hawthorne for discussion here.

[82] Thus, there is no reason to think that the ordinary use of 'proposition' outside of philosophy, on which it seems more or less equivalent to 'claim' or 'statement', tracks the theoretical notion in philosophy of the proposition expressed by a sentence (relative to a context).

[83] I certainly think that pretheoretical intuitions about when people "say the same thing" don't track any one thing. If you and I both utter 'I am hungry', there is a perfectly ordinary sense in which it is correct to say that we said the same thing.

4

Objections to Structured Propositions Generally

Having considered objections to the particular view of structured propositions I am defending, in the present chapter I address objections to structured propositions generally. For the most part, the objections considered here do not depend on idiosyncrasies of the account of structured propositions I have sketched. Of course, not all challenges to structured propositions can be considered. Thus, the present chapter comprises a sampling of challenges that I take to be important to address.

There is one prominent sort of challenge that will not be considered here. It is sometimes argued that structured propositions of the sort I am defending cannot, without some additional machinery, underwrite a proper semantics for verbs of propositional attitude. For, assuming that names and predicates have the sorts of semantic values I have assumed them to have, that verbs of propositional attitude express two-place relations between individuals and propositions, and that that-clauses designate propositions, neither of the following two sentence pairs can diverge in truth value:

1a. Lucy believes that Mark Twain is a great author.
1b. Lucy believes that Samuel Clemens is a great author.
2a. Lucy believes that a groundhog is in the shed
2b. Lucy believes that a woodchuck is in the shed.

In both cases, there is only one proposition to be believed on the present account. And some hold that this is too implausible to accept.[1]

I don't ignore this sort of challenge to structured propositions here because I take it lightly or think it isn't important. There are two reasons for setting it aside. First, the challenge is well known and has been extensively discussed in the literature, whereas, so far as I know, the objections I will be considering have not received replies. And second, as I said in Chapters 1 and 2, my *primary*

---

[1] For example, both Schiffer (2003) and Matthews (2002) give arguments of this sort against Russellian structured propositions. Interestingly, though Schiffer thinks Russellian propositions aren't what that-clauses in sentences like 1a/1b and 2a/2b designate, he nonetheless tends to think that Russellian propositions are needed because possible worlds are constructed out of them. See p. 96.

concern is not with the constituents of propositions, but rather with how those constituents are bound together. Thus, though I have adopted a view about the constituents of propositions on which 1a and 1b express the same proposition (the same goes for 2a and 2b) and I think the view is a plausible one, I at least in principle remain open to other views as long as they cohere with my account of what binds the constituents of propositions together.

That said, let me begin by considering a very general argument against any theory of structured propositions (either Fregean or Russellian) recently given by Stephen Schiffer (2003). (I'll be primarily concerned with the argument as an argument against Russellian views of structured propositions, on which their constituents are objects, properties and relations, since that is the sort of view I am defending.) Since Schiffer states the argument very concisely, let me quote him in full:

(1) If any theory of structured propositions is true, then (*a*) 'barks' in 'Ralph believes that Fido barks' functions as a *singular term* whose referent is a constituent of the structured proposition to which the that-clause refers (for all intents and purposes, that referent would either be the property of being a barker or else a concept of that property).

(2) If (*a*), then the following inference is valid:
   Ralph believes that Fido barks.
   ∴ (∃x)(Ralph believes that Fido x)

(3) But the inference isn't even coherent, let alone valid.

(4) ∴ No theory of structured propositions is true.[2]

Now the natural first reaction to the argument, which I shall argue is correct, is that premise (1) is false. However, Schiffer offers the following defense of premise (1):

Premiss (1) may strike one as surprising, but the theorist of structured propositions seems committed to it. For example, for the Russellian 'that Fido barks' in 'Ralph believes that Fido barks' is a semantically complex singular term whose referent is, or may be represented as, <Fido, the property of being a barker>. This means that both '<Fido, the property of being a barker>' and 'that Fido barks' are co-referential semantically complex singular terms, in the first of which 'the property of being a barker' refers to the property of being a barker, and in the second of which 'barks' refers to that property. This isn't a role 'barks' could perform if it were functioning as a verb; to perform its referential role in the that-clause it must be functioning as a singular term on all fours with the co-referential expression 'the property of being a barker'. Likewise, mutatis mutandis, for the Fregean, only in her case the reference is not to the property of being a barker but to a concept of it.[3]

I have to confess that I don't follow Schiffer's reasoning here as to why the structured proposition theorist is committed to premise (1).[4] Schiffer says that

---

[2] P. 30.   [3] P. 30.

[4] A minor problem with his reasoning is that he seems to assume that Russellians will claim that 'the property of being a barker' is a referring expression whose referent is the property of being a

the Russellian is committed to the following claims in defending premise (1) in the above quotation (and suggests that the Fregean is committed to analogues of them):

A. '<Fido, the property of being a barker>' and 'that Fido barks' are complex singular terms that both refer to the proposition that Fido barks.
B. 'the property of being a barker' in '<Fido, the property of being a barker>' refers to the property of being a barker.
C. 'barks' in 'that Fido barks' is a singular term referring to the property of being a barker.

Given that 'barks' is a referring expression in 'that Fido barks', as is claimed in C, it should be legitimate to existentially generalize on it. This gives us the claim in premise (2) that the inference mentioned there is valid.

One thing that puzzles me about Schiffer's defense of premise (1) here is why he brings up '<Fido, the property of being a barker>' at all. Does he think A and B above *entail* C? He doesn't say this, but if he doesn't think it, why did he bring up '<Fido, the property of being a barker>'?

I believe that Schiffer reasons that premise (1) is true as follows.[5] Assume you are a structured proposition theorist. Assume 'that Fido barks' is a referring expression whose referent is the proposition that Fido barks. Schiffer takes structured proposition theorists to endorse a principle he calls the *compositionality hypothesis (CH)* according to which 'the referent of a that-clause token is determined by its structure and the referents of its component expressions together with whatever implicit references are made in the utterance of the that-clause.'[6] We can safely ignore implicit references in the present case. Schiffer thinks that in an utterance of 'Wendy believes that it's raining' the speaker might make implicit reference to a place, say Mammoth Lakes, so that the token of 'that it's raining' in question refers to the proposition that it is raining *in Mammoth Lakes*. In the case of 'that Fido barks', we can assume no implicit references are made. So CH tells us that the referent of 'that Fido barks' is determined by its structure and the referents of its component expressions. But 'barks' is one of the component expressions and must surely help to determine the referent of the that-clause. So this means that 'barks' must have a referent.[7] For the Russellian, could this referent be the set

barker. I, like I think most Russellians, take definite descriptions to be quantificational expressions and so hold that they don't have referents at all. Or perhaps, following Fara (2001), definite descriptions should be understood as predicates. In any case, they aren't referring expressions. Because this is a minor problem, I'll set it aside.

[5] My belief is based in part on how Schiffer defends a closely related premise in a similar argument against (only) Fregeans. See pp. 27–8.

[6] P. 17. Schiffer seems to take structured proposition theorists to be committed to CH because he thinks that adherence to CH is what motivates the view that propositions are structured in so far as it is difficult to hold both CH and the view that proposition are *un*structured. See pp. 1–2; 18; 31; 46; and 88.

[7] Note that to this point, we are considering any sort of structured proposition theorist, including Fregeans. Thus, Schiffer thinks that any such theorist must hold that 'barks' has a referent in 'that

of barking things? No, because if the set of barking things and the set of things with fleas were the same, it would then follow that 'that Fido barks' and 'that Fido has fleas' refer to the same proposition. Thus, the Russellian must hold that 'barks' is a referring expression in 'that Fido barks' that refers to the property of being a barker. In order to do this, 'barks' must be a singular term referring to the property of being a barker. But then the inference in premise (2) ought to be valid. I should add that Schiffer correctly assumes that the Russellian doesn't hold that 'barks' refers to the property of being a barker in sentences like 'Fido barks'. Thus, he thinks that Russellians must hold that 'barks' functions differently semantically in that-clauses than it does in sentences like 'Fido barks', violating semantic innocence.[8]

As against Schiffer, I'll argue that there is no good reason to believe premise (1). Worse, I believe premise (1) can be shown to be false. Let me take these points in turn.

Unless the following claim is true there is no reason to believe premise 1:

i. (Putting implicit references aside) Structured proposition theorists, including Russellians, are committed to the claim that the referent of a that-clause is determined by the referents of the expressions in it and how they are combined syntactically (CH), and so all the expressions in a that-clause (including 'barks' in 'that Fido barks') must be referring expressions.[9]

For it is the claim that structured proposition theorists hold that 'that Fido barks' is a referring expression whose referent is determined by the referents of its parts, including 'barks', that allows Schiffer to conclude that structured proposition theorists are committed to the claim that 'barks' is a singular term with a referent in the that-clause. I'll argue that i is false, and so there is no reason to believe premise (1).

Second, premise (1) entails at least the following claims:

ii. Structured proposition theorists, including Russellians, are committed to the claim that that-clauses are referring expressions.

iii. Structured proposition theorists, including Russellians, are committed to the claim that 'barks' functions semantically differently in that-clauses than it does in sentences such as 'Fido barks'.

(Premise (1) entails iii in conjunction with the obvious truth that 'barks' in 'Fido barks' does not function as a singular term.) I'll show that ii and iii are false, and hence that premise (1) must be as well.

Fido barks.' Of course what the referent is depends on whether one is a Fregean or Russellian. In any case, the conclusion that 'barks' is a referring expression in that-clauses is enough to render the inference in premise (2) valid.

[8] P. 45. Presumably, Schiffer thinks Fregeans will be stuck with this conclusion as well, since he thinks they will be forced to hold that 'barks' is a referring term in 'that Fido barks' and they will not hold that it is a referring terms in 'Fido barks'.

[9] See note 6.

Taking i first, note that if ii is false, then i is false. If Russellians are not committed to the claim that that-clauses are referring expressions, then neither are they committed to the claim that the *referent* of a that-clause is determined by the referents of the expressions in it and how they are combined syntactically (CH), nor to the claim that all the expressions in a that-clause (including 'barks' in 'that Fido barks') are referring expressions. Hence since I will show that ii is false, it follows that i is false. I should add that though the Russellian is not committed to these claims, she may well hold that in some sense the semantic value of a that-clause is a function of the semantic values of its parts and how they are combined. It's just that because she is not committed to that-clauses being referring expressions, she is not committed to the *referent* of a that-clause being a function of the *referents* of its parts and how they are combined.

But I also wish to emphasize that even a Russellian who takes that-clauses to refer should reject both the claim that the referent of a that-clause is determined by the referents of the expressions in it and how they are combined syntactically, and the claim that all the expressions in a that-clause are referring expressions. To see this, consider the case of complex demonstratives. I have argued elsewhere that they are not referring expressions, but suppose one held that they are referring expressions.[10] Would one hold that the expressions in 'that man in the corner talking' are all referring expressions and that the referent of the demonstrative is a function of the *referents* of its parts and how they are combined?[11] Surely not! Otherwise, one would presumably have to admit that the following inference is valid: John knows that man in the corner talking. Therefore, $(\exists x)($John knows that man in the corner x$)$. Hence, even if one held that complex demonstratives are referring expressions, one should deny that all the expressions in a complex demonstrative are referring expressions. Those Russellians who hold that that-clauses are referring expressions should do the same. Hence, even those who accept the view that that-clauses refer should reject the claim that the referent of a that-clause is determined by the referents of the expressions in it and how they are combined syntactically (CH), and the claim that all the expressions in a that-clause (including 'barks' in 'that Fido barks') are referring expressions. So contrary to i, not only are Russellians not *committed* to these claims, but no Russellian should *endorse* them.

Turning now to ii, aren't Russellians committed to the view that that-clauses are referring expressions? They clearly are not. I think that Russellians should hold that a belief ascription such as 'Lucy believes that Fido barks' is true iff Lucy stands in the belief relation to the proposition that Fido barks. And I myself hold this. But this doesn't at all require the Russellian to hold that that-clauses are *referring* expressions. To see this, simply note that holding that a sentence

---

[10] King (2001).
[11] Presumably speaker intentions or some such thing would figure in the determination of reference as well.

like 'Michelle loves the tallest California congressman' is true iff Michelle bears the loving relation to the unique thing o that is a tallest California congressman doesn't require one to hold that 'the tallest California congressman' is a *referring* expression that refers to o. For example, one could maintain that 'the tallest California congressman' is a quantifier. In just the same way, the Russellian can hold that a belief ascription like 'Lucy believes that Fido barks' is true iff Lucy stands in the belief relation to the proposition that Fido barks, while holding that 'that Fido barks' is not a referring expression. It is true that such a person must hold that *in some way* the that-clause here has the effect of making the proposition that Fido barks and the relations it stands in relevant to the truth conditions of the sentence 'Lucy believes that Fido barks.' But she need not hold that it does so by *referring* to the proposition that Fido barks.

It is worth adding that there are some reasons for doubting that that-clauses are referring expressions. First, there are expressions that *do* appear to be singular terms referring to propositions, such as 'logicism'. Given that one believes in propositions, it is hard to think of what such expressions could be except referring expressions whose referents are propositions. Such expressions exhibit distributional differences with that-clauses:

3. Robin embraced logicism/*that arithmetic reduces to logic.
4. Robin is sure of logicism/*that arithmetic reduces to logic.
5. Robin hoped *logicism/that arithmetic reduces to logic.
6. It is necessary *logicism/that arithmetic reduces to logic.

Admittedly, the distributional differences don't *show* that that-clauses aren't singular referring terms. But they should give us pause. After all, we don't find these distributional differences between expressions that are widely acknowledged to be singular referring terms, such as names, indexicals, and demonstrative pronouns. But then if that-clauses and terms like 'logicism' are all referring expressions, why would we get distributional differences here?

Second, there seem to be semantic differences between 'logicism' and 'that arithmetic reduces to logic'. The following apparently could diverge in truth value:[12]

7a. Glenn knows that Frege believed logicism.
7b. Glenn knows that Frege believed that arithmetic reduces to logic.

Suppose that Glenn knows that logicism is a view about the relation between arithmetic and logic, and he knows that according to it they are intimately related somehow but he isn't sure exactly how. He knows that a number of philosophers held the view in the late nineteenth and early twentieth centuries. Finally, he learns that Frege held this view. Then arguably, 7a is true and 7b is false. But to hold that we must hold that there is some semantic difference between the

---

[12] I believe this point is due to Richard (1993).

that-clause 'that arithmetic reduces to logic' and 'logicism'. If 'logicism' is a referring expression, the that-clause must not be.[13]

Finally, consider a sentence in which a universal quantifier binds pronouns in a that-clause:

8. Everyone believes that he is smart.

The occurrence of the that-clause here doesn't simply refer to a proposition. At most, it could be held to refer to a proposition relative to an assignment of values to variables. In any case, it does not refer to a proposition in the sense that it cannot contribute a (single) proposition to the proposition expressed by 8. The truth of 8 requires people to believe different things! Hence the that-clause here cannot make the sort of contribution to the proposition expressed by 8 that singular referring terms make: a single referent. Further, the fact that all other expressions in natural language that one can quantify into in this way appear to be quantificational (or at any rate, not referring expressions) provides some reason for thinking that that-clauses are not referring expressions:

9. Every man loves some women he used to date.
10. Most swimmers remember the fastest swim they ever had.

In any case, the main point here is that ii is false. Russellians need not hold that that-clauses are referring expressions. I myself am a Russellian who is at least skeptical of the claim that that-clauses refer for reasons such as those just canvassed.

Finally, let's turn to iii. To show that iii is false, we'll construct a toy theory of the semantics of that-clauses that is available to the Russellian and according to which 'barks' behaves semantically in the same way in 'Shirley believes that Fido barks' and in 'Fido barks.'[14] Suppose we have a language containing n-place predicates (for arbitrary values of n); let B be a two-place predicate ("believes"). Suppose our language contains names of individuals. For any expression e, let e^* be the semantic value of e. If b is a name, b^* is an individual; and B^*, the semantic value of B ('believes'), is a two-place relation between individuals and propositions. For other n-place predicates P, P^* is an n-place relation between individuals. Assume our language contains truth functional sentential connectives, quantifiers and the complementizer 'that'. Assume the obvious syntax (an n-place predicate followed by n names is a sentence, etc.), with the addition that placing 'that' in front of a sentence yields a that-clause. We then add:

If α is a name, and C is a that-clause, then $\alpha(B(C))$ is a sentence.[15]

---

[13] Putting it this way is a little contentious, since Richard himself holds that-clauses refer. But they function differently semantically on his account than expressions like 'logicism' and as a result there is a sense in which they do more than refer in the way 'logicism' does.

[14] The account I'll sketch is essentially that of Richard (1993).

[15] Of course we would want to allow quantifiers to occur in place of α here as well, but I'll ignore that. Further, I'll not attempt to formulate things in such a way as to allow quantification

Because nothing hangs on it here, we represent propositions by ordered tuples. In what follows, let S be a sentence, let Π be an n-place predicate, and let $a, a_1, \ldots, a_n$ be names. Then some of the clauses specifying the propositions expressed by sentences are as follows:

1. $\Pi a_1, \ldots, a_n$ expresses the proposition $<\Pi^*, <a_1^*, \ldots, a_n^*>>$.
2. $a(B(\text{that } S))$ expresses the proposition $<a^*, <B^*, <g, \text{Prop } S>>>$, where g is the function that maps every proposition to itself and Prop S is the proposition expressed by S, where the constituents of Prop S are constituents of $<a^*, <B^*, <g, \text{Prop } S>>>$.

The force of the comment that the constituents of Prop S are constituents of $<a^*, <B^*, <g, \text{Prop } S>>>$ can be made clear as follows. Consider a one-place predicate of the language 'R' ("barks") and names 'f' ("Fido") and 's' ("Shirley").[16] Now consider the sentence:

11. s(B(thatRf)) ("Shirley believes that Fido barks.")

Instead of rendering the proposition expressed by this sentence as an ordered n-tuple, let's represent it in tree form. It looks thus:

11'.

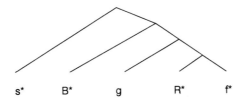

s*   B*   g   R*   f*

Note that R* and f*, the constituents of the proposition expressed by 'Rf', are at terminal nodes in this tree. That is to say, they are constituents of the proposition 11', which 11 expresses. By contrast, suppose we introduced into our language a singular term referring to the proposition expressed by 'Rf', say 'dogicism'. Call such a singular term a *proposition name (PN)*. We then add to the syntax:

If a is a name and D is a PN, then $a(B(D))$ is a sentence.

Now consider the sentence

12. s(B(dogicism))

into that-clauses. This is in part why I call the theory a toy theory. My main concern here is simply to show that there are theories of the semantics of that-clauses available to Russellians on which words like 'barks' in them function semantically in the same way they function outside them. I'm not claiming the theory I sketch in the text is ultimately precisely the correct one. Again, it is a toy theory. However, I do tend to think that something like this theory is correct.

[16] 'R' is intended to call to mind 'rrrufff'.

It expresses the following proposition:

12'.

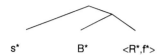

$$s^* \qquad B^* \qquad <R^*,f^*>$$

Note that though the proposition $<R^*, f^*>$ is a constituent of this proposition (since it occurs at a terminal node), neither R^* alone nor f^* alone is. What the last part of clause 2 tells us is that a sentence containing a that-clause expresses a proposition in which the proposition expressed by the sentence 'that' fronts occurs, and where the constituents of the latter occur as constituents of the larger proposition. Finally, our definition of truth for propositions includes the following clause:

1. A proposition of the form $<a^*, <B^*, <g, \text{Prop } S>>>$ is true at a circumstance of evaluation e iff $<a^*, g(\text{Prop } S)>$ is in the extension of B^* at e.[17]

I take it that on the account I have sketched words function the same way semantically in and out of that-clauses (and terms like 'barks' do not function in that-clauses as referring terms that refer to properties). To see this, consider the proposition expressed by

13. Fido barks. (Rf)

It is:

13'. $<R^*, f^*>$

Now consider the proposition expressed by

14. Shirley believes that Fido barks. (s(B(thatRf)))

It is (this time as an ordered n-tuple):

14'. $<s^*, <B^*, <g, <R^*, f^*>>>>$

In both cases, 'barks' contributes to the proposition expressed by the sentence in question R^*, the property of being a barker, and it does so in the same way in both cases. So 'barks' functions the same way semantically in both sentences. Thus on

---

[17] It would be easy enough to introduce a quantifier 'something' into our language and allow sentences such as 'something: x(s(B(x)))'. This sentence would express a proposition that is true at a circumstance e iff there is something ϕ such that $<s^*, \phi>$ is in the extension of B^* at e (i.e. iff s^* believes something in e). We would then get the result that if 'Shirley believes Fido barks' ('s(B(Rf))') expresses a proposition true at e, so does 'Shirley believes something' ('something: x(s(B(x)))').

the present view, the inference Schiffer claims the Russellian is committed to (in premise(2)):

Shirley believes that Fido barks
∴ (∃x)(Shirley believes Fido x)

is no better than this one

Fido barks.
∴ (∃x)(Fido x)

And Schiffer has offered no reason for thinking the Russellian is committed to the latter inference.

The account of that-clauses I have sketched shows that there are accounts available to the Russellian on which words like 'barks' function semantically the same way in and out of that-clauses. Hence iii above is false.

In summary, unless i above is true, there is no reason to believe premise (1) of Schiffer's argument against structured propositions. Further, Schiffer's premise (1) entails claims ii and iii mentioned above. I have now argued that i–iii are all false. I conclude that not only is there no reason for holding premise (1) of Schiffer's general argument against structured propositions (since i false), but in addition it is false (since ii and iii are). For this reason, the argument fails.

Max Cresswell (2002) has also given a general argument against structured propositions.[18] Cresswell's argument employs four "assumptions", as he calls them. First, there is what Cresswell calls the *principle of effability (PE)*:

Propositions are the semantic values of sentences, and for every proposition p there is a possible language V in which there is a sentence α such that V(α) = p.[19]

The rough idea behind the generalized version of this principle (see note 19) is that for any particular thing that is of the sort to be a semantic value of a certain kind of expression, there is a possible language in which it *is* the semantic value of an expression of that kind. The second assumption is *functional compositionality*:

The semantic value of a whole sentence if obtained by functions which are the semantic values of parts of that sentence operating on the semantic values of other parts.[20]

---

[18] I commented on an earlier version of Cresswell (2002) at the Rutgers Semantic Workshop in 2002. Much of what follows is drawn from that comment. I thank both Max Cresswell and the audience for comments on my comment.

[19] P. 643. Actually, Cresswell needs a strengthened version of what he calls the *generalized principle of effability*. Specifically, he needs the claim that for any two functions ω and ω^* from propositions to propositions, there is a language V with functors δ and δ^* such that $V(\delta) = \omega$ and $V(\delta^*) = \omega^*$ (see p. 645 and his note 8). Cresswell uses 'V' to mean both a language and the interpretation of the language (the function that maps expressions of the language to their semantic values). See his notes 3 and 8.

[20] P. 645.

As we'll see, for our purposes the important feature of FC is that it entails that if α is a one-place sentential connective that attaches to a sentence β to form the complex sentence $<\alpha,\beta>$, then the semantic value of $<\alpha,\beta>$, $V(<\alpha,\beta>)$, $= V(\alpha)(V(\beta))$. That is, the semantic value of the complex sentence is the output of the semantic value of α, a function, taking the semantic value of β as argument. The third assumption Cresswell employs is the *principle of truth conditions(TC)*:

(a) If p is a proposition and I a set of indices, then there is an associated set, I(p), which is the set of indices at which p is true.

(b) For any *a* subset of I, i.e. any set of indices, there is a proposition p such that $I(p) = a$.[21]

Indices, of course, are the circumstances at which propositions are evaluated. We don't worry here about what such circumstances of evaluation are (worlds? world/time pairs?, etc.).[22] TC claims simply that every proposition is associated with the set of indices at which it is true; and for every set of indices, there is some proposition that is true at exactly the indices in the set. The final assumption Cresswell employs is the *principle of classical negation (PCN)*:

If there are two (sentence) operators $\sim$ and $\sim^*$ in language V such that for any sentence α, $\sim\alpha$ is true at index i iff it is not the case that α is true at index i and $\sim^*\alpha$ is true at index i iff it is not the case that α is true at index i, then $V(\sim)=V(\sim^*)$.

Essentially, PCN says that any sentential operators in a given language that obey the truth table for negation have the same semantic value.

Cresswell proves that if a language obeys his four assumptions PE, FC, TC and PCN, the propositions expressed by sentences of that language that are true at exactly the same indices are identical. Cresswell dubs this result *Theorem 1*. Cresswell claims, and I agree, that for present purposes anyway, we might as well take Theorem 1 as showing that the propositions expressed by sentences of such a language just *are* sets of indices. Thus, if Cresswell's four principles hold for natural language, it follows that the propositions expressed by sentences of natural language are sets of indices. Thinking of sets of indices for the moment as sets of possible worlds, this would mean that propositions expressed by sentences of natural languages are sets of possible worlds. Cresswell writes:

The importance of Theorem 1 resides in the assumption that the conditions mentioned [PE, FC, TC and PCN] should be satisfied by any acceptable semantics for natural language which makes use of intensional entities like propositions . . . [23]

Of course, structured proposition theorists like me will want to resist this conclusion. Precisely the motivation for structured propositions is that sets of

---

[21] P. 646. Actually, instead of (b), Cresswell only needs the weaker claim that for any proposition p, there is a proposition r such that $I(r)=I-I(p)$. See his note 8.
[22] As we'll see in Chapter 6, I think they are worlds.   [23] P. 649.

worlds are not fine grained enough to play the role of propositions expressed by sentences of natural languages. If propositions are only as fine grained as sets of worlds, there are no structured propositions.

As Cresswell himself says, '. . . if you don't like the conclusion, then you must reject one of the assumptions . . .',[24] and so the question arises as to which of Cresswell's four assumptions I will want to reject. I am not completely sure about some of the other principles (especially PCN), but I am sure that I want to reject functional compositionality (FC). I believe that whether or not FC holds for natural language is the main issue between Cresswell and structured proposition theorists. Thus in responding to Cresswell I will focus solely on the question of whether a semantics for natural language must adhere to FC. If the answer is no, the proof of theorem 1 doesn't go through for natural language, and so we have no reason to think that sentences of natural language don't express structured propositions. Thus, if it can be argued that FC doesn't hold for natural language, Cresswell's argument against structured propositions fails.

The structure of my response to Cresswell runs as follows. First, I'll briefly indicate why structured proposition accounts like mine (and those of others) violate FC. Then I'll consider Cresswell's defense of FC and will respond to that defense. As we'll see, in the end Cresswell and I agree on most substantial claims at issue in his paper. It seems, however, that we view the claims in question in somewhat different terms.

Let's recall Cresswell's statement of FC:

FC: The semantic value of a whole sentence is obtained by functions which are the semantic values of parts of that sentence operating on the semantic values of other parts.

Now consider a negated sentence like:

15. It is not the case that Squaw Valley is in New Jersey.

Assume that 'It is not the case that' in 15 is a sentence operator expressing the truth function for negation or, as on Cresswell's treatment, a function from a set of indices to the complement of that set. On a structured proposition view of the sort I'm defending, 15 expresses a structured proposition that looks something like this:

15a. Neg (p)

where Neg is the truth function for negation or Cresswell's function from sets of indices to their complements, and p is the structured proposition expressed by the embedded sentence in 15. Now 15a is the semantic value of 15 on my view, but it is *not* obtained by functions that are the semantic values of the relevant parts of 15 operating on the semantic values of other parts of 15, as FC requires. In particular, 15a is not the result of applying the function Neg to p. Indeed,

[24] P. 644.

the function Neg, either a function from truth values to truth values or from sets of indices to sets of indices, *can't* operate on p since p is not a truth value or a set of indices. p, of course, is a big, structured entity. So the claim that 15 expresses the structured proposition 15a is incompatible with FC. Obviously, since I think 15 *does* express or have as its semantic value 15a, I am committed to denying FC.

Now what does Cresswell say in defense of FC? He writes:

> . . . without supplementation non-functional semantic theories cannot deliver the truth conditions of sentences. There are semantic theories which are not functionally compositional, but these theories cannot of themselves preserve the link with truth.[25]

Cresswell goes on to consider a theory of structured propositions that violates FC and assigns to the sentence 15 something like the proposition 15a.[26] Cresswell worries about how the proposition 15a determines the intuitively correct truth conditions for the sentence 15. He suggests that one could make 15a have this effect by stipulation as follows:[27]

16. $i \in I(Neg\,(p))$ iff $i \notin I(p)$.

where i is an index and $I(p)$ is the set of indices at which the proposition p is true. This says that $Neg(p)$ is true at an index i iff p is not true at i.[28] Cresswell then makes the following complaint about 16:

> What makes [16] unsatisfactory is that it turns I into an interpretation function, which *gives* a meaning to [Neg], whereas the whole point of structured propositions is supposed to be that they are not things which *have* meanings, but are things which *are* meanings. The semantic work is now done by the fact that I satisfies [16], and provided it does that, [Neg] could be *anything at all*.[29]

Cresswell's point is that nothing in the nature of Neg results in 15a having the truth conditions it does. 16 enforces the proper truth conditions, but the function Neg itself plays no role in the truth conditions coming out right. And so Neg could be anything at all, e.g. Mount Everest instead of a function, and the truth conditions would still come out right as long as 16 remains in force. Because the nature of Neg plays no role here, and 16 in effect "interprets" Neg, Cresswell complains that Neg, and the whole structured proposition 15a, acts like a linguistic expression that is *interpreted* by a clause like 16. Nothing in

---

[25] P. 651. [26] Pp. 651–2.

[27] I have changed the numbering of the principle here to accord with the numbering in the rest of the chapter.

[28] Here I will for the moment adopt Cresswell's treatment of Neg as a function from a set of indices to its complement to make things easier for the reader who wishes to look at Cresswell's paper—I actually prefer an account on which it is the truth function for negation or the property of propositions of being false.

[29] P. 652; bracketed expressions indicate changes I made to make Cresswell's quote in order to reflect my notation and numbering.

the natures of linguistic expressions themselves determine the truth conditions of a sentence—it is how they are interpreted by semantic clauses. Similarly, Cresswell says, for Neg here and its interpretation 16. This, I take it, is the sense in which theories that aren't functionally compositional require supplementation to deliver the truth conditions of sentences, according to Cresswell in the above quotation. The supplementation takes the form of clauses like 16 that serve to interpret and hence in effect *assign* meaning to things like Neg. But, Cresswell says, Neg is supposed to *be* a meaning.

In response, I wish to emphasize that 16 is not the sort of clause for negation I use. In Cresswell's notation and on his approach, it would be rather:

16a. i ∈ I(Neg p)) iff i ∈ Neg(I(p)).

Again, p is itself a structured proposition in 16a. It says that the structured proposition Neg (*p*) is true at an index i iff Neg maps the set of indices at which p is true to a set of indices that contains i. We can put this point another way, letting Neg now be the truth function for negation:

16b. Neg (p) is true at circumstance i iff Neg maps the truth value of p at i to true.

16a/16b get the right truth conditions for 15a, and here Neg *does* play a substantial role in the derivation of those truth conditions: we get the truth conditions right because Neg maps a set of indices to the right set of indices (16a) or because Neg maps truth values to the right truth values (16b). So the fact that Neg is the relevant function in 16ab/16b plays a crucial role in the derivation of the proper truth conditions for the proposition 15a and hence the sentence 15. Hence Cresswell can't complain here that the nature of Neg plays no role in determining truth conditions and that the clause for negation in the definition of truth for structured propositions interprets Neg. I think this addresses Cresswell's argument *to this point* against structured proposition theories that violate FC. Because things are about to become more complicated, let me pause to note that to this point, we have been given no reason to reject structured proposition accounts that violate FC and we have been given no reason to think that a semantics for natural language must obey FC.

Now in discussing Lewis' (1970) account of structured meanings, Cresswell notes that it violates FC in just the way that an account of structured propositions like mine does.[30] Cresswell gives a response to his argument on Lewis's behalf that is exactly similar to the one I just gave to Cresswell's argument (invoking a semantic clause for negation like 16a/16b instead of 16). Cresswell then provides a response to the response he provides on Lewis' behalf. I'll sketch a

---

[30] Roughly, on Lewis' account, a sentence expresses a (structured) meaning consisting of the intensions of its lexical items occurring at the terminal nodes of the sentence's syntactic tree in the places where those lexical items themselves occurred in the sentence.

modified version of Cresswell's response that applies to *my* response to Cresswell's argument. For the remainder of my discussion of Cresswell, I shall ignore the differences between a Lewisian structured meaning account and an account of structured propositions like mine. Both violate FC and the question I am interested in is whether this is a problem.

To recap, recall that the initial worry about theories like mine that hold that 15 expresses something like 15a was that it wasn't clear how 15a could get the right truth conditions for 15. Invoking a clause like 16 for negation was claimed to be illegitimate, because the nature of Neg played no role in getting the truth conditions right. Thus, Neg could be anything at all, so long as it was governed by 16. But then Neg, the constituent of a proposition, behaves like a linguistic expression, being interpreted by or given a meaning by 16, rather than itself being the meaning of an expression. My response was that the clause for negation I use (and Lewis uses) is 16a/16b, and here the nature of Neg, what sort of function it is, plays a crucial role in getting the truth conditions of 15a and hence 15 right.

To this Cresswell responds as follows. The primary business of semantics is assigning intensions to sentences. To do this for simple sentences such as 15, nothing more is required than that the intension of the sentence is derived from the intensions of the parts of the sentence in the function/argument way dictated by FC in accordance with the syntax of the sentence. A Lewisian structured meaning or a structured proposition like my 15a can only get the truth conditions for 15 right by having entities at the terminal nodes that either are or determine intensions corresponding to the parts of the sentences, and allowing these things to combine in such a way that the right intension for the sentence is derived. But all that is *needed* to derive the right intension for 15, and hence all that semantics *requires*, is the intensions of the parts of the sentence combining in a function/argument way, that is, according to FC, as determined by the syntax of the sentence. There is no need for a Lewisian structured meaning or a structured proposition here. Recall that on my view of structured propositions, the structure of a proposition like 15a mirrors the syntactic structure of the sentence 15 at the level of LF or at the level of whatever syntactic representations are the inputs to semantics. Suppose, as Cresswell assumes, that the intension of a complex expression is derived from the intensions of its parts in a function/argument way. Then as Cresswell notes, if you take a structured proposition like my 15a expressed by a simple sentence like 15, replace the propositional constituents by their intensions (which essentially gives you a Lewisian meaning), and let the intensions combine in a function/argument way, you will get the proper intension for the sentence 15. In this sense, what is primary for semantics, at least for a semantics of simple sentences like 15, is that it assigns intensions to sentence parts and obeys FC.

Cresswell stresses that he is not concerned to deny that there may be metaphysical reasons for holding that some entities, say properties and relations, are more basic than, but determine, intensions of expressions. Thus Cresswell writes:

I am not concerned in this paper to deny that there may be metaphysical reasons for saying that this or that kind of favoured entity is more basic, but as far as semantics is concerned anything that *does* determine an intension will do the job, and anything which does not will not. All semantics requires is the intensions themselves.[31]

Especially given this last qualification, I can't find much of substance to disagree with so far. For simple sentences like 15, of course I agree that all that is *needed* to derive its intension is the intensions of its parts combining in a function/argument way, as FC requires. But of course, those of us who favor the view that natural language sentences express structured propositions do so because of the semantics of sentences containing verbs of propositional attitude. Here, people like me think that we need more than the intensions of the parts combining in a function/argument way to get the intension of the whole sentence. A verb of attitude is sensitive to *more* than the intension of the sentence it embeds. Those of us who endorse structured propositions think that a verb of attitude is precisely sensitive to the structured proposition expressed by the sentence it embeds. So while I can agree with Cresswell's view that all that is required to derive the intensions of sentences like 15 is the intensions of their parts combining in a function/argument way, that is not so for sentences in a fragment of natural language that contains verbs of propositional attitude. In particular, to get the intension of a sentence containing a verb of propositional attitude, we need the structured meaning of or structured proposition expressed by the sentence it embeds.

Given this, consider the following sentence:

17. That first order logic is complete is necessarily true and believed by Cresswell.

If the that-clause here must have as its semantic value a structured meaning or structured proposition so that the semantics of the belief ascription comes out right, it would seem that being necessary and being true must also be predicated of a structured entity in 17.[32] But then it would appear that natural language sentences containing that-clauses in which truth or modality is ascribed, as well as sentences containing verbs of propositional attitude, must have parts whose semantic values are structured meanings or structured propositions. But since having expressions whose semantic values are structured meanings or propositions violates FC, it appears that FC fails for a large part of natural language. Indeed, it seems reasonable to think that FC fails for any fragment of natural language containing that-clauses.

Now I would have thought that this is game over: FC fails for a large portion of natural language, hence Theorem 1 doesn't go through for natural language,

[31] P. 654.

[32] In saying that the that-clause has a proposition or structured meaning as its semantic value, I mean only that the that-clause is used to ascribe properties to propositions or meanings or to assert that they stand in relations to other things. See my remarks earlier in this chapter and in Chapter 5.

and so it provides no reason to hold that sentences of natural language express *un*structured propositions. But Cresswell, the author of *Structured Meanings* after all, agrees with everything I've just said! He writes:

Does the need for structured meanings to account for propositional attitude sentences count against FC? For the semantics of such a sentence is not obtained by the meaning of the attitude verb operating on the intension of the complement sentence. If this violates FC then it would seem that English may not after all be a 'well behaved' language in the sense introduced earlier, and that Theorem 1 might therefore not apply to it.[33]

And later, after considering examples similar to my 17 above, :

But if the preceding observations are correct, it would seem that almost any contexts involving truth, necessity or what have you, which can make sentences out of *that*-clauses would seem to require structured meanings. If so, it would seem that FC fails for far more of a language than just propositional attitudes.[34]

Despite our agreement on these points, Cresswell insists that the violations of FC are deviant exceptions and that in some important sense, most of natural language does obey FC, so that Theorem 1 does apply to natural language and unstructured propositions are "primary". If Cresswell and I have any substantive disagreement regarding the issues he raises that I've discussed, it is here.

As I understand it, Cresswell's defense of the claim that in some sense FC governs natural language in spite of the violations to it engendered by verbs of attitude, modality and truth is three-pronged. First, Cresswell claims that in a language without propositional attitudes but containing modal operators and a truth predicate, FC would apply unrestrictedly.[35] So there is a sense in which verbs of propositional attitude provide the only exception to FC. Second, Cresswell claims that FC itself predicts that there will be exceptions to it.[36] Consider a language for which FC is stipulated to hold. Such a language will have syntactic structures that are the inputs to semantics and an assignment of intensions to basic expressions, where the intensions of complex expressions are determined in a function/argument way from the intensions of its parts and how they are put together. But then such a language essentially generates structured meanings, which after all are just syntactic structures whose terminal nodes are occupied by intensions. So, Cresswell thinks, since a language obeying FC essentially generates structured meanings, it isn't surprising that users of the language would want to talk about them. In so doing, they develop mechanisms that violate FC, since they will develop sentences whose intensions depend on these structured meanings, and not simply intensions, of their parts. So, again, Cresswell claims that FC itself predicts that violations to FC will occur.[37] Third, and related to the second point just mentioned, Cresswell

[33] Cresswell characterizes a 'well behaved language' as one for which his four assumptions, including FC, hold. See p. 649.
[34] Pp. 656–7.   [35] P. 657.   [36] P. 657.
[37] Of course it isn't really true that FC predicts violations to itself. Rather, the claim is that if we stipulate that a linguistic system is governed by FC, this very fact will lead us to predict that the

claims that unstructured meanings, sets of indices, are primary.[38] In his most explicit statement regarding what he means by this, he writes:

Semantic structures . . . are not an end in themselves and owe their existence to their contribution to the determination of sets of indices which *are* the end.[39]

Cresswell's remark here is immediately preceded by a reiteration of the second point above: that in any linguistic system governed by FC, its users will inevitably develop means for talking about structured meanings, leading to a violation of FC. I think the point about the primacy of unstructured meaning is that structured meanings come into play only because in some cases the intension, *unstructured meaning*, of a sentence depends on the *structured meaning*/proposition of one of its parts. Thus, the determination of sentences' intensions/unstructured meanings is the important point, and structured meanings are only justified to the extent that they contribute to the determination of unstructured meanings. In this sense, unstructured meanings are primary.

For the sake of argument, let me grant all of this. Cresswell sees in these claims a vindication of the claim that in some important sense, natural language obeys FC. But I am inclined to view things differently. The first point, that a language without verbs of propositional attitude would be governed by FC, is irrelevant. Structured proposition theorists can happily agree to this, since they think precisely that the semantics of verbs of propositional attitude require structured propositions. Their arguments in favor of structured propositions have to my knowledge always invoked this claim.[40] The third point is irrelevant as well. Again, the structured proposition theorist can happily agree that the justification for structured propositions is that they contribute to the determination of the intensions of some sentences. Indeed, the structured proposition theorist will see in this a point *in favor* of structured propositions: they are *required* to determine the intensions of some sentences. Isn't that precisely the point structured proposition theorists have been insisting on all along?

This leaves us with the second of Cresswell's points, and the one that he seems to stress the most. If Cresswell is right that FC itself *correctly* predicts that there will be exceptions to it, in the sense that a language initially governed by FC will inevitably evolve into a language in which FC is violated, then it seems to me that the proper conclusion to draw is that FC is self undermining. A language governed by it will inevitably cease to be governed by it. In short, suppose Cresswell is right about a language governed by FC *inevitably* giving rise to violations of FC via some expressions coming to have structured propositions or structured meanings as their semantic values. Then had I written Cresswell's paper, instead of being called 'Why Propositions

system will eventually produce violations to FC. When I (or Cresswell) say(s) that FC predicts that FC will be violated, I (he) should be understood as meaning this.

[38] P. 643, 658, and 659.   [39] P. 658.   [40] See e.g. Soames (1987).

Have No Structure' it would have been called 'Why Propositions *Must* Have Structure'!

In conclusion, as I said earlier, Cresswell and I appear to agree on most of the answers to the substantive questions raised by his paper that I have discussed. However, we seem intent on spinning those answers somewhat differently. Cresswell sees the claim that languages governed by FC will inevitably evolve into languages violating FC as vindicating FC. I see it as undermining FC. In my view, then, since FC doesn't govern natural language, Theorem 1 doesn't hold for it. But then Cresswell has no argument against structured propositions.

Let me turn to a different objection to structured propositions.[41] It might be thought that accounts according to which propositions are structured commits one to the view that distinct propositions may have exactly the same parts. Or at any rate, it might be thought that the current account so commits one. For consider the proposition that Carl loves Wendy and the proposition that Wendy loves Carl. If we suppose that the relation R binding together the constituents of both propositions is the same (as I believe), and we suppose that the constituents of both propositions are the same (as I believe), then it looks like we have two propositions made of exactly the same things. Both propositions are facts with precisely the same components: R, Wendy, Carl and the loving relation. Now I take the facts that are these propositions to be built out of these components, so that they are present in the proposition and so are parts of the proposition.[42] But then it looks as though I am committed to the claim that two things, the fact that is the proposition that Wendy loves Carl and the fact that is the proposition that Carl loves Wendy, are composed out of the same parts. This contradicts a principle I've touched on at a couple of points in previous chapters, which I'll call *uniqueness of composition or fusion*. According to the principle, there is only one whole composed of given parts. Now Lewis (1986b) for one finds the idea that distinct things are composed of exactly the same parts unintelligible.[43] If the present account of propositions is committed to denying uniqueness of composition and if composition that doesn't obey uniqueness is unintelligible, that spells real trouble for the account.

There are two things one might say in response to this concern. First, one might maintain uniqueness of composition and adopt a view on which the propositions that Carl loves Wendy and that Wendy loves Carl have different

---

[41] Thanks to David Manley for useful discussions of and suggestions regarding the issues about to be addressed.

[42] One could investigate the idea that components are not parts of propositions, but I'll set aside the issue of fully articulating the relation between componenthood and parthood. Though I claim here that all components of the facts that are propositions are parts of propositions, this leaves open whether all parts are components. Assuming transitivity of parthood, Wendy's nose is a part of the proposition that Wendy loves Carl. If all parts are components, this would mean that Wendy's nose is a component of that proposition. I find nothing objectionable about this. Thus, I am sympathetic to the idea that componenthood is parthood.

[43] Pp. 94–7.

parts and so are distinct. But how could the propositions have different parts? Consider both propositions in tree form:

18.

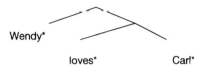

19.

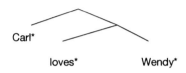

Suppose we held that 18 has only two parts, namely

18a.

and

18a'.

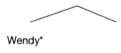

Of course, 18a and 18a' themselves have parts. Call the relation binding loves* and Carl together in 18a *R'*. Then 18a is the fusion of loves*, Carl and *R'*. Call the relation in 18a' *R"*. Then 18a' is the fusion of Wendy* and *R"*. But though 18a and 18a' have the parts mentioned, these aren't parts of 18. 18 has only two parts, 18a and 18a'. Thus, we deny that parts of parts of x are themselves parts of x (e.g. Wendy* and *R"* are parts of 18a', and 18a' is part of 18, but Wendy* and *R"* are not parts of 18). That is, we deny that parthood is transitive. But we maintain uniqueness of fusion. Wendy* and *R"* have a unique fusion (18a'), as do loves*, Carl* and *R'* (18a). And 18 is the unique fusion of 18a and 18a'. Thus, on this view, 18 is distinct from the fusion of all the parts of both 18a and 18a': Wendy*, *R"*, loves*, Carl* and *R'*. For that fusion has parts not had by

18 (e.g. Wendy*). Finally, on this sort of view 19 is the fusion of the following two parts:[44]

19a.

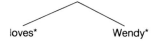

loves*   Wendy*

and

19a'.

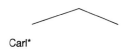

Carl*

Since neither 19a nor 19a' is a part of 18, 18 and 19 are distinct. Though I don't see anything wrong with this proposal in principle, it has the effect of making the constituents of propositions not be parts of those propositions, which to my mind is unfortunate. For example, though intuitively Wendy* is a constituent of the proposition that Wendy loves Carl, she is not a part of it on the present view.[45]

A second way of addressing the present worry, which I favor, is to deny uniqueness of fusion or composition for facts and hence propositions, and hold that both 18 and 19 have exactly the same parts: Wendy*, R", loves*, Carl* and R'. Those parts are simply composed differently in the two propositions. Now is composition that denies uniqueness of fusion unintelligible, as Lewis asserts? I don't want to claim that I can make completely clear what composition of this sort is, but it seems to me the claim that it is unintelligible is clearly too strong. In the first place, there are those who think that in the case of material constitution, a statue and piece of bronze might share all the same parts and yet be distinct.[46] In this case, the parts are even arranged in the same way. But still, there must be two things made of the same parts because they have different properties.

[44] I assume that the relations holding together the parts of 19a and 19a' are the same as those holding together the parts of 18a and 18a'.

[45] Delia Graff Fara pointed out to me that another way to get 18 and 19 to have different parts is to assign semantic values to non-terminal nodes in certain ways and claim these actually occur in the propositions. So, for example, one could assign to the non-terminal (non-root) node on the right side of 18 the relational property of loving Carl and claim it occurs in that proposition; and assign to the corresponding node in 19 the relational property of loving Wendy and claim it occurs in that proposition. Then the proposition 18 would have a part (the relational property of loving Carl) that the proposition 19 doesn't have (and vice versa). However, I don't see any reason to claim that such properties occur in propositions except to get this result. Thus, doing so looks somewhat ad hoc to me.

[46] E.g. Doepke (1982) holds that you and your body are distinct but share all the same parts. See pp. 10 and 17.

Theorists who hold this view then try to explain how two things made of the same parts arranged the same way can nonetheless have different properties. Now I reject such accounts of material constitution, but I feel as though I *understand* the accounts. They aren't literally unintelligible!

Secondly, I think we have an intuitive idea of what non unique composition is like. I think this intuition is reflected in recurring talk of facts or states of affairs in philosophy. The intuitive idea is something like this. There are relations and things stand in them to other things. A given two-place relation R may be such that though a stands in R to b, b doesn't stand in R to a. Consider such a relation R and suppose c stands in R to d and d stands in R to c. c standing in R to d is one fact and d standing in R to c is a different fact, as witnessed by the fact that the former could have existed without the latter existing. However, these facts have exactly the same parts: c, d and R. Somehow, these parts combine two different ways to yield different facts. At this point, one is likely to picture R having argument places—literally positions things can occupy—and to think that one fact results from c occupying the "first" argument position in R and d occupying the second; whereas the other fact results from d occupying the first argument position and c the second. We can make intuitive sense of how the same parts can combine to yield multiple complexes by invoking some notion of a relation having different positions that the relata can occupy. Different complexes can result from the same relata occupying different positions. But if we can make some sort of intuitive sense of the idea that the same parts can be combined to yield different objects, the idea cannot be unintelligible. Let me add that if, never having thought about it before, one were asked whether combining a given group of parts always yields a unique object, I suspect one would not be certain what to answer. But if the claim that two different objects could be composed out of exactly the same parts is really unintelligible, one should on reflection think the answer to the above question has to be 'yes'. But many people do not think that this is so even on reflection.

Finally, Lewis (1986b) writes the following about a notion of composition that denies uniqueness of composition (which he calls *unmereological composition* in virtue of it violating uniqueness of composition—see p. 96) :

What is the *general* notion of composition, of which the mereological form is supposed to be a special case? I would have thought that mereology already describes composition in full generality. If sets were composed in some unmereological way out of their members, that would do as a precedent to show that there can be unmereological forms of composition: but I have challenged that precedent already.[47]

There are two important points here. The first is that Lewis thinks he is owed an account of the general notion of composition of which composition obeying uniqueness of fusion is a special case. Very well: composition is the combining

---

[47] P. 97.

of parts to form an object with those parts. Composition obeying uniqueness is a special way of doing this that results in the complex object being unique. As to the second point, Lewis suggests that sets are not composed by means of a mode of composition that violates uniqueness of composition, and so cannot serve as a precedent showing that there are such modes of composition. What is not clear to me is whether Lewis means to be claiming that there must be such a precedent if composition violating uniqueness is to be accepted. Does he mean to suggest that unless we can give an uncontroversial example of something that is composed in a way that violates uniqueness of composition, we should not accept that there is such composition? Whether Lewis is suggesting this or not, it would be wrong to do so. Suppose one were to claim that qualia don't supervene on the totality of purely physical facts about the world. For this claim to be acceptable, should one be *required* to give an uncontroversial example of something that doesn't supervene on the totality of purely physical facts? Obviously not. Or suppose you are arguing with someone who denies that *mereological* composition *ever* occurs. This person holds that there are only mereological atoms, so that nothing is a part of anything else. Can such a person demand of those who hold that mereological composition occurs that she be given an uncontroversial example of a case in which things are composed mereologically as a precedent? Obviously not. Similar remarks apply in the present case. Those who deny that composition violating uniqueness of fusion occurs cannot require that those who hold that it does provide an uncontroversial example of things composing in a way that violates uniqueness of fusion as a precedent.[48]

In conclusion, then, composition that violates uniqueness of fusion is not unintelligible. Hence the advocate of the account of propositions I am defending may embrace it without fear.

I wish to close this chapter with a brief discussion of a very different sort of concern about structured propositions when they are taken to be the objects

---

[48] Some might feel that there is a tension between my claim that those who endorse composition violating uniqueness of fusion are not required to give an uncontroversial example of it as a precedent and my claim in Chapter 3 that absent uncontroversial examples of things possessing properties at times when they don't exist, those who claim that things *can* possess properties at times when they don't exist shoulder the burden of proof and so must give some argument for their claim. But there is no tension for two reasons. First, in Chapter 3 I pointed out that there *are* uncontroversial examples of properties that require a thing to exist at a time in order to be possessed at that time, whereas there are *no* uncontroversial examples of things possessing properties at time when they don't exist. Further, I pointed out that the idea of a thing not existing at a time and possessing a property then is puzzling. This generated the burden of proof. I don't think either of these claims is true in the present case. I don't think that there are *uncontroversial* examples of composition obeying uniqueness of fusion. And I don't think that the idea of composition not obeying uniqueness is very puzzling (as I have discussed). Second, and more importantly, in Chapter 3 I merely argued that the lack of an uncontroversial example of a thing possessing a property at a time when it doesn't exist shifted the burden of proof to those who think this can happen. Here I am asking whether an uncontroversial example of composition violating uniqueness of fusion is *required for the doctrine to be accepted*. The answer is no, both in this case and in the case of things allegedly possessing properties at times when they don't exist. Thanks to an anonymous referee for raising this issue.

of certain attitudes.[49] David Kaplan and Richard Montague (1960) consider a language L that contains Robinson's Arithmetic (Q) and assume some scheme of Gödel numbering that allows one to say things in the language about expressions of the language. Where A is an expression of the language, $^<A^>$ is the numeral in the language that stands for the Gödel number of A. Assume we add to the language a one-place predicate K. The intended interpretation is that K is true of a number just in case that number is the Gödel number of a sentence that is known. Since L contains Q, we know by the Diagonal Lemma that there is a sentence D such that the following is provable in L:

20. $D \Leftrightarrow (K(^<\sim D^>)$

But then Kaplan and Montague are able to show that given the following three assumptions, we are able to derive a contradiction:

A1 $K(^<\sim D^>) \rightarrow \sim D$
A2 $K(^<K(^<\sim D^>) \rightarrow \sim D^>)$
A3 $[I(^<K(^<\sim D^>) \rightarrow \sim D^>, {}^<\sim D^>) \& K(^<K(^<\sim D^>) \rightarrow \sim D^>)]$
     $\rightarrow K(^<\sim D^>)$

where the predicate I(x,y) in A3 means that the sentence with Gödel number y is derivable in L from the sentence with Gödel number x. (This relation is definable in L.) A1 intuitively says that if $\sim$D is known, it is true. A2 says that A1 is known. And A3 is a single instance of a closure principle. It says that if $\sim$D is derivable from A1 and A1 is known, $\sim$D is known. Again, taking A1–A3 as assumptions allows one to derive a contradiction in L.

As interesting as this is, so far there is no problem for me, since K is a predicate of (Gödel numbers of) *sentences*. But I, of course, take the things to be known to be propositions, and so have no commitment to predicates that say of sentences that they are known. Hence I thus far have no need to decide which of A1–A3 I must give up. However, Rich Thomason (1980, ms.) considers a language (again containing Q) that has a predicate K* of *structured propositions* whose intuitive interpretation is 'It is known that'. Given certain assumptions that are hard to deny (e.g. the expression relation between a sentence and the proposition it expresses is recursive), Thomason is able to show that one can use K* to define a predicate of sentences K such that A1–A3 hold.[50] Thus, it appears that the structured proposition theorist does have to say which of A1–A3 he would deny.

The obvious first thought is to deny the instance of the closure principle A3. Since it seems that quite often I know something A that entails something B, but I don't know B, denying an instance of this seems to come with virtually

---

[49] Thanks to Rich Thomason for raising this worry.
[50] Thomason actually considers the slightly different paradox in Montague (1963). But as far as I can tell, his reasoning goes through for the paradox in Kaplan and Montague (1960) which uses only A1–A3.

no price.[51] However, Cross (2001) appears to show that there is a closely related paradox that makes use of only (the analogues of) A1 and A2, so that denying closure won't rid us of paradox here. Though Uzquiano (2004) challenges Cross' conclusion by arguing that Cross' new paradox requires a more controversial assumption than A3, Cross' argument is sufficiently worrisome to make me uncomfortable resting the resolution here on the denial of A3 or its analogue.[52] Further, Anderson (1983) has offered a spirited defense of the claim that Closure (A3) can't be the problem. What else to do?

I don't see that A1 (or its analogue) can be denied. To do so seems tantamount to giving up the claim that if a sentence is known, then what it says is true. Surely we can't deny that! But then, assuming we are banning blaming closure at least for the moment, A2 must be the problem. But what exactly is the problem? Following Anderson (1983), one might reason as follows. Just as one may think that the Liar paradox showed that 'true' has some sort of hidden hierarchical structure, so the paradox of the knower shows this about 'It is known'. Anderson shows how to implement a resolution of the paradox of the knower by introducing different subscripted predicates K_0, K_1, ... On Anderson's treatment, A2, on which the subscripts on K must be the same, comes out false. Anderson advocates thinking of the subscripted predicates not as actually distinct lexical items (it certainly doesn't seem we have those in English), but rather as representing different extensions of the expression 'It is known' as fixed by features of context. If this is right, essentially the resolution of the paradox involves giving up the view that 'It is known' has a fixed, context independent interpretation.[53] I assume, then, that the advocate of the view that structured propositions are the objects of knowledge can avoid paradox either by denying closure (A3) or by adopting a hierarchical/context sensitive view of 'It is known' on which A2 (where K has the same index twice) comes out false.

---

[51] Max Cresswell (1985) takes Thomason's argument to show that in a community of beings for whom closure holds (or for whom the instance A3 holds), the objects of knowledge are not structured meanings/propositions (see. p. 41).

[52] See also Cross' (2004) response to Uzquiano.

[53] Cross (2001) notes that this is one way to avoid the paradox as well.

5

Objections to Propositions Generally

In the previous chapter, we looked at arguments against structured propositions. In the present chapter, we consider arguments against propositions generally. As was the case in Chapter 4, I am specifically concerned to consider objections here that are recent and have not yet received responses in the literature.

Michael Jubien (2001) provides a number of very interesting arguments against propositions. Jubien distinguishes between different types of theories of propositions. He then argues against all the types of theories he discusses, concluding that there are no propositions. Here we shall confine our attention to what Jubien calls *mathematical theories* and *ontological theories*. As we will see, Jubien considers the theory I am defending an ontological theory (though see below). So in fact, only his discussion of ontological theories is relevant to us. However, it is hard to understand that discussion without seeing what Jubien has to say about mathematical theories. Hence, we begin there.

According to Jubien, mathematical theories of propositions are accounts that have set theoretic or other mathematical constructions play the role of propositions. The primary example of such a theory Jubien considers is the account of propositions as functions from possible worlds to truth values. Essentially, Jubien argues that either mathematical theories aren't intended to be theories of what propositions *are*, instead simply providing *models* of propositions in which the mathematical constructions are "proposition surrogates", or they are to be taken as claiming that the mathematical constructions *really are* propositions. If a mathematical theorist is merely claiming the former, then we are still owed an account of what propositions really are. For all we have been given so far are models of or surrogates for propositions. Hence on this way of understanding mathematical theories, they aren't really theories of what propositions are. By contrast, if the mathematical theorist claims that her mathematical constructions really are propositions, Jubien thinks she is subject to what he calls a "Benacerraf dilemma". For example, suppose she claims that propositions *really are* functions from worlds to truth values. The problem is that there are other entities that are equally well suited to be propositions: in the present case, sets of worlds. Both types of entities have equal claim to really be propositions, and so it seems that no principled reason could favor the choice of one over another. This suggests that neither mathematical construction really is a proposition.[1] On the basis of this reasoning, Jubien concludes that either a mathematical account is not an account of what propositions are at all; or it is such an account but can be refuted by a Benacerraf dilemma. I find Jubien's argument here compelling.

Having disposed of mathematical theories of propositions in this way, Jubien turns to ontological theories. Such theories really purport to tell us what propositions are, instead of offering up proposition surrogates or models as do mathematical theories on one understanding of them. Jubien considers the theory of propositions I defend to be an example of an ontological theory.[2] Jubien characterizes ontological theories as follows:

A second type of theory would try to provide a more plausible account of the intrinsic nature of Platonic propositions, one that doesn't treat them as mathematical entities of some antecedently familiar sort, but as entities of their own special kind. To succeed, such a theory must mesh well with our intuitions about propositional constituency, and hence with our intuitive conception of propositions as complex entities that stand on their own. Inevitably, it would include an account of how propositions are composed of entities like properties and relations, which after all are the intuitive constituents of propositions.[3]

Note that Jubien understands ontological accounts of propositions to be accounts according to which propositions are structured and have constituents. Ontological accounts explain how propositions are composed of properties, relations and so on. Though, as indicated, Jubien himself considers my account of propositions to be ontological, presumably because it does provide an account of how propositions are composed of properties, relations and individuals, there is some room for doubt as to whether it is an ontological account in Jubien's sense.[4] Jubien makes clear that he is talking about *Platonic* propositions, which he takes to 'exist independently of minds and the spatiotemporal realm'.[5] As we have seen, propositions as I construe them would not have existed had minds failed to exist (though now that they do exist, they don't exist "only in our minds") and they are certain sorts of facts in the actual world. So there is reason to believe that propositions as I understand them are not Platonic propositions in Jubien's sense and hence that the arguments Jubien gives against ontological accounts of Platonic propositions do not include accounts such as mine among their intended targets. But I believe it is worthwhile to see whether and how my account can get around Jubien's arguments, both because he does say my

---

[1] Though we have here used only one example of a mathematical theory (propositions as functions from worlds to truth values), Jubien thinks that any mathematical theory will be subject to this objection. Of course in Chapter 1, I gave precisely this sort of argument against the view that propositions are ordered n-tuples. Jubien would certainly consider that view a mathematical theory as well.

[2] See Jubien's note 17.   [3] P. 50.

[4] I surmise that this doubt is reflected in Jubien's own remark in note 17 that he suspects that behind my account lurks an account like his that rejects propositions.

[5] P. 47.

account is an ontological account and because of the intrinsic interest of his arguments. Further, doing so will shed light on ways in which a theory of the sort I am defending differs from traditional Platonic accounts of the sort Jubien intends to criticize and so is immune to certain arguments against such Platonic accounts.

Jubien's first argument against ontological accounts of propositions begins with an argument that propositions represent or have truth conditions as a result of their "internal make up". The argument is as follows:

> Propositions represent the world as being one way or another. If they didn't represent in this way, it would be utterly implausible to view them as the ultimate bearers of truth values. Now, in an ontological account, the representing a proposition does must be the result of its internal makeup—it must somehow emerge from the constituents of the proposition itself. To ground the representational force *outside* the propositions, say in the intentions of conscious agents, would sabotage the motivating "ontological" idea that the entity really *is* a proposition, not a mere surrogate. So it must emerge from a successful ontological account that no *other* entity could be the proposition in question. If its "propositionality" were derived from representational activity outside the entity, then the hope of uniqueness would be lost. In effect, we would merely have a philosophically more enticing *mathematical* account, with parallel surrogate accounts in the wings.[6]

Jubien seems to be reasoning as follows. If the fact that a proposition represents/has truth conditions were due to something outside the proposition, such as the intentions of conscious agents, then some entity other than the proposition could be or could have been the proposition.[7] In effect, whatever activities of conscious agents resulted in the proposition having truth conditions could (or could have) also result(ed) in some other entity having those truth conditions and hence being the proposition. But then we would again face a Benacerraf dilemma: there would be no principled reason to claim that one entity or the other really is the proposition. So neither entity is. Jubien concludes that the fact that a proposition has the truth conditions it does must be due to its constituents representing, where whatever it is about its constituents that results in the proposition having truth conditions presumably must not itself be bestowed upon the constituents by something outside them. Call this the *argument for internal representation*.

On the basis of this argument, Jubien holds that the representational capacity of propositions must be grounded in the representational capacity of its constituents, where the latter is grounded in the nature of the constituents themselves (and so not bestowed from outside). He then goes about trying to construct an account according to which this is so. He assumes that properties represent their instances, and that propositions are mereological fusions or sums of properties

---

[6] P. 50.

[7] Note that Jubien says that a successful ontological account must hold that no other entity `could be` the proposition' (my emphasis).

and relations. Jubien also assumes the principal that in Chapter 4 I called *uniqueness of composition or fusion*: that given parts have a unique mereological sum or fusion. Thus, the proposition that some dogs are swimming must be *the* mereological fusion of the property of being a dog, the property of swimming and the relation between properties of being coinstantiated (the latter is supposed to make the proposition true iff being a dog and swimming are coinstantiated—i.e. iff some dogs are swimming).

The problem Jubien finds with this suggestion is that the account identifies distinct propositions. For consider the property of being a swimming dog. Jubien thinks this is the mereological sum of the properties of being a dog and swimming. But now consider the proposition that some swimming dogs are swimming dogs. This must be the mereological sum of the property of being a swimming dog and the property of coinstantiation. But this in turn is the mereological sum of the property of being a dog, the property of swimming and coinstantiation. The problem is that that mereological sum was also supposed to be the proposition that some dogs are swimming. But then the one mereological sum of the properties of being a dog, swimming and the relation of coinstantiation is both the proposition that some dogs swim and the proposition that some swimming dogs are swimming dogs. But that means the latter two propositions are identical. And this is clearly incorrect. Thus, Jubien's first argument against ontological theories of propositions.

Now two things got the ontological theorist into this trouble. The first was the argument for internal representation.[8] The second was the assumption that propositions are mereological sums of their constituent properties and relations, and that there is a unique mereological sum of given parts. Of course, I reject the latter. I also reject the argument for internal representation. Recall that this argument claimed that if the capacity to represent was derived from something outside a proposition, then some other entity could be or could have been the proposition in question, presumably because the representational force could be or could have been bestowed on this other thing. But then this other entity has or could have just as much claim to being the proposition as the thing being claimed to be the proposition. This in turn means that both are simply proposition surrogates and neither is really the proposition.

Now consider my account of propositions. Propositions exist and have the truth conditions they do because of the intentions and actions of conscious agents. Had there been no such agents, there would have been no propositions.

---

[8] It may appear that only the claim that propositions are mereological sums of properties and relations and that there is a unique fusion of given parts got the ontological theorist into this trouble. But Jubien only considered an account of that sort plausible to the extent that he thought that properties and relations can represent things as a result of their natures. And it was the argument for internal representation that made him think that the capacity of a proposition to represent had to be derived from the capacity of its constituents to represent (as a result of their natures).

And had the agents done different things, different facts could have had the truth conditions that the facts that are actually propositions have.[9] So it seems that at least in some sense, on my account the representational capacity of propositions is derived from something outside them. But the matter is complex, because as we noted in Chapter 2, on my account having the truth conditions it has is an intrinsic (and essential) property of a proposition. So it isn't clear to me whether Jubien would hold that on my account the representational capacity of a proposition comes from outside it or not.

Does Jubien's argument cut against my view and show that propositions as I understand them are subject to a Benacerraf dilemma? The key claim in Jubien's argument is that if the capacity to represent was derived from something outside a proposition, then some other entity could be or could have been the proposition in question. We saw that it isn't clear whether Jubien would hold that on my view, the representational capacity of propositions comes from outside them. If it doesn't, then my account already satisfies Jubien's constraint that the representational force of a proposition can't come from outside it. And since I hold that distinct propositions may have exactly the same parts, my view will not be subject to the second stage of the argument in which Jubien claims to show that ontological theories will be forced to identify distinct propositions.

So let's suppose that Jubien would hold that on my view the representational force of propositions *is* derived from something outside them and that he will use the considerations adduced in the argument for internal representation to argue against the view. What is not clear to me is whether in that argument Jubien is claiming: 1) that if the representational force of a proposition derives from something outside it, something else *actually has an equal claim* to be the proposition (presumably because it too had representional force bestowed on it from outside); or 2) that if the representational force of a proposition derives from something outside it, something else *could have been the proposition*, (presumably because it could have had representational force bestowed on it from outside).

I think my view shows that claim 1 is false (assuming, as we currently are, that on my view the representational force of propositions comes from outside them). Speakers in fact did things that brought the facts I claim are propositions into existence with the result that they have the truth conditions they have. Further, as I argued in Chapter 2, even if they also brought into existence other facts that are also eligible to play the role of propositions, the facts I claim are propositions are intrinsically the most eligible facts for that role. So the fact that the representational force of propositions comes from outside them, in the sense that speakers brought propositions into existence with the truth conditions they

---

[9] For example, if the syntax of English had been different, different facts would be the propositions expressed by the sentences of what would have been English (or something similar to English). I discuss this below.

have, did not result in other entities *actually having* an equal claim to being propositions as well. So if Jubien intends to employ claim 1 as a premise in the argument for internal representation, (and if on my account the representational force of propositions comes from outside them), then the argument fails against my view because this premise is false.

By contrast, if Jubien intends to employ claim 2 as a premise in the argument, the premise is true but it won't support the rest of his argument. In particular, the truth of premise 2 is not enough to saddle me with a Benacerraf dilemma. It is true on my view that "something else could have been the proposition that snow is white" in the sense that some different fact could have had as components the property of being snow and the property of being white, could have been true iff snow is white, (for example, the sentential relation, which is part of the propositional relation, might have been different) and could have been intrinsically most eligible to play the role of the proposition that snow is white.[10] If speakers had behaved somewhat differently and language had developed somewhat differently, this would have been so. But from this, no Benacerraf dilemma follows. The fact that I identify with the proposition that snow is white actually exists, has the truth conditions it has, and is the most eligible. This other entity that might have been that proposition doesn't exist, though it might have. So there aren't two entities with equal claim to being the proposition that snow is white. There is only one. So though claim 2 is true (on one way of understanding it), its truth doesn't lead to any Benacerraf dilemma. Thus Jubien's first argument against ontological accounts of propositions doesn't tell against the account of propositions I am defending. The argument requires the claim that given certain constituents, there is only one proposition with those constituents, which I reject; and it requires that the argument for internal representation succeeds, which it does not, either because it has a false premise or because the conclusion, that views on which the representational force of propositions comes from outside them are subject to a Benacerraf dilemma, doesn't follow.

Jubien's second argument against ontological accounts of propositions begins by considering the proposition that all canines are dogs. Jubien calls the relation between properties expressed by 'all' *subextensiveness*. He thinks that the proposition that all canines are dogs just is the proposition that being canine is subextensive to being a dog.[11] As we now know, one cannot take this proposition to be the mereological fusion of being a dog, being canine and being subextensive if we hold there is only one such fusion. For there are two different propositions

---

[10] I use scare quotes here because I am uncertain whether this means that something else literally could have been the proposition that snow is white. It may only mean that the proposition that snow is white might not have existed and another thing might have existed that was true iff snow is white. Speaking loosely, I'll say here that something else might have been the proposition that snow is white. See note 21.

[11] P. 52.

with the constituents in question: the proposition that all canines are dogs and the proposition that all dogs are canines. So Jubien thinks we must somehow code into the proposition the order in which we must take the properties of being a dog and being canine with respect to the subextensiveness relation. Inspired by taking the set {a,{a,b}} to be the ordered pair <a,b>, Jubien notes that one might take the mereological sum of *the property* of being the property of being canine, the property of being a dog, and subextensiveness to be the proposition that all canines are dogs; whereas the sum of the property of being the property of being a dog, the property of being canine and subextensiveness is the proposition that all dogs are canines. We thus mark which property is said to be subextensive to which in the proposition by taking the property of being that property rather than the property itself. But Jubien correctly notes that this seems arbitrary and stipulative. Why not do things exactly the other way around, and identify the proposition that all dogs are canine with the mereological sum of the property of being a dog, the property of being the property of being canine, and subextensiveness? Neither mereological sum has more of a claim to be the proposition that all dogs are canines than the other. Thus, once again, we face a Benacerraf dilemma and we are forced to conclude that neither mereological sum is the proposition that all dogs are canines. And again, this leaves us without any account of propositions.

Now it appears that this is only a problem for those who view propositions as mereological sums of properties, relations and so on, and who hold that there is only one sum of given parts. For the problem is that subextensiveness is not a symmetric relation between properties. Thus the proposition that the property A bears subextensiveness to the property B may differ in truth value from the proposition that B bears subextensiveness to A. Hence the propositions must be different. But assuming uniqueness of mereological fusions, there is only one mereological fusion of subextensiveness, A and B. Thus, some trick of the sort Jubien considers is necessary to get *two* mereological sums to be the two propositions in question. If, as on a theory like mine, the properties A and B can occupy different positions in the proposition, the proposition that all As are Bs will be different from the proposition that all Bs are As in virtue of the properties A and B occupying different positions in the propositions. The former looks roughly as follows:

[[ALL [A]] [B]]

and the latter as follows:

[[ALL[B]][A]]

(where ALL is subextensiveness). So Jubien's argument here appears to be only an argument against ontological accounts of propositions that hold that propositions are mereological fusions of their constituents and that there is only one mereological fusion of given parts.

But Jubien denies that his argument only cuts against such views. He writes:

Now, this sort of situation is going to arise whether we take constituency mereologically or not. For consider again the proposition *that all canines are dogs*. We're trying to see it as a Platonic entity having the properties *being canine* and *being a dog* as constituents. Of course we would finally have to say something about constituency. But whatever we might say, the constituents would have to be bound together in the right way with logical glue, glue that is itself Platonic in nature. So the glue would have to include something more or less like the *subextensiveness* relation. It is clear, for the reason just given in the mereological case, that it won't be enough merely for this relation to be a further constituent. For each of the two properties has to be associated with the correct "position" in the relation.

What's crucial here is that no particular way to bring about the positional association is mandated by our prior conceptions of properties, relations and the Platonic realm at large. We're faced with a very general, sophisticated coding problem, essentially like the simpler ordered-pair problem, and therefore one to which our ingenuity may be applied in any number of different but ultimately interchangeable ways...If there is a multiplicity of interchangeable systems of proposition-like complexes, then we have a Benacerraf dilemma, and the fact that we need positional coding *guarantees* such a multiplicity.[12]

Jubien's claim here is that regardless of how we understand constituency, we need to somehow assign "positions" to the properties of being canine and being a dog in the proposition that all canines are dogs. We need to do this in order to distinguish the proposition that all canines are dogs from the proposition that all dogs are canines. These propositions have precisely the same constituents and are claimed to differ only in the "positions" occupied by the property of being canine and the property of being a dog in the two propositions. But Jubien in effect claims that for any way of assigning these properties different positions in propositions, there will be some other way to do so. And the "proposition-like complexes" resulting from different ways of assigning properties positions in these "proposition-like complexes" all have equal claim to be the propositions in question. But then this Benacerraf dilemma gives us reason to think none of them is really a proposition.

The crucial claim here is that for any way of assigning properties positions in propositions, there is another that results in entities that have just as much claim to be propositions as do the entities that result from the previous assignment of positions. Is this claim correct when applied to the account I am defending? What assigns positions to properties in propositions on the present account? It is the relations that bind together the constituents of propositions, what I called *propositional relations* (represented by the brackets in [[ALL[A]][B]] and [[ALL[B]][A]]) in Chapter 2. The difference between the proposition that all

---

[12] P. 52–3. Jubien uses 'mereology' in such a way that a mereological account of constituency is committed to there being a unique fusion or sum of given parts.

Surely positioning
implied by the type of
R
coding is

canines are dogs and the proposition that all dogs are canines is that the property of being a dog and the property of being canine occupy different argument places in the propositional relation in the two propositions. Is there, then, another way of assigning these properties different positions in "proposition-like complexes" such that the resulting complexes have as much claim to being propositions as the things that I am calling propositions, as Jubien claims? No. The argument of Chapter 2 rules these other pretenders out. I there argued that the particular relations that I claim hold together the constituents of propositions have a special claim to be the relations that do this. First, the things I claim are propositional relations endow propositions with the appropriate degree and type of structure. Second, the actions of conscious agents resulted in the constituents of propositions actually standing in these propositional relations, so that we know that propositions as I understand them exist. Third, and perhaps most importantly, we can see how/why the entities bound together by my propositional relations have truth conditions and so represent. Finally, I argued that any other alleged propositional relations satisfying these conditions as well as any others that must be satisfied, and that give rise to facts that are eligible to play the role of propositions, deliver facts that are intrinsically less eligible to play that role than the facts that I claim are propositions. These features of my propositional relations uniquely suit them to be *the* relations that bind together the constituents of propositions. Thus, there simply are no other relations that bind together the constituents of propositions yielding "proposition-like complexes" that have as much claim to being propositions as the things I claim are propositions. Hence there is nothing to generate a Benacerraf dilemma for me and I am immune to Jubien's objection here.

Jubien's final argument against ontological accounts of propositions concerns the very idea that Platonic entities of any sort can represent other things.[13] As we saw, based on the argument for internal representation, Jubien holds that on an ontological view, a proposition represents in virtue of its constituents—properties and relations—themselves representing. But Jubien now claims that things like properties and relations can't, on their own, represent other things:

> I think the project was doomed from the start by the illusion that, for example, the property of *being canine* represents canines. It doesn't follow from the fact that a property has instances that it *represents* those instances . . . Of course, if we like, *we* may utilize a property to represent its instances, but then the representational oomph is coming from us. *We*, after all, can use anything to represent anything else. If, employing a prearranged code, a spy displays a lemon to signal the presence of dogs, there's no illusion that the lemon *itself* is doing any representing *on its own*. With a property and it instances, the illusion is more likely, but it's still an illusion.[14]

---

[13] Jubien also thinks that this argument refutes what he calls *primitive-entity* theories of propositions, of which Bealer (1998) is a paradigm.
[14] P. 54.

So Jubien claims here that Platonic properties and relations aren't things that by their nature represent other things. As with words or anything else, *we* could use them to represent other things. But in and of themselves they don't represent anything. I completely agree with Jubien here. Indeed, this is one reason I have always found it odd that properties, relations and propositions are often grouped together as things of the same kind (with propositions perhaps being thought of as zero-place properties). Propositions are importantly different from properties and relations in that they represent.[15] As Jubien says, properties and relations don't unless we use them to represent. Next, Jubien extends this point to all Platonic entities:

> But there's nothing special here about properties. In the end, it's implausible to think that *any* genuine Platonic entity could represent on its own cuff. *Representation* is an "intentional" or "outer-directed" relation. If x represents y, then x has a part that "stands for", "refers to", or is otherwise "about" y. This is the admittedly vague but undeniable heart of the notion. It borders on the absurd to suppose that any inert, non-spatiotemporal entity could have a part that, in itself, plays any such referential or quasi-referential role . . . Representation is ultimately the business of beings with intentional capacities, in short, thinkers. So Bealer's *primitive* Platonic propositions are no better off than those of the ontological theorist.[16]

Here Jubien rejects the idea that *any* Platonic entity (mind independent and existing outside of the spatio-temporal realm), whether property, relation or primitive proposition (a sui generis entity, not "reducible" to anything like a set of possible worlds, a structured entity with properties and relations as constituents, etc.) could represent *on its own*. Any representing done by such a thing must be due to conscious creatures employing the thing as a representation.

It should be clear that none of these claims cuts against the present view of propositions. It is no part of the present view that any Platonic entity represents other things *on its own*. Propositions as I construe them were brought into existence by conscious creatures and represent other things (have truth conditions) because of the actions of conscious creatures. Had there been no conscious creatures, there would have been no propositions representing anything. Thus, we can happily agree with Jubien here and the considerations he adduces do not do any damage to the present view.

We have now seen that the arguments Jubien presents against ontological accounts of propositions do not work against the view of propositions defended here. I remind the reader that it is not clear that Jubien intended the arguments to apply to this view. In fact, Jubien has at least some tendency to see the present view as similar in spirit to the sort of view he ends up endorsing.[17] Nonetheless, I believe consideration of Jubien's arguments has been instructive. It shows how the present view can avoid difficulties with more traditional conceptions of propositions.

---

[15] I briefly touched in these issues in Chapter 2.
[16] P. 54.   [17] Again, see his note 17.

I now wish to consider an argument against a view that endorses the claim that there are propositions as well as certain other claims. Indeed, those who have given the argument disagree to some extent as to what it is an argument against. However, it appears that I hold all the claims that together are supposed to lead to trouble. Hence, I am compelled to consider the argument in question

As mentioned in Chapter 2 and elsewhere, I take propositions to be the things we believe, doubt and so on. I also think that verbs of attitude express two-place relations between individuals and propositions. We can state that an individual stands in one of these relations to a proposition by using a name of the individual, a verb of propositional attitude and an expression designating the proposition, in this case a that-clause, and forming a sentence such as: 'Oriana believes that philosophy is hard'.[18]

Of course, as was suggested in Chapter 4, there are various linguistic devices that appear to designate propositions. The following examples illustrate three of them:[19]

1. 'logicism'
2. 'the proposition that arithmetic reduces to logic'
3. 'that arithmetic reduces to logic'

For ease of subsequent reference, let us call expressions like 2 *proposition descriptions* (henceforth *PDs*); and as we did in Chapter 4, we'll call expressions like 1 *proposition names* (henceforth *PNs*). We'll also continue to call expressions like 3 *that-clauses* (henceforth *TCs*). Further, when a PD and TC are related as are 2 and 3 (in that 2 is the result of prefixing 'the proposition' to 3) I shall say that the PD and the TC *correspond*. One caveat before continuing: I shall not consider PDs or TCs containing contextually sensitive expressions or pronouns anaphoric on expressions outside the PDs or TCs. As far as I can see, they have no important bearing on the issues I am interested in and handling them would require complications in many formulations I give.

Because it will be important later, let me say a bit about what I mean when I say that 1, 2, and 3 *designate* the proposition that arithmetic reduces to logic. I intend this in a pre-theoretical, neutral sense that allows that these expressions may function in different ways semantically while ultimately designating the same thing, (for example, in the way in which, in my view at least, a definite description and a name function differently in designating the same thing).[20]

---

[18] The material that follows is from King (2002). I thank *The Philosophical Review* and Duke University Press for their kind permission to use the material.

[19] There appear to be other devices for designating propositions, for example 'what David said', (as well as others).

[20] In Chapter 4 I indicated that I thought that PNs and TCs probably *do* in fact function differently semantically. But I'll remain neutral on that point here since I didn't and won't give an account of how PNs and TCs (and PDs) function semantically. Recall that the "theory" of TCs given in Chapter 4 was an illustrative *toy* theory.

Indeed, all I really mean when I say that 1, 2, and 3 designate the proposition that arithmetic reduces to logic is that these expressions are *in some way or other* (and possibly different ways for 1, 2, and 3) semantically associated with the proposition that arithmetic reduces to logic with the result that when they occur in sentences, as a result of their so-occurring, the sentences express propositions whose truth and falsity depend on the properties possessed by the proposition that arithmetic reduces to logic and the relations it stands in. Since I wish to allow that different occurrences of the same expression might designate different things, I really need to characterize designation for *occurrences* of expressions in sentences as follows: an occurrence of expression e in sentence S designates o iff this occurrence of e is via some semantic mechanism associated with o and as a result, in virtue of containing this occurrence of e, S expresses a proposition P whose truth or falsity at a circumstance of evaluation depends in part on the properties of o and the relations it stands there.[21] I shall sometimes talk of an

[21] I intend the notion of an occurrence of an expression e being associated with an object o via *some semantic mechanism* in such a way that supposing that, for example, an occurrence of 'that grass is green' is associated via a semantic mechanism with the proposition that grass is green does not entail that this occurrence of this TC is associated with a *constituent* of that proposition (for example, grass) via a semantic mechanism, (and so from the fact that the TC designates the proposition, it does not follow that it designates any constituent of the proposition). For the TC is associated with grass by being *semantically* associated with the proposition that grass is green, *and* by grass being a constituent of this proposition. But this latter relation (constituency) between grass and the proposition that grass is green is not a *semantic* relation (presumably, it is some sort of part/whole relation), and so the TC is not associated with grass via 'purely' semantic means, (of course, a *part* of the TC, 'grass', is purely semantically associated with grass, but again the *TC* is only associated with grass by *having a syntactic part* that is semantically associated with grass, and again this is not a purely semantic relation between the TC and grass). Thus, the way I intend the notion, the TC is not associated with grass via a semantic mechanism. For an occurrence of an expression e to be associated with an object o via a *semantic mechanism* requires the relation between the two to be "purely" semantic. Roughly, this means that either o is "directly" associated with e via semantic rules, so that o is a semantic value of e; or some other entity o' is so associated with e, and o' bears a purely semantic relation to o. This latter would be the case if, for example, e had associated with it by semantic rules some descriptive conditions, which o in turn satisfies (the satisfaction of descriptive conditions here being understood as a semantic relation). Note that in addition to requiring such a semantic relation between e and o, designation requires that as a result of this relation, the truth or falsity of the proposition expressed by the sentence containing this occurrence of e depends in part on the properties of o and the relations it stands in. Finally, let me note that designation really should be relativized to a circumstance of evaluation to allow for the possibility of an occurrence of an expression designating different things at different circumstances of evaluation. It may even be that PDs and TCs *do* designate different things at different circumstances. Consider the following PD and TC: 'the proposition that snow is white'; 'that snow is white'. Certainly, these designate the proposition that snow is white at any world where the fact that is that proposition exists. But what about a world where that fact doesn't exist, but a slightly different fact whose constituents are the same exists (because of language evolving slightly differently) and is true iff snow is white? I am not sure whether the above PD and TC do not designate anything at this world or whether they designate the fact in question and so are not rigid. Despite this, I have not chosen to relativize designation to circumstances due to the fact that at all the circumstances relevant to my discussion here, the PDs and TCs I'll consider designate the same fact/proposition. Thus, relativizing designation to circumstances would make for additional wordiness with no benefit. All this said, I recognize that the characterization of 'designation' given is fairly loose. Still, I believe

expression designating something, instead of talking of its *occurrences* designating something, when I take all occurrences of the expression to designate the same thing. I wish to note that my rather loose characterization of designation does not rule out an occurrence of an expression designating more than one thing. This would occur if the occurrence of the expression were semantically associated with more than one thing *and as a result of this*, the sentence expressed a proposition whose truth or falsity (at a circumstance) depended on the properties of more than one entity and the relations they stand in (at the circumstance). Intuitively, in such a case, the single occurrence of the expression affects the truth conditions of the proposition expressed by the sentence by making the truth value of the proposition depend on the properties possessed by more than one thing. Perhaps no expression does designate more than one thing (though a more precise generalization of the notion of designation might have it that some plural definite descriptions or plural pronouns used deictically do), but nothing in my characterization of designation rules this out.

It should be clear that the claim that occurrences of 1, 2, and 3 designate propositions is compatible with a wide variety of theories as to how occurrences of these expressions function semantically. And as I said, it is compatible with the claim that they all function differently semantically.

My primary concern will be with corresponding PDs and TCs. Of course, there are syntactic differences between these expressions. PDs are noun phrases (NPs) and TCs are clauses (really, complementizer phrases). And so there are distributional differences between PDs and TCs.[22] For example, some verbs take sentential complements but don't take NP complements. Thus, TCs can follow such verbs while PDs cannot:

4. Russell said/hoped/wished that arithmetic reduces to logic/*the proposition that arithmetic reduces to logic.

On the other hand, certain verbs take NP but not sentential complements, and so allow PDs but not TCs as complements:

5. Connie embraced the proposition that arithmetic reduces to logic/*that arithmetic reduces to logic.

However, there are environments in which (PNs and) both PDs and TCs can grammatically occur. One such environment, and the one that will be of interest to us, is following certain verbs of propositional attitude. For certain verbs of propositional attitude take both sentential and NP complements:[23]

---

it is sufficiently precise for present concerns. I am indebted to the comments of an anonymous referee here.

[22] I noted in Chapter 4 that there are also distributional differences between PNs and TCs.

[23] In the present work, I presuppose that in 6a below (and similar examples), the complement of 'believed' really is an NP as it appears to be, and not, as is claimed by Den Dikken et al. (1996,

6a. Russell believed the proposition that arithmetic reduces to logic.
6b. Russell believed that arithmetic reduces to logic.

Not only are 6a and 6b grammatical, but they appear to express propositions that share the same truth value at any circumstance of evaluation.[24] This is probably what one would expect. After all, if, as seems plausible, the occurrences of 2 and 3 in 6a and 6b (respectively) both designate the proposition that arithmetic reduces to logic and if, as we are assuming, 'believes' expresses a two-place relation between individuals and propositions, one would probably expect that 6a and 6b would each be true relative to a circumstance of evaluation iff Russell stands in the belief relation to the proposition that arithmetic reduces to logic in that circumstance.

However, if we use some verbs of propositional attitude other than 'believes', we get sentences like 6a and 6b that fail to be necessarily equivalent:

7a. Amy remembers the proposition that first order logic is undecidable.
7b. Amy remembers that first order logic is undecidable.

These sentences can differ in truth value and so must express different propositions. Suppose that Amy took a class that covered decidability results. She may well remember what first order logic is and what it is to be decidable, and so remember the claim that first order logic is undecidable. So 7a is true. But Amy may well have forgotten whether this claim is true or false. She recalls it being discussed, but can't remember if it or its negation was proved. Then 7b is false. Sentence pairs involving other verbs of propositional attitude behave in the same way. For example,

8a. Jody heard that first order logic is undecidable.
8b. Jody heard the proposition that first order logic is undecidable.
9a. Jody fears that first order logic is undecidable.
9b. Jody fears the proposition that first order logic is undecidable.

8a and 9a might be true, while 8b and 9b are not. For example, Jody might believe with some alarm that first order logic is undecidable, so that 9a is true. And having shaken off Quinean worries about intensional entities, she may not be afraid of any proposition, so that 9b is false. Of course, some might take 8b and 9b to be gibberish. My own view is that they make perfect sense, but are very

---

2002) with respect to similar examples, a "covert" clause. It would be interesting to investigate the phenomenon discussed in the present paper from the standpoint of the view of Den Dikken et al.

[24] I am deliberately skirting the issue of whether 6a and 6b express the same proposition, though they wouldn't on the view of propositions I have been advocating. On views of the semantics of sentences like 6a and 6b according to which they are contextually sensitive, we must consider 6a and 6b as uttered in the same context. The claim would then be that the sentences, so uttered, express propositions that have the same truth value at every circumstance of evaluation. Henceforth, I shall ignore the possibility that 6a and 6b and sentences like them are contextually sensitive, since it seems to me that the question of whether they are or not is orthogonal to present concerns.

unlikely to be true. But even if they are gibberish, since 8a and 9a are not, this shows that 8a and 8b and 9a and 9b may differ in truth value, (in the sense that allows something without a truth value to differ in truth value from something with a truth value). So 7a and 7b (and 8a and 8b; and 9a and 9b) must fail to express the same proposition.

Let us call the phenomenon illustrated by the sentence pairs 7a/7b, 8a/8b and 9a/9b (i.e. that the members of sentence pairs that differ only in that one has a TC where and only where the other has a corresponding PD may differ in truth value (where this includes one having a truth value and the other being gibberish) and so must fail to express the same proposition) *substitution failure*.

We are finally in a position to state the objection that is our present concern. Some authors claim that substitution failure provides an argument against a combination of views I endorse. Kent Bach (1997) claims that it provides evidence against what he calls the *relational analysis of belief reports* (*RABR*). RABR as Bach understands it includes the claim that 'believes' expresses a relation between persons and propositions; the claim that 'the semantic value of a "that" clause is a proposition'; and the claim that in a true belief report, a proposition that the subject of the report believes must be specified (presumably by the complement of 'believes').[25] Michael McKinsey (1999) makes the radical claim that substitution failure cannot be explained on the view that verbs of propositional attitude express relations between persons and propositions.[26] Since I am an advocate of RABR, and so hold that verbs of attitude express

---

[25] Bach does not spell out *precisely* why substitution failure provides evidence against RABR. But what is important here is that he thinks substitution failure supports the radical conclusion that RABR is false. Bach noted (p.c.) that though he thinks substitution failure provides evidence against RABR, he draws the radical conclusion that RABR is false from other arguments. Still, I intend to show that substitution failure can be explained from the perspective of (a version of) RABR, and so it doesn't even provide evidence for Bach's radical conclusion.

[26] McKinsey calls such a view *the relation theory*. Sometimes McKinsey appears to claim only that substitution failure undermines an argument in favor of the relation theory (see the first three paragraphs of his section 6, beginning on p. 529). But he also writes:

(17) Monica thinks that Jimmy is cute.

If 'think' expresses a relation in (17), then the result of replacing the 'that' clause in (17) with a term that refers to the proposition expressed by the imbedded sentence should make sense:

(18) *Monica thinks the proposition that Jimmy is cute.

But to my ear (18) does not make sense. (p. 530)

This certainly makes it sound as though he is claiming that the relation theory cannot explain the substitution failure exemplified by (17) and (18). Actually, McKinsey has chosen a poor example. For it seems to me that the explanation of (17) and (18) is particularly straightforward: 'thinks' takes complementizer (TC) complements but does not take NP complements, (though see next note). Note that 'thinks' does not allow any of the following NPs as complements:

Monica thinks *every student/*flowers/*Logicism/*Sue/*her

Thus (18) is simply ungrammatical. But we could replace his sentence pair with one employing a verb like 'remember' that takes both NP and TC complements, and for which we get substitution failure.

relations between persons and propositions, I must provide some response to the arguments of Bach and McKinsey. I shall argue that substitution failure *can* be explained while maintaining the views that verbs of propositional attitude express relations between individuals and propositions, that that-clauses designate propositions, and that sentences containing verbs of propositional attitude assert that an individual stands in a relation to a proposition. Thus the phenomenon does not undermine what McKinsey calls 'the relation theory' or Bach's RABR.

Before proceeding, let me re-emphasize a point mentioned earlier. As I noted earlier in discussing the syntactic distributions of PDs qua NPs and TCs qua sentential complements, some verbs of attitude take TC complements and do not take NP complements. Earlier, in citing 4, repeated here, I said that 'said', 'hoped' and 'wished' are of this sort:

4. Russell said/hoped/wished that arithmetic reduces to logic/*the proposition that arithmetic reduces to logic.

And indeed, when we look at other NPs, it seems clear that these verbs simply do not take (most) NP complements:[27]

4a. Russell said/hoped/wished *every girl/*Julie/*Logicism/*snakes/*her/*gold.

So though 4 strictly constitutes an instance of substitution failure (since we included the case where one sentence has a truth value and the other is gibberish), substitution failure of *this* sort is very easily explained within our, and virtually any, framework: when we substitute an NP complement for a TC complement where the verb whose complement it is takes only TC complements, we go from a grammatical sentence to an ungrammatical sentence.[28] Of course, this

---

[27] Gilbert Harman, Paul Pietroski and Ernie Lepore noted that 'said', 'wished' and 'hope' (and 'think'—see previous note) can take certain (apparent) NP complements:

Russell hoped/wished/said that.
Russell hoped/wished/said the same thing I did.
Russell said a few words/the only sensible thing that was said all day/the words we were hoping he would say.

That these verbs allow a very small, idiosyncratic range of NP complements doesn't undermine the point made in the text, which is that they syntactically don't allow any other NP complements, (let me remark cryptically that Anthony Everett pointed out to me that one might challenge the claim that the complements in the sentences cited by Pietroski, Lepore and Harman really are NPs; since my point here doesn't require that they aren't, I will not pursue this here). This gives us good reason to think that they syntactically don't allow PNs and PDs, and that this is the reason for substitution failure with such verbs.

[28] Schiffer (2003) claims that this doesn't really explain the substitution failure in question when he writes:

. . . I don't see that [King] provides the kind of explanation of the [substitution] failures I was in search of. For example, as regards 'Jane hopes that Slovenia will win the World Cup', King says that verbs like 'hopes' 'simply do not take (most) NP complements' and that therefore 'substitution failure . . . is very easily explained . . . when we substitute an NP complement for a [that-clause] complement where the verb whose complement it is takes only [that-clause] complements, we go from a grammatical sentence to an ungrammatical sentence.' But I don't see how this explains what

isn't very interesting. Thus, we wish to consider and explain cases in which we get substitution failure, where there is independent reason to think the verbs in question take both TC and NP complements. The pairs 7a/7b, 8a/8b, and 9a/9b are cases of this sort, since these sentences together with the following show that the verbs of attitude in them take both NP and TC complements:

7c. Amy remembers Carl/some friends/snakes/him.
8c. Jody heard Carl/some friends/snakes/him.
9c. Jody fears Carl/some friends/snakes/him.

needs to be explained. If, as the report claims, Jane stands in the hope relation to the proposition to which the *that-clause refers*, then one would expect 'Jane hopes x' to express a property which that proposition has and that, accordingly, a truth will be expressed by any sentence that results from replacing the free variable 'x' with a *singular term that refers to that proposition*. But, even though 'the proposition that Slovenia wins the World Cup' *refers to* the same proposition as 'that Slovenia wins the World Cup', we don't get a true sentence when we put the first *singular term* in place of 'x', and what requires explanation is precisely why that should be. Merely pointing out that 'hopes' takes only that-clause complements exacerbates rather than explains the mystery.' (My emphasis; pp. 95–6, note 36).

There are a couple of problems here. First, Schiffer has failed to grasp my explanation. As is clear from the emphasized portions of the quotation, Schiffer assumes that I am assuming that both TCs and PDs are referring expressions, (or at least he makes this part of the explanation he attributes to me). In fact, I don't hold that either is. Both, I claim, *designate* propositions, where this is consistent with the claim that they function differently semantically and that neither refers (as I in fact think). Now my explanation is that when you have two expressions that designate the same thing, but are of different syntactic categories, you can get substitution failure substituting one expression for the other simply because the "syntactic location" in which the substitution is performed allows only expressions of one of the two syntactic categories. Surely this does explain the substitution failure! Consider an analogous case. As I use the term, both 'now' and 'the present moment' (taken relative to a context whose time is t) designate the same time t, (i.e. both these expressions are *in some way or other* (and possibly different ways) semantically associated with t with the result that when they occur in sentences, as a result of their so-occurring, the sentences express propositions whose truth and falsity depend on the properties possessed by t (including what happened then) and the relations it stands in). But they are of different syntactic categories (at least on some uses of 'now'). Thus, when we take a sentence containing an expression that takes NP complements but not adverbial complements, such as 'at' in the following sentence:

i John is happy at the present moment.

and attempt to substitute 'now' for the NP 'the present moment':

ii *John is happy at now.

we get substitution failure (remember that this includes the case where one thing has a truth value (i) and the other is gibberish (ii)). Surely this *is* an explanation of the substitution failure in i and ii, and indeed it is the correct explanation. I am claiming that the substitution failures in Schiffer's 'hope' examples (see the above quotation) and my 4 in the body of the text are explained in exactly the same way. If the explanation is good in the case of i and ii (it is!) and we have evidence that 'hopes' etc. don't take NP complements (we do!—see 4a) and 'the proposition that p' is an NP and 'that p' isn't, then the explanation looks awfully good for the substitution failures in 4 and Schiffer's 'hopes' examples, contrary to what Schiffer suggests. A second problem is that Schiffer seems unaware that I claim that substitution failure occurs for at least two, and possibly three, different reasons. So there will be two or three different ways of explaining the different kinds of substitution failure, (this will be discussed subsequently). And in the relevant portion of his text (pp. 92-5) Schiffer considers different cases for which I *would* offer different explanations.

We wish to explain substitution failure involving verbs of attitude of *this* sort from the standpoint of our framework.

It is worth stressing that because substitution failure of the sort exhibited by 4 has a purely syntactical explanation, whereas substitution failure of the sort exhibited by 7–9 does not, substitution failure is not a homogeneous phenomenon. Indeed, as I discuss below, there may be three (or even more) different types of substitution failure.

As I said at the outset, it appears that occurrences of PDs and TCs can be used to designate propositions. For example, the PDs in the following sentences certainly appear to designate a proposition:

10. The proposition that first order logic is undecidable is true.
11. Gödel's first incompleteness theorem entails the proposition that first order logic is undecidable.

Surely, 10 attributes the property of being true to the proposition that first order logic is undecidable; and 11 affirms that Gödel's first incompleteness theorem stands in the relation of entailment to the proposition that first order logic is undecidable. Thus, presumably as a result of containing the PD 'the proposition that first order logic is undecidable' and of that PD being in some way semantically associated with the proposition that first order logic is undecidable, the truth or falsity of the propositions expressed by 10–11 (in a circumstance) depends on the properties possessed by the proposition that first order logic is undecidable and the relations it stands in (in that circumstance). But then given the neutral sense in which I am using the terms 'designate', this is just to say that the PDs in those sentences designate this proposition.

Similarly, the TCs in the following sentences also appear to designate a proposition:

12. That first order logic is undecidable is true.
13. Gödel's first incompleteness theorem entails that first order logic is unde- cidable.

Again, surely 12 attributes the property of being true to the proposition that first order logic is undecidable; and 13 affirms that Gödel's first incompleteness theorem stands in the relation of entailment to the proposition that first order logic is undecidable. Thus, just as with 11–12, the truth or falsity of the propositions expressed by 12–13 (in a circumstance) depends on the properties possessed by the proposition that first order logic is undecidable and the relations it stands in (in that circumstance), and does so because of containing the TC 'that first order logic is undecidable' and this TC being in some way semantically associated with the proposition that first order logic is undecidable. As before, this is just to say that the TCs in these sentences designate this proposition.

Though we shall reconsider this assumption later (see our discussion of ATC and ATC+ below), we begin our investigation of substitution failure by assuming that PDs and TCs in all their occurrences designate propositions (and that all occurrences of a given PD or TC designate the same proposition), as they appear to do in 10–13. We also assume that all occurrences of a given PD or TC function semantically in the same way. Adopting these assumptions at the outset just seems to make good methodological sense. We might end up being *forced* to hold that a PD like 'the proposition that first order logic is undecidable' or a TC like 'that first order logic is undecidable' sometimes designates one thing and sometimes another. Or we might be *forced* to hold that some occurrences of this PD or TC function semantically in one way, while other occurrences of the same PD or TC function semantically in another way. But surely a simpler theory of these expressions holds that all occurrences of a given PD or TC designate the same thing, and do so in the same way. It makes good sense to begin by assuming that this simple theory is correct.

These assumptions, together with our observation that e.g. the PD in 10 and the corresponding TC in 12 both designate the proposition that first order logic is undecidable, require that occurrences of this TC and the corresponding PD always designate this same proposition, (and that each occurrence of the PD or TC does so in the same way as every other occurrence of that PD or TC). However, recall that the way we are using the term, that a *PD and TC* designate the same proposition does not require that *they* do so in the same way. In particular, we need not hold that a PD and corresponding TC make the same contributions to propositions expressed by sentences in which they occur. This naturally suggests a way we might try to explain substitution failure. Since 7a and 7b differ only in that 7a has an occurrence of 'the proposition that first order logic is undecidable' where 7b has an occurrence of 'that first order logic is undecidable' (similarly for 8a/8b; 9a/9b), it is tempting to suppose that these must make different contributions to the propositions expressed by 7a and 7b; and that this is how/why 7a and 7b express different propositions and so may diverge in truth value.

Unfortunately, given the assumptions we have made, supposing that 'the proposition that first order logic is undecidable' and 'that first order logic is undecidable' make different contributions to the propositions expressed by 7a and 7b (respectively) won't by itself happily explain how they can differ in truth value. Here is why.

Suppose 'the proposition that first order logic is undecidable' contributes to the proposition expressed by 7a something, say p; and suppose that 'that first order logic is undecidable' contributes to the proposition expressed by 7b something, say q, where *not* $(p = q)$. One or both of p and q may fail to be the proposition that first order logic is undecidable, as long as not $(p = q)$. At any rate, at least one of them must fail to be this proposition. Say it is p. Given our view that the structures of propositions mirror the structures of the sentences expressing them, 7a and 7b express propositions that can be represented as follows:

7a'. [o [R [p]]]
7b'. [o [R [q]]]

(where o is Amy, R is the relation expressed by 'remembers' and p is the propositional contribution of 'the proposition that first order logic is undecidable' and q is the propositional contribution of 'that first order logic is undecidable'). Though p isn't the proposition that first order logic is undecidable, the following must be true: since p is the propositional contribution of 'the proposition that first order logic is undecidable' and since this latter expression designates the proposition that first order logic is undecidable in 7a, p must have the effect of making the truth value of 7a' (at a circumstance) depend on the properties of the proposition that first order logic is undecidable and the relations it stands in (in that circumstance). For to say that in 7a 'the proposition that first order logic is undecidable' designates the proposition that first order logic is undecidable is to say that this occurrence of the expression is in some way semantically associated with the proposition that first order logic is undecidable, so that as a result of its occurring in 7a this sentence expresses a proposition whose truth or falsity at a circumstance depends on the properties of the proposition that first order logic is undecidable and the relations it stands in in that circumstance. But we are now assuming it has this effect by contributing p to the proposition expressed by 7a (i.e. 7a'). Thus p must affect the truth conditions of 7a' by making its truth or falsity at a circumstance depend on the properties of the proposition that first order logic is undecidable and the relations it stands in in that circumstance.

Since 'that first order logic is undecidable' also designates the proposition that first order logic is undecidable, similar remarks apply to q and 7b'. q must have the effect of making the truth or falsity of 7b' (at a circumstance) depend on the properties possessed by the proposition that first order logic is undecidable and the relations it stands in (at that circumstance—though q might have this effect by *being* that proposition since we have assumed only that *p* is not the proposition that first order logic is undecidable). Let us put this by saying that p and q *determine* the proposition that first order logic is undecidable, (this is so even if the *way* that q makes the truth or falsity of 7b' at a circumstance depend on the properties of the proposition that first order logic is undecidable and the relations it stands in in that circumstance is by *being* the proposition that first order logic is undecidable—in that case, q determines itself). Because it will be relevant in a moment, recall that given the way I am using the term 'designate', 'the proposition that first order logic is undecidable' and 'that first order logic is undecidable' may designate things in addition to the proposition that first order logic is undecidable in 7a and 7b. That is, as a result of these expressions occurring in 7a and 7b, the truth or falsity of the propositions expressed by those sentences (at a circumstance) may also depend on the properties possessed by some other entity o* and the relations it stands in (in the circumstance). If this were so, since p and q are the contributions that these expressions make to 7a' and 7b', it must be p and q that have the effect of making the truth or falsity of 7a' and 7b' (at a circumstance) depend on the properties possessed by o* and the relations it stands in (at the circumstance). In such a case we shall also say that p and q determine o* (in addition to the proposition that first order logic is undecidable). Thus, though p and q must both determine the proposition that first order logic is undecidable, one or both of them can determine some other entities as well (and they may determine *different* other entities).

Now looking at 7a' and 7b', it seems that whether they are true or false at a circumstance must depend on how o, R and the things determined by p and q are configured at the circumstance. That is, these propositions represent o, R and the things determined by p and q as being arranged in a certain way. The propositions are true at a circumstance of evaluation if these things are arranged there in the way the propositions represent them as being arranged, false otherwise. In much the same way, a sentence like 'Chris loves the successor of 1' expresses a proposition that can be represented as follows:

[c [L[s]]]

where c is Chris, L is the relation of loving and s is the propositional contribution of the definite description 'the successor of 1'. This proposition represents Chris, the loving relation and the thing determined by s (i.e. 2) as being arranged in a certain way. It is true at a circumstance if those things are arranged in the relevant way, false otherwise.

Returning to 7a' and 7b' then, 7a' is true at a circumstance iff o, R and the thing(s) determined by p are arranged in a certain way there; and 7b' is true iff o, R and the thing(s) determined by q are arranged in a certain way. But then it appears that there are only two ways that 7a' and 7b' could diverge in truth value at a circumstance: 1) one of p or q determines some entity (or entities) o* (in addition to the proposition that first order logic is undecidable) not determined by the other, so that one but not the other of 7a' and 7b' requires for its truth (at a circumstance) that o, R, the proposition that first order logic is undecidable, *and* o* are arranged in a certain way (at the circumstance); or 2) p and q determine the same entities (either only the proposition that first order logic is undecidable or this proposition *and* some additional entities), but 7a' requires that o, R and those entities be arranged one way (at a circumstance) for its truth (at the circumstance), and 7b' requires that *those same things* be arranged a *different way* (at a circumstance) for its truth (at the circumstance).[29] Unfortunately for the

[29] One could of course combine both options, but the arguments I give against each option would apply to the view that combines both options. Presumably an advocate of option 2) would want to hold that there is some difference in the *structures* of the propositions expressed by 7a and

view under consideration, neither of these options seems attractive. If 1) is right, the reason that 7a' and 7b' can differ in truth value at a circumstance is that either p or q determines, and so either 'the proposition that first order logic is undecidable' or 'that first order logic is undecidable' designates, some entity (or entities) o* (in addition to the proposition that first order logic is undecidable) that the other doesn't designate. But this suggestion strikes me as mysterious and ad hoc. The claim is that both of these expressions designate the proposition that first order logic is undecidable and one of them designates in addition something else. But what in the world could this additional entity (or entities) be that is designated by one of these expressions and not the other? Unless some non-ad hoc and philosophically motivated account of what this entity is and why only one of these expressions designates it can be given, this option is unacceptable. And I can think of no such entity and account.

The second option fares no better. On this option, p and q determine the same entities, and so 'the proposition that first order logic is undecidable' and 'that first order logic is undecidable' designate the same entities. Thus, we may as well assume that they both designate only the proposition that first order logic is undecidable, (as seems independently plausible, especially in light of what was said about the first option above). So 2) claims that 7a' and 7b' may differ in truth value at a circumstance because 7a' requires for its truth at a circumstance that o, R and the proposition that first order logic is undecidable be arranged one way at the circumstance; and 7b' requires for its truth at a circumstance that o, R and the proposition that first order logic is undecidable be arranged in a different way at the circumstance. But this is implausible in the extreme! This would mean that these propositions may differ in truth value (at a circumstance) for the same reason that the proposition that Tom loves Sue and the proposition that Sue loves Tom (sadly) may differ in truth value at a circumstance. In both cases, the two propositions require for their truth (at a circumstance) that the *same* things be arranged *differently* (at the circumstance). But in the case of 7a' and 7b', what could these two different arrangements of the *same things* (Amy, the remembers relation and the proposition that first order logic is undecidable) be? One of these arrangements presumably would be Amy standing in the remembers relation to the proposition that first order logic is undecidable. But what would the *other* arrangement of these elements be? It seems to me there is no remotely plausible answer to this question.

Supposing that 'the proposition that first order logic is undecidable' and 'that first order logic is undecidable' make different contributions to the propositions expressed by 7a and 7b (respectively) and that this is how/why the propositions

---

7b that explains why the two propositions require for their truth at a circumstance that the same things be arranged *differently* at the circumstance. This makes no difference to my argument here, so I ignore it. Thanks to John MacFarlane and an anonymous referee for insightful criticism and discussion that resulted in significant improvements in the argument I am giving here.

expressed by those sentences may differ in truth value (at a circumstance) leads to options 1) and 2) above as to *precisely how* the difference may come about. We have now seen that neither option is viable. I conclude that holding that the propositional contributions of 'the proposition that first order logic is undecidable' and 'that first order logic is undecidable' are distinct does not explain why 7a and 7b can diverge in truth value.

It is worth pausing to note that invoking *guises* for, or *modes of presentation* of, propositions does not appear to help explain *our* substitution failure at all. For first, even if we were to invoke such things, it does not seem as though 'the proposition that first order logic is undecidable' and 'that first order logic is undecidable' differ in terms of the guise or mode of presentation under which they present something. Second, in any case, it certainly does not seem as though the difference in truth value between 7a and 7b (in the situation as described) has to do with Amy having multiple modes of presentation of the proposition that first order logic is undecidable. Indeed, we can simply stipulate that Amy has only one way of thinking of this proposition, and we still have the result that 7a and 7b diverge in truth value. Amy remembers the proposition that first order logic is undecidable (presented in way m), but cannot remember whether it (presented in way m) is true or false. Thus she doesn't remember that first order logic is undecidable (when presented in way m).

Before turning to *our* explanation of substitution failure, let us briefly consider a final way one might be tempted to explain it. Though, as we have mentioned, the propositions expressed by 7a and 7b are not necessarily equivalent, those expressed by 7b and 7d appear to be:

7a. Amy remembers the proposition that first order logic is undecidable.
7b. Amy remembers that first order logic is undecidable.
7d. Amy remembers the fact that first order logic is undecidable.

Thus, one might reason as follows. The reason that we get substitution failure in the case of 7a and 7b is that the TC in 7b does not designate the proposition that first order logic is undecidable in that construction, contrary to what we have assumed to this point. Rather, it designates the *fact* that first order logic is undecidable.[30] Thus, substituting 'the fact that first order logic is undecidable', which (presumably in all of its occurrences) designates the fact that first order logic is undecidable, for 'that first order logic is undecidable' gives us a sentence 7d necessarily equivalent to the original sentence 7b. However, when we substitute 'the proposition that first order logic is undecidable' for 'that first order logic is

---

[30] I am not assuming that expressions of the form 'the fact that p' designate what I have called *facts* throughout the book. It is a substantive claim that they do so. I'll remain neutral on that question here. But I shall call the things they designate 'facts' in this chapter and assume that they are not propositions (not even true propositions). So what I call facts henceforth in this chapter may not be the things I have called facts throughout the book. I realize this is a bit awkward, but I couldn't figure out what else to call the things designated by expressions of the form 'the fact that p'.

undecidable', we are substituting an expression designating the *proposition* that first order logic is undecidable for an occurrence of an expression designating the *fact* that first order logic is undecidable. Thus the resulting sentence 7a asserts that Amy stands in the remembering relation to the *proposition* that first order logic is undecidable; whereas the original sentence asserted that Amy stands in the remembering relation to the *fact* that first order logic is undecidable, (of course, one must hold that facts are not simply true propositions). So, the sentences are not necessarily equivalent.

This explanation of substitution failure apparently requires us to say that one can bear the remembers relation to both facts and propositions, (7a affirms that Amy bears the relation to a proposition; 7b affirms that she bears the relation to a fact—of course, one would have to supplement the explanation of substitution failure just given with an account of how/why one can stand in the remembers relation to a (true) proposition without standing in the remembers relation to the relevant fact). It also requires us to say that TCs sometimes designate propositions (for example, when embedded with respect to 'believes') and sometimes designate facts (for example, when embedded with respect to 'remembers').[31] Since a given TC may designate a fact or a proposition depending on the verb of attitude it is embedded with respect to, the explanation posits an ambiguity in TCs. Let us call this way of explaining substitution failure the *ambiguity in that-clause* account, (henceforth *ATC*).[32]

ATC fails to provide the correct explanation of the *general* phenomenon of substitution failure. And if we try to extend it so that we do get a general explanation of the phenomenon, we are left with an empty, unsatisfactory explanation of many cases. Let me take these points in turn.

To see that ATC cannot provide an explanation of the general phenomenon of substitution failure, note that there are cases of substitution failure in which substituting 'the fact that p' for 'that p' does *not* result in a sentence necessarily equivalent to the original sentence. For example, consider the following:

---

[31] Of course, I have claimed throughout the present work that propositions are certain kinds of facts. But as I said in the previous note, I am not assuming that expressions like 'the fact that . . . ' designate what I have called facts throughout the book. Further, the point is that on the view I am describing, 'that first order logic is undecidable' sometimes designates the proposition that first order logic is undecidable and sometimes designates the fact that first order logic is undecidable. Even if this latter fact is the sort of thing I have been calling a fact throughout the book, it is not the fact that I claim is the proposition that first order logic is undecidable. Thus, I'll continue to talk about occurrences of TCs designating facts rather than propositions on the present view, where that means that e.g. an occurrence of the TC 'that p' designates the fact that p and not the proposition that p, (even though the latter is itself a fact in my sense, though not the fact that p).

[32] Terry Parsons (1993) tentatively endorses ATC. See p. 455. From the fact noted here, that ATC must hold that different occurrences of a given TC designate different things, it does not strictly *follow* that ATC must posit an ambiguity in TCs. One could try to assign TCs a univocal semantics that allows some occurrences of TCs to designate facts and other occurrences to designate propositions. But I don't see any motivated way of doing this. And in any case, my argument against ATC and ATC+ would apply to a theory that assigns TCs a univocal semantics.

14a. Ken felt that Nicole was lying.
14b. Ken felt the proposition that Nicole was lying.
14c. Ken felt the fact that Nicole was lying.

Since 14a may be true while 14b is not, we have a case of substitution failure.[33] But clearly 14a might be true while 14c is not. However, if the substitution failure exhibited in 14a/14b were a result of the TC in 14a designating a fact rather than a proposition, as ATC claimed for the previous case 7a/7b/7d, we would expect 14c to be necessarily equivalent to 14a. But it is not. Further, since 14a can be true even if Nicole wasn't lying, 14a cannot assert that Ken stands in some relation to the *fact* that Nicole was lying. But if ATC were correct, this is what 14a would assert. Thus ATC cannot explain the substitution failure here.

We could try to extend ATC to include the claim that the TC in 14a designates some other entity that is *neither* a fact *nor* a proposition; and that this is why 14b and 14c fail to be necessarily equivalent to 14a. Let us call this extension of ATC *ATC+*. It seems to me that the explanation ATC+ gives of examples of substitution failure such as 14a/14b above is very unsatisfactory. ATC+ claims that the TC in 14a designates some non-fact, non-proposition. However, crucially there appears to be *no* definite description such as 'the fact/possibility/state of affairs/circumstance that Nicole was lying' that can be substituted for 'that Nicole was lying' in 14a yielding a sentence necessarily equivalent to 14a. Surely this should make us extremely suspicious. For the evidence in favor of *ATC* (that is, in favor of thinking that TCs sometimes designate facts) was precisely that substituting 'the fact that first order logic is undecidable' for 'that first order logic is undecidable' in 7b yielded a sentence necessarily equivalent to 7b. But in the case of 14a we have no comparable evidence that the TC designates some non-fact/non-proposition. We simply have the substitution failure itself. And if the TC in 14a does designate some non-proposition/non-fact as the ATC+ theorist has to claim, surely it must be some sort of thing like a possibility, state of affairs or whatever. *But then why can't we find a description such as 'the possibility/state of affairs/that Nicole was lying' that can be substituted for the TC in (14a) yielding a sentence necessarily equivalent to it?* These considerations, it seems to me, render ATC+ implausible. In particular, its explanation of cases like 14a–14c is empty, claiming as it does that the that-clauses in such examples designate some we-know-not-what non-fact/non-proposition that cannot be designated by any definite description. And cases like 14a–14c arise with many other verbs, including 'suspect', 'heard', 'expect', 'imagine', 'indicate' and 'explain'.[34] Thus, ATC+ can give no satisfactory explanation for *many* cases of substitution failure.

---

[33] Since 'felt' takes NP complements ('Ken felt a peach/snakes/Marilyn Monroe/her'), the substitution failure here is not a result of 'felt' not taking NP complements.

[34] For 'imagine' to exhibit the relevant behavior, it must be understood in the sense in which imagining that p is thinking or conjecturing that p, (for example, someone asks me where Jay is and I say that I imagine that he is at the movies. I am not here reporting simply that I have formed a mental image of Jay being at the movies). Also, with respect to the verb 'explain', I am assuming

There is a further reason for rejecting ATC+. The following inferences seem valid:

1. Jimmy doubts that first order logic is undecidable and Heather suspects that first order logic is undecidable.
2. So, there is something that Jimmy doubts and that Heather suspects.

1.' Jimmy denies that first order logic is undecidable but Heather knows that first order logic is undecidable

2.' So, there is something that Heather knows and that Jimmy denies.

Yet it does not appear that ATC+ can explain this. For since, according to ATC+, the TC in the first conjunct of each premise designates a proposition and the TC in the second conjunct designates a fact or non-proposition/non-fact, the conclusions should not follow from the premises. But they certainly appear to.[35]

On the basis of these considerations, I reject ATC+. "Officially" I shall leave open the possibility that *ATC* explains substitution failures such as that exhibited in 7a/7b/7d in which the description 'the fact that first order logic is undecidable' can be substituted for a corresponding TC yielding a sentence necessarily equivalent to the original. But this would still leave us without an account of substitution failures such as 14a/14b. Thus, the official position of the present paper is that there are certainly two, and *may* be three, different kinds of substitution failure: 1) substitution failure in which an NP complement is substituted for a TC complement where the verb whose complement it is takes only TC complements, resulting in ungrammaticality (see example 4); 2) substitution failure of the sort exhibited by 14a–14c, which we are about to explain; and 3) substitution failure resulting from substituting a PD for a

---

that explaining that p is different from explaining the fact that p. If John simply told some people that quantifiers take scope, John explained that quantifiers take scope. But he did not thereby explain *the fact* that quantifiers take scope. The latter requires more than simply telling someone that quantifiers take scope.

[35] Admittedly, as noted in Parsons (1993), other similar inferences seem bad in the sense that the conclusions seem somewhat infelicitous. For example,

1". Jimmy believes that first order logic is undecidable and Heather regrets that first order logic is undecidable.
2". So there is something that Jimmy believes and that Heather regrets.

Some explanation needs to be given for why this conclusion sounds odd. Parsons takes the oddness of sentences like the conclusion here to support ATC. The idea is that since, according to ATC, TCs embedded with respect to factives like 'regrets' designate facts, and TCs embedded with respect to non-factives like 'believes' designate propositions, when we try to quantify across both the factive and non-factive context, the result is odd. I don't think data of this sort support ATC, because we can get comparable oddness even attempting to quantify across *two factive* contexts (suppose Joe confessed that he hated Sue and John saw that Joe hated Sue):

*There is something that John saw and that Joe confessed.

It seems to me plausible that whatever explains the oddness in these cases would also explain the oddness of our conclusion above.

corresponding TC, where the TC designates a fact and the PD designates a proposition (see 7a/7b).[36] I am committed to there being substitution failures of types 1 and 2; and I allow that there *may* be substitution failures of type 3. However, I also think that it is possible that alleged instances of type 3 are instances of type 2. Whether this is so or not depends upon how much independent evidence there is for thinking that TCs sometimes designate facts (which are not simply true propositions); and how much independent evidence there is for thinking that they do so in sentences like 7b. Precisely because I think the considerations here are rather subtle, I leave open the possibility that ATC is correct about cases like 7a/7b. However, since we have rejected *ATC+*, we henceforth once again assume that occurrences of TCs (in nonfactive contexts) designate propositions, (unless otherwise indicated).

To return to where we were before digressing to consider ATC and ATC+, whether 'the proposition that first order logic is undecidable' contributes the proposition that first order logic is undecidable to the propositions expressed by 8b/9b ('Jody heard the proposition that first order logic is undecidable.'/'Jody fears the proposition that first order logic is undecidable.') or not, this PD designates this proposition. And this makes it almost inevitable that 9b is true iff Jody stands in a certain relation to the proposition that first order logic is undecidable. Similarly, whether 'that first order logic is undecidable' contributes the proposition that first order logic is undecidable to the proposition expressed by 9a ('Jody fears that first order logic is undecidable.') or not, this TC designates this proposition. And this makes it almost inevitable that 9a is true iff Jody stands in a certain relation to the proposition that first order logic is undecidable, (note that since 9a/9b is not a case to which ATC would apply, the foregoing remarks hold even if ATC is correct). But then it appears that (from the standpoint of our framework) the *only* way for 9a and 9b to diverge in truth value, and hence express different propositions, is for their truth to require that Jody stands in *different relations* to the proposition that first order logic is undecidable. And now that we have mentioned it, this seems *intuitively* correct. In fearing the proposition that first order logic is undecidable, Jody is related to it by being scared of it, (of course, one might think that it is impossible to be scared of propositions, so that 9b is anomalous—but this is to agree that for 9b to be true, Jody *per impossible* must be scared of a proposition). Note that she need not believe that the proposition might be true for 9b to be true. By contrast, in fearing *that* first order logic is undecidable Jody must more or less anxiously believe that the proposition might be true. Note that she need not be scared *of* the proposition for 9a to be true. But then it really does seem that in fearing *the proposition* that first order logic is undecidable intuitively one stands to it in a different relation

---

[36] Schiffer (2003) fails to see that I claim that there are at least two and possibly three kinds of substitution failure, each with a different explanation. He only sees that I claim there is substitution failure of the first type mentioned here. See his p. 95 note 36 and my note 28.

than one stands to it in fearing *that* first order logic is undecidable. Thus, it would appear that 'fears' contributes different relations to the propositions expressed by 9a and 9b and so is ambiguous (or polysemous—see below). By contrast, that 6a and 6b (repeated here for convenience):

6a. Russell believed the proposition that arithmetic reduces to logic
6b. Russell believed that arithmetic reduces to logic.

are necessarily equivalent suggests that 'believe', unlike 'fears', is univocal and expresses the *same* relation in 6a and 6b.

To summarize, I claim that 'fears' is ambiguous (or polysemous), contributing different relations to the propositions expressed by 9a and 9b; and 'believed' is univocal, expressing the same relation in 6a and 6b. This in turn explains why 9a and 9b can diverge in truth value and 6a and 6b cannot. More generally, I claim that there are two classes of verbs of propositional attitude (that take both NP and S complements) where the members of one class are ambiguous in the way that we have claimed 'fears' is and where members of the other are univocal in the way that we have claimed 'believed' is. In particular, here are some examples of members of the first class, ambiguous verbs of propositional attitude (henceforth *AVPs*): 'remember'; 'fear'; 'feel'; 'understand'; 'explain'; 'expect'; 'hear'; 'mention'; 'indicate'; 'suspect'; 'demand'; 'desire'; 'suggest'; 'request'; 'imagine'; 'know'; and 'recommend', (though if ATC is correct, some of these verbs—for example, 'remembers' and 'understand'—are not AVPs). What is characteristic of verbs of this class is that the analogues of 9a and 9b containing them may exhibit substitution failure and so must express different propositions, as we saw in the case of 8a/8b and 7a/7b. I claim that the reason such sentence pairs exhibit substitution failure is that the AVPs in them contribute different relations to the propositions expressed by the a examples than to the propositions expressed by the b examples.

A question that arises here is what determines which relation an AVP contributes to the proposition expressed by the sentence in which it occurs. I incline towards the view that it is the *syntactic category* of the complement of the verb that determines which relation it contributes.[37] The alternative is to claim

---

[37] An astute anonymous referee noted that the phenomenon of substitution failure (or something similar to it) arises in certain cases with predicates as well (assuming, as we have been, that one-place predicates express properties): 'This apple is red' and 'This apple is the property of being red' are not equivalent. The referee suggested that I might argue that the substitution failure arises because 'is' expresses two different relations something can bear to a property: instantiation and identity. He/she further noted that I might claim that the disambiguation is governed by syntax, as I suggest here with respect to AVPs. This account fits very well with the view being defended here, and I thank the referee for this helpful comment and suggestion. Also, Zoltan Szabo noted that in Hungarian, it is not the syntactic *category* of the complement that determines which relation an AVP expresses. This is because in Hungarian we have examples such as:

(a) Amy emlekszik arra az allitasra hogy

Amy remembers to-that the proposition that . . .

that it is the nature of the *semantic value* of the complement of an AVP that determines which relation it contributes to a proposition. On this view, 'that p' and 'the proposition that p' must be assigned different semantic values. Note that this would allow one of the values to be the proposition that p and the other to be an entity that determines (only) the proposition that p. For ease of exposition, let us call the relation an AVP expresses when it has an NP complement its *NP relation* and the relation it expresses when it has a TC complement its *TC relation*.

Here are some members of the second class of verbs, univocal verbs of propositional attitude (henceforth *UVPs*): 'believe'; 'doubt'; 'deny'; 'prove'; 'accept'; 'assert'; 'state'; and 'assume'. The characteristic feature of these verbs is that analogues of 9a and 9b containing them are necessarily equivalent. Thus,

15a. Cari doubts the proposition that first order logic is undecidable.
15b. Cari doubts that first order logic is undecidable.
16a. Cari asserts the proposition that first order logic is undecidable.
16b. Cari asserts that first order logic is undecidable.

Positing two classes of verbs of propositional attitude, the members of one of which are ambiguous, accounts for the data we have looked at. However, positing ambiguity to explain recalcitrant data in semantic theorizing is rightly looked upon with suspicion. Of course, *independent evidence* of ambiguity in such a case ought to allay any such suspicions. And it appears to me that there is independent evidence that members of our one class of verbs really are ambiguous (or polysemous—see below) and the members of the other class are not.

First, as I hinted above, there is a strong *pre-theoretical* intuition that in sentence pairs containing AVPs such as 9a and 9b, the verbs in question have different meanings. As we said in discussing 9a and 9b, fearing the proposition that first order logic is undecidable intuitively involves being scared and does not involve belief; whereas fearing that first order logic is undecidable intuitively involves (anxiously) believing something might be the case and does not involve being scared of anything. But then intuitively, we feel as though 'fear' in 9a

(b) Amy emlekszkik arra hogy . . .

Amy remembers to-that that . . .
where these exhibit the readings corresponding to the English pair:

(a') Amy remembers the proposition that . . .
(b') Amy remembers that . . .

But the Hungarian examples have complements of the *same* syntactic category, since both are headed by the demonstrative pronoun 'arra' and so are NPs. Here we can claim that it is *all* the syntactic *properties* of the complement (including their internal syntactic structures) that trigger the verb expressing one relation rather than another. Of course, the claim that it is the syntactic *category* of the complement that triggers the verb expressing the relation it does may still be correct for English. But since this doesn't appear to be correct cross-linguistically, perhaps even for English we should put the point in terms of *all* syntactic *properties* of the complements, which of course includes their syntactic categories.

and 9b has two different meanings, one of which involves being scared but not believing anything, and the other of which involves believing something but not being scared. Similarly, there is a pre-theoretical intuition that in the following two sentences, the AVP 'felt' means different things:

17a. Steve felt the proposition that arithmetic reduces to logic.
17b. Steve felt that arithmetic reduces to logic.

The truth of 17a requires Steve to have had a tactile experience, and does not require that Steve was positively disposed toward the view that arithmetic reduces to logic (again here, one might hold that 17a is anomalous because it is impossible to feel propositions—but again this is to agree that the truth of the sentence requires that Steve feel a proposition). The truth of 17b requires Steve to be positively disposed toward the view that arithmetic reduces to logic, but does not require that he had a tactile experience. So here again we have a pre-theoretical intuition that the meaning of the verb in 17a involves things that the meaning of the verb in 17b does not involve, and vice versa. By contrast, there is *no* pre-theoretical intuition that in the sentence pairs containing UVPs (6a/6b; 15a/15b; 16a;16b) the verbs have different meanings. That *even pre-theoretically* we feel as though in sentence pairs such as 9a/9b and 17a/17b the verbs have different meanings, and that we don't feel this way about sentence pairs such as 6a/6b, 15a/15b and 16a/16b, *strongly* supports the claim that AVPs really are ambiguous and UVPs are not.

Second, it is suggestive that AVPs generally allow a much wider range of NP complements than do UVPs. As the following examples show, AVPs can take as NP complements referring expressions, bare plurals, mass nouns, and quantifier phrases of all sorts.[38]

18. I fear Cari/snakes/water/every car/her.
19. I desire Cari/snakes/water/every car/her.

By contrast, UVPs allow a very limited range of NP complements:

20. I deny *Cari/*snakes/*water/*every car/the proposition that arithmetic reduces to logic.

---

[38] Some AVPs are more limited than others in the sorts of NP complements they can take. For example, 'suspect' can take as complements NPs "denoting" people ('John', 'every student'), and NP's denoting something like action types ('arson', 'treason'). But it isn't entirely clear what to make of sentences like 'I suspect rocks.' (though as Delia Graff Fara and an anonymous referee pointed out, if one thinks rocks are sentient one can felicitously utter this sentence). Presumably this variation is explained by the NP relation a given AVP expresses. Some AVPs express NP relations that can hold between people and all sorts of things (for example, 'fear'). Other AVPs express NP relations that persons can bear only to a limited class of things (for example, 'suspect'), and so the sorts of NP complements such verbs felicitously allow is more restricted. Still, AVPs allow a wider range of NP complements than UVPs.

21. I assert *Cari/*snakes/*water/*every car/the proposition that arithmetic reduces to logic.

Indeed, many and perhaps most UVPs appear to allow only NP complements that designate propositions or quantify over them ('logicism'; 'the proposition that arithmetic reduces to logic'; 'what John said'; 'every theorem of Peano arithmetic'; etc.). Exceptions to this seem primarily to involve cases like 'believe' and 'doubt', where NPs denoting things that in some sense can (or are thought to) *give expression to* propositions, or contain expressions expressing propositions, are also allowed:

22. Cari believes/doubts Terry/the Tarot cards/the Bible/*furniture.

However, even in these exceptional cases, the truth value of the sentence is determined by whether the subject of the ascription bears the belief relation to some proposition, (for example, to believe Terry presumably is to believe something Terry said, wrote or etc.).[39]

This data, it seems to me, is quite suggestive. If UVPs really are univocal and express relations between individuals and propositions, then this would explain why the NP complements allowed by such verbs would be restricted to those that designate propositions (or designate things that give expression to or contain expressions expressing propositions). By contrast, if AVPs express two

---

[39] There still is a question as to the precise semantics of sentences containing UVPs like 'believes' or 'doubts', where the NP complement designates something that can give expression to propositions (or contains expressions expressing propositions, etc.). It seems to me that there are at least three accounts one might give. Consider the sentence

(i) Cari believes Terry.

The first account one might offer is that 'Terry' here at the relevant level of syntactic representation is something like 'what Terry said'. The latter is an NP designating a proposition, and so (i) is true iff Cari bears the belief relation to the proposition denoted by the latter NP. Thus, on such a view NP complements of 'believes', etc. that apparently designate non-propositions are at the relevant level of syntax NPs that designate propositions. A second account would hold that 'believes' expresses a relation between individuals and propositions or things that can assertively express propositions (or things that contain expressions assertively expressing propositions, etc.). Necessarily, this relation holds between an individual and a thing that can express a proposition iff it holds between that individual and a certain proposition assertively expressed by the thing that can express a proposition, where the individual knows that the thing that can express a proposition assertively expressed the proposition in question. A third view holds that UVPs such as 'believes' are ambiguous: they express relations between individuals and propositions and relations between individuals and things that can assertively express propositions. However, necessarily an individual stands in the latter relation to a thing that can express a proposition iff she stands in the former relation to a certain proposition assertively expressed by the thing that can express propositions, and knows that the thing in question assertively expressed the proposition in question. Of course, on this third option such UVPs are ambiguous. Still, on all three of these options, an individual standing in the relation expressed by such a verb to a proposition is in some sense "basic", since the truth of a sentence containing such a verb and an NP complement that (apparently) doesn't designate a proposition is explicated in terms of an individual standing in the relation in question to a proposition. In this sense, the UVPs in question are still importantly different from AVPs. Thanks to Jason Stanley for insightful comments on these issues that helped me see some of the possibilities here.

different relations, one of which obtains between individuals and propositions (their TC relations) and the other of which obtains between individuals and objects of various sorts (their NP relations), this would explain why the class of NP complements such verbs allow is so much wider than the class allowed by UVPs.

The third bit of evidence that AVPs are ambiguous and that UVPs are not concerns data involving gapping. Consider a sentence such as:

22. Tom fears snakes and John bears.

Such sentences are a bit awkward, but the idea is that the second conjunct verb has been ellipsed. Thus the second conjunct contains a null verb with the semantic properties of its antecedent ('fears'). So the second conjunct means that John fears bears. Now suppose that Bert and Dave are deranged and that they have come to think that certain abstract objects, including properties and propositions, might visit them. I make this supposition so that sentences such as 'Dave expects the property of being red' or 'Dave expects the Pythagorean theorem.' should not sound completely anomalous in this context. Now consider the following sentences:

*23. Bert expects that arithmetic reduces to logic and Dave the proposition that set theory is consistent.

24. Bert believes that arithmetic reduces to logic and Dave the proposition that set theory is consistent.

Though both sentences, like 22 itself, are somewhat awkward, my judgment is that 23 is significantly worse than 24, (and I find most people make the same judgment). The claim that AVPs are ambiguous and UVPs are not would explain this. The first conjunct of 23 asserts that Bert stands in a certain relation R to the proposition that arithmetic reduces to logic. R here is the relation we claim that 'expects' expresses that obtains between individuals and propositions (its TC relation). 'Expects' expresses this relation because its so doing is triggered by its having a TC complement in the first conjunct. The ellipsed verb in the second conjunct should express the same relation, (we assume that the ellipsed verb must express the same relation as its antecedent). But here the object of the verb is an NP. Thus, we have a sort of conflict. The ellipsed verb is constrained to be interpreted the same way as its antecedent, as expressing R; but it takes an NP complement, which triggers the ellipsed verb expressing a relation other than R. Thus the sentence is very awkward. Presumably, the awkwardness of 'Bert threw a party and Tom a baseball.' has a similar explanation. By contrast, in 24 the antecedent verb and the ellipsed verb both will be interpreted in the same way, since they are univocal and so there is no triggering of the expression of different relations by complements of different categories. Thus the conflict present in 23 is not present here. So we predict that 24 will be significantly less awkward than 23. And so it seems to be.

This point is supported by the following consideration. Consider the result of substituting PNs for PDs in 23–4:

*25. Bert expects that set theory is consistent and Dave logicism.
26. Bert believes that set theory is consistent and Dave logicism.

Here again the example with the AVP is significantly worse. And as before, we attribute this to the fact that the first and second conjuncts have complements of different syntactic categories and so "trigger" the AVP expressing different relations in those conjuncts. At the same time, the ellipsed verb is constrained to be interpreted the same way as its antecedent. Thus, an unresolvable conflict arises. Not so in the case of 26.

Admittedly, these judgments regarding 23–6 are a bit subtle. My suspicion is that this *may be* because AVPs are really polysemous rather than ambiguous. For with polysemous verbs, it appears that sentences such as 23 and 25 can range from quite awkward to almost impeccable. As I've already said, I do think that 23 and 25 are much more awkward than 24 and 26. But if AVPs really are polysemous, they may do significantly better on traditional ambiguity tests (such as the gapping just considered) than truly ambiguous expressions. Thus the subtlety of the judgments here. For simplicity, I shall continue to talk of AVPs being ambiguous; but I should be taken to mean *ambiguous or polysemous*. And indeed, I currently lean towards the view that AVPs are polysemous.[40]

A loose end remains to be tied up, and it is related to my claim that some verbs of propositional attitude are ambiguous and that which relation they express in a given sentence is determined by the syntactic category of their complements.[41]

---

[40] Roughly, polysemy is the phenomenon whereby a word has two or more *significantly related* meanings (in this it distinguishes itself from straight ambiguity), as perhaps does 'eye' in examples such as 'eye of a person', 'eye of the hurricane'. An anonymous referee worried that if the translations of AVPs into other languages behave like AVPs, this would undermine the position being defended here. I take it the worry is that if a verb really is ambiguous (or polysemous), we would expect there to be languages in which the verb is disambiguated. Hence, if AVPs are not disambiguated in other languages, this would be a blow to the present view. Two comments on this. First, I claim 'know' is an AVP and it *is* disambiguated in other languages. So presumably this is evidence *for* the current view. Second, sometimes polysemous words are not "dispolysemated" in other languages. E.g. in English, the polysemous word 'mouth' can apply both to human orifices and places where rivers meet the ocean. The same is true for the Spanish 'boca'. Presumably the question of whether we should expect disambiguation/dispolysemation in other languages depends on how closely related the distinct meanings are. Since AVPs may, and I think do, differ in this regard, we might expect cross linguistic disambiguation/dispolysemation in some cases and not others. Thus, it seems to me subtle questions are involved in interpreting the cross linguistic data here.

[41] In discussing this above, I said that we should hold either that it is the syntactic category of the complement of an AVP that determines which relation it expresses or that it is the nature of the *semantic value* of the complement of an AVP that determines which relation it expresses. If the latter, then expressions of the different syntactic categories have different sorts of semantic value. But then the syntactic category of the complement indirectly determines which relation an AVP expresses. The syntactic category determines the nature of the semantic value, where that nature determines which relation an AVP expresses. So here I shall just talk about the syntactic category of the complement determining which relation an AVP expresses.

It concerns sentences in which AVPs have 'something', 'everything' or 'nothing' as their complements.[42] Thus consider the following sentence:

27. Tara mentioned something.

Given what has been said to this point, since 'something' is an NP it results in 'mentioned' expressing its NP relation. However, the following inference appears to be valid:[43]

1'''. Tara mentioned that first order logic is undecidable.
2'''. So, Tara mentioned something

But on my account, the argument is not valid. Since the complement of 'mentioned' in the premise is a TC, the view we have outlined claims that 'mentioned' in the premise expresses its TC relation. But from the fact that Tara stands in this TC relation to the proposition that first order logic is undecidable, it doesn't follow that Tara stands in the quite different NP relation to anything! Thus, the truth of the premise does not force the truth of the conclusion given what I have said.[44]

Of course, 27 also has a reading on which 'mentioned' expresses its NP relation. For the following argument is valid:

1''''. Tara mentioned the proposition first order logic is undecidable.
2''''. So, Tara mentioned something

'Mentioned' in the premise expresses its NP relation. Thus, for the conclusion to follow from the premise, 'mentioned' in the conclusion must express its NP

---

[42] Friederike Moltmann (2002) brought data of this sort to my attention.

[43] When I say that the argument is valid, I mean that the premise and conclusion have readings on which the conclusion follows from the premise, (or perhaps that on the readings in question, the truth of the premises makes the truth of the conclusion metaphysically impossible).

[44] It might be thought that we could explain why the inference is valid in the following way. Suppose the premise is true, so that Tara mentioned that first order logic is undecidable, (that is, Tara stands in the TC relation expressed by 'mentioned' to the proposition that first order logic is undecidable). For Tara to do this, she must mention logic, (that is, stand in the NP relation expressed by 'mentioned' to logic). (The underlying assumption here is that it is impossible to mention that first order logic is undecidable without mentioning logic—of course one could do the latter without doing the former.) But since Tara stands in the NP relation expressed by 'mentioned' to logic, she stands in the NP relation expressed by 'mentioned' to something. That is, she mentioned something. So the conclusion is true. Though such an explanation *may* explain the validity of such inferences containing AVPs like 'mentioned', it can't explain the validity of the following inference involving another AVP:

(i) George suspects that John is rich.
(ii) So, George suspects something.

Here the above explanation won't work, because we can't move from the truth of the premise to the truth of the claim that George suspects John, or . . . (as we did from the truth of 'Tara mentioned that first order logic is undecidable' to the truth of 'Tara mentioned logic'). Thus, there are at any rate some valid inferences of this sort involving AVPs that are not explained in the way suggested.

relation. Of course our account does predict that 27 has a reading on which 'mentioned' expresses its NP relation.

To summarize the main point here, it appears that 27 has a reading on which 'mentioned' expresses its TC relation even though it has an NP as its complement; and so our claim that it is the syntactic category of the complement that determines which relation an AVP expresses is incorrect. Similar considerations suggest that when an AVP has 'everything' or 'nothing' as its complement, it can express its TC relation.

The interesting thing about this phenomenon is that it appears that 'everything', 'nothing' and 'something' are unique among NPs in this respect. That is, when an AVP has *virtually any other NP as its complement*, it expresses (only) its NP relation. To illustrate, consider the following sentences:

28. Tara mentioned Michelle.
29. Tara mentioned most past presidents.
30. Tara mentioned the Goldbach conjecture.

The NP relation expressed by 'mentioned' is a relation an individual can bear to many sorts of objects; and one bears this relation to an object by referring to it in an incidental manner. By contrast when one mentions that first order logic is undecidable, and so stands in the *TC* relation expressed by 'mentions' to the proposition that first order logic is undecidable, one bears a relation to the proposition that one cannot bear to non-propositions and that requires one to assertively utter a sentence that expresses the proposition. Now it should be clear that in 28–30 'mentioned' expresses its NP relation. For each sentence merely asserts that Tara referred to something in an incidental manner. This is so even when the NP complement designates a proposition, as in 30. 30 doesn't entail that Tara mentioned *that* an even number greater than two is the sum of two primes (and thus that she committed herself to the truth of Goldbach's conjecture), and so doesn't entail that Tara stands in the TC relation expressed by 'mentioned' to the Goldbach conjecture.[45]

In addition, whenever 'mentioned' has a TC complement, it expresses its TC relation; and so the truth of the sentence in which it occurs requires the subject of the ascription to have assertively uttered a sentence expressing the proposition designated by the TC.

Thus, the NPs 'something', 'everything' and 'nothing' appear to provide singular exceptions to our claim that an AVP expresses its NP relation when and only when it has an NP complement; and that it expresses its TC relation when and only when it has a TC complement.[46] I am not at all sure why 'something',

[45] Similar remarks apply to 'know'. The truth of the sentence 'Tara knows the Goldbach conjecture' does not require Tara to know that an even number greater than two is the sum of two primes. Rather, it requires Tara to be familiar with the (the content of the) conjecture.

[46] 'That' is another exception. 'Tara mentioned that' can be true if Tara stands in the TC relation expressed by 'mentioned' to the proposition 'that' designates (in the context of utterance). At any

'everything', and 'nothing' behave in this exceptional way. But there is a bit of data that is both suggestive and comforting. Earlier, I noted that certain verbs of propositional attitude do not take NP complements. Among them are 'say', 'wish', and 'hope'. I cited the following as evidence that these verbs do not take NP complements:[47]

4a. Russell said/hoped/wished *every girl/*Cara/*some fish/*snakes/*her/*gold.

Curiously, these verbs can take 'something', 'everything' and 'nothing' as complements:[48]

4a'. Russell said/hoped/wished something/nothing/everything.

This is comforting, because we are forced to claim that 'something', 'everything' and 'nothing' behave unlike other NPs when they are complements of AVPs in that the TC readings of AVPs are available in such cases. However, 4a and 4a' show that 'something', 'everything' and 'nothing' exhibit other behavior that is unlike that exhibited by other NPs. That 'something', 'everything' and 'nothing' behave unlike other NPs in sentences like 4 makes our claim that they behave exceptionally in sentences like 27 more plausible and less ad hoc.[49]

Further, the data comprising 4a and 4a' are suggestive. Given that here 'something', 'everything' and 'nothing' behave syntactically in a most un-NP-like fashion, perhaps it is not surprising that they don't, as "normal" NPs do, require the AVPs whose complements they are to express NP relations. After all, if NPs require AVPs to express NP relations, then it is reasonable to suppose that NPs that behave syntactically in un-NP-like ways would not require this. This is

---

rate, 'that', 'something', 'everything' and 'nothing' are singular exceptions to our claim that an AVP expresses its NP relation when and only when it has an NP complement.

[47] Of course a sentence like 'Russell said snakes' can be given in response to a question such as 'What is the most common animal around here?' But here 'snakes' in the complement is elliptical for something like 'Snakes are the most common animal around here'. The point is that 'said' cannot take an NP complement that is not elliptical for a full clause, (except for the NPs already noted).

[48] Some of these can sound a bit odd, for example, 'Russell hoped everything'. But this is simply because it is hard to see how one could hope *everything*. As noted earlier, these verbs can also take 'that' as complements. See notes 27 and 46.

[49] Jason Stanley and Delia Graff Fara independently noted another apparently related respect in which 'everything', 'something' and 'nothing' behave unlike other quantificational NPs. The sentence 'John is everything his mother wanted him to be: a doctor, a good father, kind, and handsome.' is fine even though the "substitution instances" of 'everything' include expressions from different syntactic categories (for example, 'a good father'; 'kind'—similar examples can be constructed with 'something' and 'nothing'). By contrast, other quantifiers don't allow this, as witnessed by the anomalousness of 'John has every property his mother wanted him to have: a doctor, a good father, kind, and handsome.' (the only expressions that would work here are 'kindness', etc.). That 'everything' etc. allow "substitution instances" from different syntactic categories is probably related to their odd behavior noted in the text, since here 'Tara mentioned something' follows from sentences with complements of different syntactic categories, (though it expresses different propositions in the two cases). This all supports the claim made in the text that these NPs behave quite unlike other NPs in various respects.

especially so, if, as we claim, it is the *syntactic category* of the complement of an AVP that determines which relation it expresses.

In summary, I have explained substitution failure from the standpoint of a framework that includes the assumptions that verbs of propositional attitude express relations between individuals and propositions; that TCs and PDs designate propositions; and that in a true belief report the subject of the report bears the belief relation to the proposition designated by the TC (or PD) in it. I have thus shown that the radical conclusions Bach, McKinsey and others draw from the phenomenon of substitution failure are unwarranted. The phenomenon of substitution failure threatens neither what Bach calls RABR nor the claim that verbs of propositional attitude express relations between individuals and propositions. Thus, those, like me, who accept both these views having nothing to fear from this phenomenon.

6

Tense, Modality, and Propositions

Though we have lately considered some issues in the philosophy of language, much of the material in the previous chapters was metaphysics. It is now time to step back and consider structured propositions in their role as semantic values of sentences. Specifically, I want to consider the assignment of propositions to sentences of a language, like English, that contains modal locutions, locational expressions, tense and temporal expressions, and verbs of propositional attitude. The emphasis in the present chapter will not be on the particular account of structured propositions I have been defending, nor even on accounts of structured propositions as opposed to accounts according to which they are unstructured. My goals here are to clarify the nature of propositions considered as semantic values, the nature of a compositional assignment of semantic values to sentences, and the nature of circumstances at which propositions are evaluated for truth and falsity. Further, as I'll discuss below, I want to meet a challenge to the motivation for positing propositions mentioned in the Introduction. Those goals are best served by abstracting from the details of particular accounts of propositions.[1]

The relevant issues are best brought out by beginning with a rough sketch of what I take to be an attractive, albeit naïve, picture. The attractiveness I take to be obvious; its naiveté, though perhaps also obvious, will come out shortly and bring the relevant issues into sharp focus. A primary purpose of a semantics for a natural language is to compositionally assign to sentences semantic values that determine whether the sentences are true or false. Since natural languages contain contextually sensitive expressions, semantic values must be assigned to sentences relative to contexts. These semantic values are *propositions.* Sentence types may also be associated with higher level semantic values that are or determine functions from contexts to propositions (something like what David Kaplan calls "character").[2]

---

[1] What follows is drawn from King (2003). Thanks to Blackwell Publishing for their kind permission to use this material.

[2] Actually, things may be a bit more complicated than this. First, some word types may not be associated with characters. For example, a demonstrative pronoun like 'he' may not have a character. It would seem that only tokens accompanied by demonstrations or accompanying intentions have characters (perhaps such word types are associated with something like functions from demonstrations or intentions to characters). But then a sentence type containing such a pronoun will not have the character level semantic value I mention here, since the sentence type by

As has been discussed, these propositions play a number of roles. Propositions are bearers of truth and falsity; and they are also the objects of our attitudes: they are things we doubt, believe, and assume. Further, sentences that contain verbs of propositional attitude, such as

1. Julia believes that Squaw Valley is a skier's paradise.

assert that an individual stands in a certain relation to a proposition. In addition, there are various expressions that embed sentences, which I shall call *sentence operators*, that are such that the truth values of sentences containing them (relative to a context) depend in part on the propositions expressed by the sentences they embed (relative to the context).[3] I shall put this by saying that the sentence operators in question *operate* on the propositions expressed by the sentences they embed. For example, the truth value of a sentence (relative to a context) like:

2. Necessarily, a skier is an athlete.

depends in part on the proposition expressed by the embedded sentence (relative to the context) (and not merely on the truth value of the embedded sentence (relative to the context)).

Finally, in addition to modal operators there are other sentence operators, most notably tenses and temporal expressions such as 'Sometimes' as well as location expressions such as 'In Carnelian Bay', that operate on propositions: again, the truth value of a whole sentence containing such an expression (relative to a context) depends in part on the proposition expressed by the embedded sentence (relative to that context).

A nice, neat story if ever there was one! Yet it involves a quite significant and not very well concealed tension. According to the story, propositions are the objects of our attitudes and verbs of propositional attitude express relations between individuals and propositions. In addition modal operators, tense operators, and location operators all operate on propositions. For all this to be so, (at least

---

itself is not associated with a function from contexts to propositions. So perhaps only a sentence type taken together with appropriate demonstrations or intentions has this character level semantic value. I ignore this complication here. Second, I am in fact somewhat skeptical as to whether a semantics assigns to *sentences* (and other syntactically complex expressions) characters at all, and I have expressed that skepticism elsewhere (King and Stanley 2005). It may be that only the syntactically simple parts of sentences are assigned characters by the semantics. One might hold this because one doesn't think that the characters of sentence parts are combined compositionally by the semantics to yield the character of a whole sentence. I shall nonetheless speak of sentence characters in the present work, because doing so will facilitate making contact with the work of other philosophers I discuss. Thanks to Jason Stanley for helping me get clear on these issues.

[3] Unless explicitly indicated, I use the term 'sentence operator' for certain non-truth-functional expressions that embed sentences. I am suppressing explicit reference to circumstances of evaluation here, and assuming that a feature or features of the context is/are used as the circumstance of evaluation. In Chapter 3, I used the term *propositional connective* to refer to the class of expressions that includes what I am here calling *sentence operators* as well as things like 'John believes', and other expressions.

some) propositions must vary in truth value across worlds, times and locations *and* be the objects of our attitudes. For if e.g. a location operator such as 'In Carnelian Bay' operates on propositions and is not vacuous, then the truth value of a sentence containing it (in a context) must depend on the truth value of the proposition expressed by the sentence it embeds (in that context) *at Carnelian Bay*. In particular, whether a sentence like:

3. In Carnelian Bay there is a boat launching ramp.

is true or false (relative to a context) depends on whether 'there is a boat launching ramp' expresses a proposition (in that context) that is true or false relative to or at Carnelian Bay. If 'there is a boat launching ramp' expressed a proposition (relative to that context) that didn't vary its truth value over locations, the location operator 'In Carnelian Bay' would be vacuous, and the sentence would "feel" like 'In Carnelian Bay arithmetic is incomplete.' But it doesn't! In an exactly similar way, if tense and modal operators operate on propositions and are not vacuous, propositions must vary their truth values across times and worlds. And finally, again, propositions are the things we believe, doubt and so on.

But now the tension present in our neat story is all too clear.[4] On the one hand, as we have seen, if the relevant tense, location and modal operators operate on propositions and are non-vacuous, propositions must vary in truth value across times, locations and worlds. On the other hand, though it seems correct to hold that the things I believe, doubt, etc. can change truth value across *worlds* (i.e. some of the things I believe are true though they would have been false had the world been different), it is hard to make sense of the idea that the things I believe may change truth value across time and location. What would it be e.g. to believe that the sun is shining, where what I believe is something that varies in truth value across times and locations in the actual world? It seems clear that when I believe that the sun is shining, I believe something about a particular time and location, so that what I believe precisely does not vary in truth value over times and locations. Right now I am in Santa Monica looking out the window. I believe the sun is shining. Is it really credible to think that my belief is *not* about Santa Monica now? If that is so, why do I take my current perceptual experience of Santa Monica as the basis for my belief? Further, powerful arguments have been given against the view that the objects of belief are things that change truth value over time.[5] So it appears that propositions must and must not change truth value across time and location. Something has to give.

---

[4] For many of us, certainly for me, this tension was made manifest by some of David Kaplan's remarks in Kaplan (1989). See pp. 502–4 including footnote 28, and p. 546. Kaplan talks primarily about modal and tense operators, but he does at least flirt with the idea of location operators (p. 504). Still, his formal fragment doesn't contain location operators, though it does contain the "position constant" 'here'. It is interesting that in Kaplan's formalism, 'now' is a sentence operator and 'here' is a position constant.

[5] See Richard (1981). I should add that I don't object to the idea that there are temporally neutral contents. I object to the idea that they are the objects of our attitudes. See note 36.

On the basis of considerations such as these, David Lewis (1980) argues that in an important sense, propositions aren't semantic values of sentences at all, not even relative to context. Lewis agrees that for a variety of reasons, we need to assign propositions to sentences in contexts.[6] But he claims that even if we adopt an approach to semantics that assigns semantic values to sentences relative to contexts, these can't be propositions, the things that are objects of our attitudes.[7] They will, however, be the things that modal, tense and location operators operate on. Further, on this way of doing semantics, the assignment of these non-propositional semantic values to sentences (relative to context) is its primary task. The assignment of propositions to sentences relative to contexts is quite secondary and is not even a job for compositional semantics! In addition, if Lewis is right, the motivation for propositions discussed in the Introduction will be to some extent undermined. For among the jobs to be performed that motivated the positing of propositions were being the objects of the attitudes and being the things on which modal operators operate. But if Lewis is right, no one thing can do both jobs. It's true that Lewis himself still allows that we need propositions to be the objects of the attitudes. But the fewer roles there are for them to play, the greater the chance that other foes of proposition will claim we should get by without them.

Friends of propositions will not be happy to see propositions demoted in this way nor to see their motivation threatened. But if we go this far with Lewis, much more radical and unhappy conclusions threaten to follow. As indicated, on an approach to semantics on which we assign sentences semantic values relative to contexts, Lewis argues these values cannot be propositions. As the above comments suggest and as we will see below, the reason is that in many cases in which a sentence is embedded in a larger sentence, what the embedded sentence taken relative to context contributes to the semantic value of the larger sentence in that context cannot be a proposition. So assigning sentences propositions relative to contexts won't in the general case capture the contribution sentences make to the semantic values relative to contexts of larger sentences in which they occur. Thus in addition to assigning sentences propositions relative to contexts, we must assign sentences semantic values relative to those contexts that *do* capture the contributions such sentences make to the semantic values relative to the context of larger sentences in which they occur. Let us call the latter *compositional semantic values*, since they are the values that sentences contribute to the semantic values of larger sentences of which they are parts.

So according to Lewis, on the one hand, we assign to sentences relative to contexts *propositions*, which capture the beliefs sincere speakers express by means

---

[6] At least Lewis (1980) agrees with this—see p.37. Of course, Lewis (1979) may not agree.

[7] Nor, of course, can they be *un*relativized character level semantic values, since we are talking of the assignment to sentences of semantic values *relative to context*.

of their utterances and what it is that they assert. On the other hand, we also need to assign to sentences relative to contexts (non-propositional) *compositional semantic values*, to capture the semantic contribution sentences relative to contexts make to the semantic values relative to contexts of larger sentences in which they occur. These two kinds of semantic values appear to be close analogues of Michael Dummett's (1991) *assertoric content* and *ingredient sense*. Roughly, the former captures what is asserted by an utterance of an unembedded sentence; and the latter captures the semantic contribution embedded sentences make to the semantic values of the larger sentences of which they are parts. Though semanticists have not been quick to embrace Dummett's view that sentences have both of these two kinds of semantic values (and that they are distinct), Lewis can be construed as providing an *argument* that this is in fact the case. Now this is where the real trouble begins.

Jason Stanley (1997a) precisely construes Lewis as providing an argument to the effect we need to assign to sentences both ingredient senses, Lewis's compositional semantic values, and assertoric contents, Lewis's propositions.[8] Further, Stanley argues that once we see that what a sentence contributes to the semantic value of larger sentences containing it cannot in general be identical to what the same sentence taken unembedded asserts, the reasons for adopting a well entrenched semantic thesis are undermined. The thesis Stanley calls *the rigidity thesis (RT)*: no rigid term ever has the same content as a non-rigid term.[9] Why believe RT? Well suppose 'Aristotle' (which I assume is rigid) and 'the greatest student of Plato' (which I assume is not rigid) have the same content. Then the sentences:

4. Aristotle is Plato's greatest student.
5. The greatest student of Plato is Plato's greatest student

also have the same content.[10] But 4 and 5 can't have the same content, because they have different modal profiles. So 'Aristotle' and 'the greatest student of Plato' don't have the same content. Thus, RT. But wait, Stanley says. Lewis has shown that each of 4 and 5 needs to be assigned a semantic value that captures what it asserts unembedded (relative to a context): something like Dummett's *assertoric content*. And they need to be assigned semantic values (relative to a context) that capture what they contribute to the semantic values (relative to a context) of larger sentences in which e.g. temporal and locational operators embed them: something like Dummett's *ingredient sense*. Now when we consider the modal profile of sentences such as 4 and 5, the question is: are we considering a property of the sentences' assertoric contents or of their ingredient senses? If the

---

[8] See pp. 575–6 and note 48.
[9] This is the formulation from Stanley (1997b). The formulation in Stanley (1997a) is slightly different in various respects, but the underlying general idea is clearly the same.
[10] I here assume a thesis about compositionality of content.

latter and if we assign assertoric contents and ingredient senses to sub-sentential expressions, we can consistently hold that a rigid and non-rigid term have the same assertoric content and that so do sentences such as 4 and 5.[11] Thus, we can hold that 4 and 5 have different ingredient senses, and our intuitions about their modal profiles track this, while having the same assertoric contents. This contradicts RT, *if* we understand 'content' in RT to be assertoric content. But it appears proper to understand it this way, since the contents of rigid and non-rigid terms are supposed to be what they contribute to the contents of sentences containing them. And the contents of sentences are what is asserted by utterances of them.

Now Stanley wouldn't actually want to rest his case against RT on an example like 4 and 5. For the claim that 4 and 5 have the same assertoric content and so "assert the same thing" (when uttered in the same context) doesn't look very plausible. Stanley would prefer to consider a case like:

6. The actual President of the US came by.
7. The President of the US came by.

in which it is at least somewhat plausible to hold that utterances of the sentences in the same context "assert the same thing". Or consider a case in which a (rigid) name is introduced by a (non-rigid) reference fixing description thus: let 'Julius' denote the inventor of the zipper. Further suppose that competence with the name requires knowing this. Then again it is not implausible to hold that the following sentences have the same assertoric content, so that utterances of them "assert the same thing":

8. Julius was born in New York.
9. The inventor of the zipper was born in New York.

If any such pair of sentences can be held to have the same assertoric content, RT is refuted.

One way of summarizing Stanley's point here is this. If, as Lewis argues, in addition to assigning to sentences (relative to contexts) elements that capture what they assert when unembedded ("assertoric contents"), we need to assign to sentences (relative to contexts) elements for tense and locational operators to operate on ("ingredient senses"), why not think that modal operators operate on these latter as well, and that these ingredient senses are the things with modal profiles?[12] If that were the case, then sentences (relative to context) that have

[11] Here I assume a principle of compositionality regarding assertoric content.
[12] Note that Stanley need not deny that assertoric contents also determine modal profiles e.g. by being propositions construed as sets of worlds. What he is committed to is the claim that our *intuitions* about the modal profiles of sentence pairs such as 6/7 and 8/9 are intuitions about properties of ingredient senses and not assertoric contents. Stanley tells me (p.c.) that he intended to be neutral on the question of whether assertoric contents themselves determine modal profiles.

different modal profiles may nevertheless have the same assertoric contents and so assert the same thing. If we identify a sentence's content (relative to a context) with what an utterance of it is used to assert (in that context), then sentences with differing modal profiles may have the same content, and sub-sentential expressions with different modal properties (rigid vs. nonrigid) may have the same content, contrary to RT.

Even while seeing the abstract possibility here, some readers may wonder how "what is asserted" by a sentence in fact can fail to be what modal operators operate on. We are so used to thinking of "what is asserted" as being what modal operators operate on that this may sound almost incoherent to some. Here it is worth noting that *one* way of developing a "two dimensional semantics" would be to hold that often what is asserted by a sentence in a context is the *diagonal proposition* expressed by the sentence in that context; but it is the *horizontal proposition* expressed by the sentence in the context that is operated on by modal operators. On such a view, "what is asserted" by an utterance of a sentence is one thing and what modal operators operate on is another.

And indeed, having broached the issue of two dimensionalism, I should say that Stanley is properly construed as arguing that there is a very direct route to a version of a two dimensionalist semantics that is based straightforwardly on purely semantic considerations. For he should be understood as claiming that Lewis has shown that given the proper semantics for tense, modal and location operators, we are forced to posit two sorts of content, or two "semantic dimensions" for sentences: one that captures what a sentence asserts and one that captures what a sentence contributes to a larger sentence of which it is a part when it is embedded under operators. I believe that Stanley took this argument in favor of a sort of two dimensionalist view to be particularly hard for philosophers of language to resist, since it is based only on considerations having to do with the proper semantics for modal, tense and location expressions, and e.g. doesn't make assumptions, which are controversial to many, about capturing epistemic properties by semantic means.[13] In this, I think Stanley is right: if considerations having to do with the semantics of modal, tense and location expressions drive us to a two dimensional semantics, then we philosophers of language are stuck with two dimensionalism.[14]

---

[13] For example, David Chalmers (2003) motivates his two dimensional semantics by assuming that some aspect of meaning needs to capture epistemic notions like a priority and two expressions differing in cognitive significance. Many philosophers, including me, are skeptical as to whether these notions should be captured/explained by semantics, and so see no reason here to embrace a two dimensional semantic framework. As I go on to say, this is why Stanley's way of motivating a two dimensional semantic approach is hard to resist. It rests on claims only about the proper semantics for tenses etc., and everyone agrees that semantics needs to capture the proper semantics for tenses, etc.!

[14] Thanks to Jason Stanley for much help with the last three paragraphs. Stanley's view still may be importantly different from the two dimensionalist's described in the previous paragraph in the following two respects. First, Stanley certainly does not claim that what is asserted by a sentence

Now recall that Stanley's attack on RT and defense of a version of two dimensionalism was predicated on Lewis having provided an argument to the effect that we need to assign to sentences both propositions/assertoric contents and compositional semantic values/ingredient senses. Further, the attack on the motivation for propositions as being both the objects of our attitudes and the things modal operators operate on, as well as their demotion to objects of secondary importance in semantics and the correlative enshrinement of non-propositional compositional semantic values as objects of primary importance, was similarly predicated. One point of the present chapter is to show that friends of RT and of propositions, and opponents of the sort of two dimensionalism defended by Stanley, need not worry on this account. Contrary to what Lewis claims, we need not assign to sentences relative to contexts both propositions *and* compositional semantic values. Propositions can be compositionally assigned to sentences relative to contexts, and no second semantic value of the sort countenanced by Lewis is needed. With this background in mind, let's turn to Lewis's argument.

Lewis's argument that propositions cannot be compositional semantic values comes in the context of a discussion of more general issues. To avoid distorting Lewis, I think it wise to sketch the issues Lewis is addressing. So let us begin with this task.

Lewis claims, and I agree, that it is the (or at least, *a*) job of a syntax and semantics for English (roughly what Lewis calls *grammar*) to deliver a characterization of truth-in-English. Lewis notes that whether truth-in-English is achieved by the utterance of a sentence depends not just on the sentence uttered and what the facts are, but also on various features of the context of the utterance of the sentence, such as who is speaking, who is being addressed, what time it is, and so on. Since English sentences are contextually sensitive in all sorts of ways, in order to characterize truth-in-English, we *at the very least* need a characterization of what it is for a sentence to be *true relative to a context*.

But Lewis argues that a characterization of truth in a context for sentences, or making the truth of sentences context dependent, is not enough. The problem is that often, whether a sentence is true in a context depends upon whether some other sentence is true relative to the result of shifting just one feature of the context. That is, languages contain "feature shifting" sentence operators. For example, whether 'It is possible that the Earth is flat' is true relative to my present context depends on whether 'the Earth is flat' is true relative to some

relative to a context (its assertoric content in that context) is the diagonal proposition expressed by the sentence in that context, (see note 12). Second, Stanley must hold that our intuitions about modal profiles of sentences like 6/7 and 8/9 track properties of the ingredient sense and not what is asserted (see note 12). Two dimensionalists may hold that intuitions about modal profiles track properties of what is asserted, even if modal operators operate on something else. Lewis's own view is interesting here. The proposition expressed by a sentence relative to a context has/determines a modal profile, since it is a set of worlds. But modal operators, like other operators, operate on the compositional semantic values of the sentences they embed.

result of shifting only the world feature of my present context. But now what sort of thing *is* a result of shifting only the world feature of my present context? Lewis thinks that this thing is not itself a context. According to Lewis, a context is a space-time location in a possible world. But the result of shifting just one feature of a context will not be a space-time location in a possible world and hence won't be a context. Indeed, Lewis claims that the result of shifting just one feature of a context is *never* a context.[15] Whether this is so or not, it is at any rate clear that *sometimes* the result of shifting just one feature of a context is not a space-time location in a possible world and hence not a Lewis context. For example, consider a context containing a speaker and addressee, and shift the world feature of this context to a world where people don't, never have, and never will exist. Then the result of this shift can't be a space-time location in a possible world, since it would consist of a speaker and an addressee and a world in which no one ever exists.

Further, there is another reason to think that the result of shifting just one feature of a context is at least sometimes not a context that is independent of whether contexts are space-time locations in possible worlds. As David Kaplan pointed out, and as was mentioned earlier, if we want sentences like 'I am here now' (or insert your favorite example) to be true in all contexts, contexts must be *proper*: the speaker of the context must be at the location of the context at the time of the context in the world of the context. But the result of shifting just one feature of a context may result in something improper: as in the case described above, the speaker of the context may not exist in the world that results from shifting only the world feature of the context. Thus, I think we should at least agree with Lewis that the result of shifting one feature of a context *may* not itself be a context.

But then since, as pointed out above, the truth of a sentence in a context often depends on the truth of a different sentence in the result of shifting one feature of the context, in the general case, the truth of a sentence in a context often depends on the truth of another sentence in something that isn't a context. Thus it appears that our characterization of truth must be a characterization not simply of a sentence being true in a context, but of a sentence being true in a context with respect to these things that result from shifting only one feature of a context. Though I have sometimes called these latter things *circumstances of evaluation* in the present work, I'll follow Lewis here and call them *indices*. Then we need to characterize a sentence being *true in a context with respect to an index*.

Of course, as I hinted above, there is other pressure to have this double dependence of truth on context and index. On the one hand, we need contexts to provide the semantic values (in that context) of contextually sensitive expressions.

---

[15] Lewis (1980) writes: 'No two contexts differ by only one feature. Shift one feature only and the result of the shift is not a context at all.' (p. 29).

On the other hand, we need indices so that the sentence operators in our language have something to shift. And so in languages, such as English, containing contextually sensitive expressions that designate and sentence operators that shift *the same kind of thing* (in the way 'actual' and 'It is possible' do), we need context to be *un*shiftable and to provide the semantic values to contextually sensitive expressions (even if they occur deeply embedded with respect to various operators) and we need indices whose features are shifted by our operators. So again, in such languages, we need truth to depend on both context and index. Thus, whether or not I agree with the details of Lewis's argument that we need to characterize the notion of a sentence being true with respect to a context and index, I do agree that we need to characterize this notion and that this is one of the primary tasks for semantics.

We should remind ourselves at this point that what *features* or *coordinates* indices must have will be determined by the sorts of sentence operators that are present in the language. For indices are the things whose features are shifted by operators, and thus whether an index must have a given feature depends on whether there are operators in the language that shift that feature.[16] Thus, if, as Lewis believes, English contains temporal, modal, location and standard of precision sentence operators, indices must have as coordinates times, worlds, locations and standards of precision. This point will be important later.

So, we wish to assign semantic values to sentences in a compositional way, so that the semantic value of a sentence is a function of the semantic values of its parts and how they are put together, and in so doing characterize a sentence's being true with respect to a context and index. Now, Lewis asks, given this, what sorts of semantic values should we assign to sentences? There appear to be two options, he says. Our syntax and semantics could assign semantic values to sentences relative to contexts, so that what semantic value a sentence has varies with context. This semantic value would then be, or determine, a function from indices to truth values. Following Lewis, call these *variable but simple semantic values*. Lewis provides the following picture:

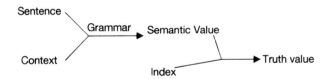

The other option is to have our syntax and semantics assign to a sentence a semantic value once and for all, and let this semantic value be, or determine, a

---

[16] For the sake of brevity, I shall sometimes speak of operators shifting indices, but this should be understood as shorthand for the claim that operators shift *coordinates* of indices.

function from indices *and* contexts to truth values. Following Lewis, call these *constant but complicated semantic values*. Again, Lewis provides a picture:

It should be clear that the assignment of either sort of semantic value allows us to characterize the notion of a sentence being true with respect to a context and index. And Lewis notes that given either sort of semantic value, it is easy to define the other in terms of it. Thus, one can easily convert the one sort of semantic approach into the other.[17] Lewis writes:

Given the ease of conversion, how could anything of importance possibly turn on the choice between our two options? . . . How could the choice between the options possibly be a serious issue?[18]

Lewis then notes that both Stalnaker and Kaplan have defended the first option on which semantic values are variable but simple. Lewis goes on to argue that neither Kaplan nor Stalnaker succeeds in showing that this option is preferable. Because I want to defend something like Stalnaker's view against Lewis, I shall only discuss Stalnaker's defense of variable but simple semantic values and Lewis' response to it.

On Stalnaker's (1970) view, syntax and semantics 'determine an interpreted sentence', which, together with a context, determine a proposition. A proposition together with a possible world determine a truth value. Thus, we can see that Stalnaker's account is a version of the variable but simple semantic value option, with propositions as semantic values. We can make this clear by annotating Lewis's picture of variable but simple semantic values with labels indicating what Stalnaker takes semantic values and indices to be:

---

[17] Converting one approach into the other in the way sketched by Lewis requires understanding both types of semantic values as functions (from indices to truth values; or from context/index pairs to truth values), and hence as *unstructured*. As indicated, in the present chapter I am abstracting from the details of particular accounts of propositions and am even suppressing the question of whether they are structured or not. See note 20.

[18] P. 35.

Stalnaker defends this account against an account that merges context and index, and assigns to sentences a semantic value that is, or determines, a function that maps these merged contexts/indices to truth values. This would be a version of the constant but complicated semantic value option (actually, not quite—see note 19).

Stalnaker's argument in favor of variable but simple semantic values is extremely straightforward. On this view, there is an 'extra step on the road from sentences to truth values'. That is, (on Stalnaker's version of this view) we map a sentence and a context to a proposition, which is something that maps a world to a truth value. On the opposing view, we map a sentence from a merged context/index straight to a truth value. So, Stalnaker says, the former approach, which involves the "extra step", is only justified if what the extra step delivers, namely, propositions, are of some "independent interest". And obviously Stalnaker thinks they are: they are objects of the attitudes and the bearers of modal properties. On the constant but complicated semantic value option, there are no entities that could plausibly be held to be the objects of the attitudes. The semantic values on this option are functions from context-index pairs to truth values. Clearly such functions from speakers, addressees, times, locations, worlds, etc. to truth values are not the sorts of things that we believe, doubt and so on.[19]

Lewis's argument against Stalnaker is also extremely simple. Variable but simple semantic values of sentences cannot be identified with propositions, as they are on Stalnaker's view. For as mentioned earlier, what coordinates an index has is determined by what sorts of sentence operators are present in the language, since these work semantically by shifting coordinates of indices. And Lewis claims that there are tense operators ('It has been that'), location operators ('Somewhere'), modal operators and standard of precision operators ('Strictly speaking'). But then indices must have at least time, location, world and standard of precision coordinates. This means that variable but simple semantic values of at least some

[19] The dialectic here is actually somewhat more complex than Lewis represents it as being. For Stalnaker (1970) is defending the view that we must keep separate two different determinants of the truth values of sentences: contexts and possible worlds (as points of evaluation). Thus, the theory he is arguing against is one that doesn't distinguish contexts from worlds of evaluation, since it merges the two into what Stalnaker calls *points of reference*. The view he opposes, then, assigns sentences semantic values that map points of reference to truth values. Thus, it is not strictly a version of Lewis's constant but complicated semantic values option, since even that option distinguishes context and index (here, possible world) as Stalnaker argues we must do. At the end of Lewis (1980), Lewis makes clear that he too opposes a view that merges contexts and indices, and assigns sentences semantic values that are or determine functions from points of reference to truth values (see third paragraph of section 12 of Lewis (1980)). I ignore this complication in the dialectic, as did Lewis. For if Stalnaker successfully argues that a theory that has propositions as middlemen is superior to one that maps points of reference straight to truth values (because of the independent interest of propositions), then this same argument will show that Stalnaker's account is superior to one that maps context-index pairs straight to truth values. For here too we fail to have the independently interesting propositional middlemen.

sentences, those embedded with respect to such operators, are, or determine, functions from an n-tuple of at least a time, location, world and standard of precision to a truth value. But such things, which change truth value across times, locations, etc. are not *propositions* and do not seem to be the right sorts of things to be the object of the attitudes; and any way, Stalnaker is clear that propositions *are* functions from (only) possible worlds to truth values. So at least some sentences must be assigned variable but simple semantic values that are not propositions. Of course, one could assign to sentences that are *not* embedded with respect to operators (i.e. either they contain no operators, or they do but are not themselves embedded with respect to any operators) propositions as variable but simple semantic values. But then the assignment of variable but simple semantic values would be noncompositional: the semantic value of an unembedded sentence containing operators in a context (i.e. the proposition it expresses in that context) would be a function in part of some *non*-propositional semantic value (in that context) of a constituent sentence (i.e. would be a function in part of something that is, or determines, a function from worlds, times, locations and standards of precision to truth values).

Thus, at least some sentences cannot have propositions as their variable but simple semantic values; and the price of assigning to the others propositions as variable but simple semantic values is a noncompositional assignment of semantic values. It is worth emphasizing that what bars the identification of Lewis's variable but simple semantic values with Stalnaker's propositions is the presence in the language of e.g. time and location operators, which bring with them the requirement that indices contain times and locations (in addition to worlds).

So Stalnaker's propositions cannot be Lewis's variable but simple semantic values. But then the need for or interest in propositions cannot constitute an argument for the variable but simple semantic value option over the constant but complicated semantic value option. And so Stalnaker has given no reason for favoring variable but simple semantic values over constant but complicated semantic values.

As I remarked earlier, Lewis (1980) endorses the view that we need propositions. He just doesn't think they can be identified with variable but simple semantic values for the reasons given. As we have indicated, using either variable but simple *or* constant but complicated semantic values we can define the relation *sentence S is true with respect to context c and index i*. Given this relation, Lewis's idea is that we can associate a proposition, construed as a set of possible worlds, with a sentence as follows: the proposition expressed by S in c is the set of worlds that contains w iff S is true with respect to c and i_c^w, where i_c^w is the result of taking the index whose coordinates are the time, location, world and standards of precision of the context c, and shifting the index's world component to w. So either variable but simple semantic values or constant but complicated semantic values can be used to assign propositions, understood as sets of possible worlds, to sentences in contexts.[20] But propositions cannot be *identified* with variable but simple semantic values (nor constant but complicated semantic values) for the reasons given. So again, that we need propositions or that they are independently interesting gives us no reason to favor variable but simple semantic values over constant but complicated semantic values. We need one or another of these types of semantic values, and Lewis is indifferent as to which, *in addition to* the assignment of propositions to sentences in contexts.

Put in the most general terms, the issue Lewis has raised is how to assign propositions to sentences relative to contexts, when your language contains modal, tense, location and standard of precision operators. As we have seen, Lewis makes essentially two points. First, if the semantic values you assign to sentences relative to contexts are propositions, the assignment will have to be noncompositional. For the proposition assigned to a sentence like 'Sometimes, Doug is happy' relative to a context cannot be determined in part by the *proposition* assigned to 'Doug is happy' relative to the context. The latter cannot vary in truth value over time, whereas the "tense operator" 'Sometimes' must operate on something that varies its truth value over time. The proposition assigned to the whole sentence relative to a context is partly determined by this thing that varies over time and is associated with 'Doug is happy' relative to the context, and not the *proposition* expressed by 'Doug is happy' relative to the context. So the proposition assigned to the whole is not a function of the proposition assigned to the embedded part. That is non-compositional. Second, as this suggests, some other sort of semantic value needs to be assigned to sentences relative to contexts, and this value needs to vary in truth value over times, locations, etc. There is no barrier to this assignment being compositional, which is why these things are the "real" semantic values, propositions being derivative and secondary.[21]

As I indicated at the outset, I intend to argue against Lewis (and so to some extent in defense of Stalnaker) that neither of the above two points is correct: sentences *can* be assigned semantic values relative to contexts in such a way that propositions are compositionally assigned to sentences relative to context and are the semantic values relative to those contexts of the sentences in question.[22] And we need not assign sentences any second sort of semantic value. Thus

---

[20] The qualification that propositions be sets of worlds is important here. If propositions are structured, a definition of the relation *S is true wrt to i and c* won't allow for an assignment of propositions to sentences. The problem is that sentences that are true with respect to the same context/index pairs may express different structured propositions. In Appendix 1 of King (2003) I discuss another claim made by Lewis that may fail if propositions (qua variable but simple semantic values) are structured.

[21] Lewis supposes, reasonably, that "real" semantic values are assigned compositionally.

[22] In King (2003) I argue that both Richard (1981, 1982) and Salmon (1986, 1989) were wrong to concede these two points to Lewis. I also argue that Salmon's accounts of tense cannot handle complex data involving tense that motivates current research in that area. See King (2003): section 3 and Appendix 2.

the independent interest in propositions noted by Stalnaker *does* provide an argument in favor of variable but simple semantic values as opposed to constant but complicated semantic values.

Like Stalnaker's argument in favor of variable but simple semantic values and Lewis's response to that argument, my response to Lewis is very simple. In effect, Lewis argues that variable but simple semantic values can't be propositions, because in the general case such semantic values must be or determine functions from indices to truth values. Since indices must include times, locations, worlds, and standards of precision, variable but simple semantic values of at least some sentences must be or determine functions from times, locations, worlds and standards of precision to truth values. If we then identify propositions with such functions (or with things that determine such functions), we must say that propositions can change truth value over times, locations, worlds, and standards of precision. But things of that sort don't seem the right sorts of things to be the objects of the attitudes. And Stalnaker's argument for variable but simple semantic values was that they are things that are suitable objects of the attitudes. Thus, to repeat, Lewis claims that Stalnaker has given no reason for preferring variable but simple semantic values to complex but constant semantic values.

By contrast, I shall argue that temporal expressions (including tenses), location expressions and expressions such as 'strictly speaking' are not best understood as sentence operators that shift features of the index of evaluation. If this is correct, then indices do not need to contain times, locations or standards of precision for such purported operators to shift. But then there is no reason to have times, locations and standards of precision as coordinates of indices. This leaves only worlds as coordinates of indices. And this, in turn, leaves us with the view that variable but simple semantic values of sentences are, or determine, functions from worlds to truth values. But such entities *are* appropriate objects of the attitudes, and possessors of modal properties. So given that we need entities that are objects of the attitudes and possessors of modal properties, this gives us reason to prefer variable but simple semantic values to constant but complex semantic values. Thus, the need for these propositional middlemen does, as Stalnaker claimed, provide a reason for preferring variable but simple semantic values.

Before turning to the argument that temporal expressions and location expressions are not to be understood as feature-of-index shifting sentence operators, a few qualifications are in order. First, I will confine my discussion here to simple tenses (present, past, and future), and temporal adverbs such as 'yesterday', 'in a week', etc. I shall not, for example, consider aspect here. As far as I can see, limiting my discussion in this way has no effect on my argument. Indeed, I suspect that a less limited inquiry would strengthen my argument. Second, I assume that we are working in a syntactic and semantic framework in which there are both index shifting sentence operators (whose semantic clauses are spelled out in terms of quantification over coordinates of indices in the metalanguage) and object language quantifiers. Certainly most current semantic and syntactic theorizing takes place within such a framework. More importantly for present concerns, the disputants involved all make use of such frameworks: Lewis, Kaplan and Stalnaker all theorize within frameworks in which one has both feature-of-index shifting operators (e.g. modal operators) and object language quantifiers (e.g. over individuals—e.g. 'every pig'). Thus, in making this assumption, I beg no questions against Lewis.

With these qualifications in mind, let us turn to tenses and temporal expressions. It is important to be clear at the outset that the claim that tenses are operators that shift features of the index of evaluation is an empirical claim about natural language. It is a claim to the effect that in the best syntax and semantics for natural language, tenses will be treated syntactically and semantically as such operators. I shall argue that given the available evidence, this is an implausible empirical claim.

Let us begin by noting various ways in which tenses don't behave as do the standard operators of standard tense logic. Standard treatments of operators of tense logic go something like the following. Taking the operator 'P' for a past tense sentence operator as an example, the relevant clause runs as follows:

(Past) 'P(ϕ)' (where 'ϕ' is a formula) is true at time t iff for some t'<t, 'ϕ' is true at t'.

Thus, 'P' is understood as effecting existential quantification over times in the metalanguage. But as Partee (1973) observed, the English past tense doesn't seem to work this way. A sentence like:

10. John turned off the stove.

uttered in a particular context (at a particular time t) will be interpreted to mean not that for some time t' prior to t, John turned off the stove at t', but rather that at some particular contextually determined time t' prior to t, John turned off the stove at t'. Thus, it looks as though here the tense in some way picks out a particular contextually determined past time (or interval of time). But in so doing, it is hardly behaving like a standard past tense operator.

Second, and related to the first point, tenses and temporal adverbs interact in ways that make little sense on standard operator conceptions of tense. As Dowty (1982) observes, if we treat temporal adverbs like 'yesterday' and past tense morphemes as standard operators, we get incorrect predictions. Thus consider what might seem the natural operator clause for the operator 'Y' (for 'yesterday'):

(Yesterday) 'Y(ϕ)' is true at t iff 'ϕ' is true at some t' such that t' is within the day preceding the day that includes t.

Now consider a sentence like:

11. Yesterday, John turned off the stove.

We have a past tense and 'yesterday', so combining (Past) and (Yesterday), we get two possibilities for readings for 11, depending on which operator takes widest scope:

11a. Y (P (John turns off the stove))
11b. P (Y (John turns off the stove))

Supposing 11 uttered at a certain time t on day d, the reading corresponding to 11a would be true in a situation in which at *any* time prior to a time included in the day before d, John turned off the stove. 11 certainly does not seem to have this reading. 11b would be true in a situation in which there is some past time t'(any past time t'!) such that John turned off the stove on the day d' that precedes the day that includes t'. Again, 11 has no such reading. So given the natural operator treatments of 'Yesterday' and past tense, we can't correctly predict their interaction in simple sentences like 11. And indeed, the prediction that 11 has two readings corresponding to 11a and 11b, whatever those readings are, is itself incorrect: 11 isn't ambiguous![23]

Thinking about the natural interpretation of 10, and now looking at 11, intuitively what seems to be going on is that 'Yesterday' in some sense picks out an interval of time, as does the past tense of 10 (both considered alone and as embedded in 11). The truth of 11 requires the interval picked out by the past tense to fall within the interval picked out by 'Yesterday'. But obviously, to understand the past tense and 'Yesterday' as working in this sort of way is not to understand them as anything like standard tense operators.

Third, and related to the first two points, consider examples such as:

12. Yesterday John gave a party. Annie got drunk.

As we have already seen, it would seem intuitively that in the first sentence (when it is uttered in a context), 'Yesterday' picks out a day and the past tense picks out

---

[23] Sophisticated readers might be thinking that the problem here is that I have assumed a semantics with a single time index. It is well known that in a language that contains temporal indexicals like 'Yesterday' and time index shifting operators like past tense, we need to have *two* time indices. And so in assuming a single time index I am making the operator treatment fail. But double indexing does not solve the problem. Kaplan's (1989) semantics, which has double indexing to context (which includes a time) and time, doesn't get the interaction of 'yesterday' and past tense right either. Kaplan's account would allow two readings of 11 corresponding to 11a and 11b. 11a is true with respect to time t context c and world w iff given the day d prior to the day that includes the time of the context of utterance, 'John turns off the stove' is true with respect to a time prior to d, c and w. 11 does not have this reading. 11b is true with respect to c, t and w iff on the day d prior to the time of the context, 'John turns off the stove' is true with respect to d (c and w). See. p. 545. The second truth conditions here are actually correct! However, this is just an odd coincidence. The truth conditions are correct only because the semantics of 'Y' (yesterday) results in its ignoring the shift in the time index induced by the wide scope 'P' (past) operator. But this means that on Kaplan's semantics, for a formula 'ϕ', 'P(Y(ϕ))' and 'F(Y(ϕ))' (where 'F' is the future operator) should have the same truth value with respect to c, t, w, since 'Y' ignores the shifting induced by 'F' *and* 'P'. Applied to English and the present case, this means that 11 (on the reading in question) should have the same truth conditions (taken in the same context) as 'Yesterday, John will turn off the stove'. Obviously, this is not correct. Also, as indicated, Kaplan's theory predicts that 11 is ambiguous, and, again, it is not.

an interval that is required to fall within that day. But further, as Partee (1973) noted, it seems that the second sentence has a reading (its most natural reading) on which the past tense in it picks out the same interval that is picked out by the past tense in the first sentence (or a closely related interval). So here, there seems to be a sort of anaphoric phenomenon: the second sentence past tense takes on the same value as its "antecedent" past tense in the first sentence. Again, no account of the tenses as standard operators gives us any insight into this behavior.

Thus far, I have discussed three respects in which tenses don't appear to behave like operators. I am not claiming that data of the sort discussed could not be handled by some modification of the operator approach to tense, and I will discuss this point below. But since data of this sort shows that tense in natural language does not work the way tense operators in standard tense logic work, researchers began to question whether viewing tenses as operators of any sort was illuminating.

Recent work on tense in philosophy and linguistics has concentrated on so-called "sequence of tense" and related phenomena. The data of concern here involve sentences with verbs that take sentential complements, such as 'believe', 'say' etc., and sentences with noun phrases that have relative clauses. Let's take a brief look at some of this data that motivates current research on tense. To begin with, consider a sentence containing a noun phrase with a relative clause, such as:

13. Peter saw a man who was a cyclist.

The matrix verb is past tense, as is the verb in the relative clause. It appears as though 13 could be true when uttered at t in any of the following three cases:

(i) Peter saw at t' prior to t a man who prior to t' was a cyclist.
(ii) Peter saw at t' prior to t a man who was a cyclist at t'.
(iii) Peter saw at t' prior to t a man who was a cyclist after t' and before t.

(This last reading can be made prominent by inserting temporal adverbs: 'Ten years ago, Peter saw a man who was a cyclist from two years ago until last week') By contrast, consider:

14. Peter heard that Liz was ill.

Again, the matrix verb is past tense, as is the verb of its sentential complement. 14 could be true when uttered at t in either of the following two cases:

(i) Peter heard at t' prior to t that Liz was ill at t'.
(ii) Peter heard at t' prior to t that Liz was ill prior to t'.

But 14 would not be true in the following case:

(iii) Peter heard at t' prior to t that Liz was ill after t' and before t.

To get a sentence true in that case, one requires:

(14a) Peter heard that Liz would be ill.

Thus 14 is not true in case (iii), which is the analogue of case (iii) above in which 13 would be true. Hence the past tenses in 13 and 14 interact differently, and this needs explaining by a proper theory of tense. This has proved to be not a simple matter.

All the past tenses in 13 and 14 at any rate require that certain things obtain in the past (i.e. corresponding to its two past tenses, 13 requires that both the seeing and the cycling occurred in the past; 14 requires that both the hearing and the purported illness occurred in the past). But the following example, due to Abusch (1997), who attributes a similar example to Kamp and Rohrer, shows that sometimes a past tense doesn't require this:

15. John decided a week ago that in ten days at breakfast he would say to his mother that they were having their last meal together.

Consider the past tense on the verb in the most embedded complement ('were having'). Though it is in the past tense, the time of the alleged last meal lies in the future of the time of utterance. How the tense works here and why it is past needs some explanation.

Finally, there are sentences that exhibit so-called "double access" readings:

16. Peter said that Liz is ill.

Put roughly, the embedded present tense here makes the alleged illness relevant both to the (past) time of Peter's saying and to the (present) time of utterance. It is hard to even state exactly what the truth of 16 does require, but it seems that it requires that Peter's saying was a past, present tense statement that Liz was ill (so that Peter in the past said 'Liz is ill'); and that in some sense Peter's statement committed him to Liz's being presently ill. The former properly rules out 16 being true if yesterday Peter said 'Liz will be ill tomorrow'. And the latter, again I think properly, rules out 16 being true if Peter said two days ago 'Liz is sick but will be better tomorrow.' Again here, formulating a theory that gets this data right has not proved easy. There is much more data of this sort to consider if we bring in more examples with present and future tense. The reader will be happy to hear that I won't do so.

The crucial point about the complex data involving tense we have just surveyed is this. Virtually every recent theory of tense that attempts to treat this data fails to view tenses as index shifting operators. Let's consider a few examples.

Enc (1987) explicitly opposes an operator account of tense and holds that tenses are devices that refer to time intervals. Her view is that tenses can be anaphoric on or 'bound' by other tenses, in which case they refer to what their antecedents refer to.[24] Obviously, then, tenses are not index shifting operators on her view.

---

[24] Enc holds that Comp optionally carries an index, and when it does the index is assigned a time interval as its referent. Tenses can be bound by other tenses or by an indexed Comp.

Abusch (1997) holds a complex theory on which some tenses are interpreted "de re" (as she puts it). Abstracting from certain complexities of her framework, in such cases tenses are rather like anaphoric pronouns on E-type theories of anaphora: they are in effect interpreted as definite descriptions denoting time intervals, where the descriptive material in the description is determined by context, including elements of the discourse/sentence the tense occurs in.[25] Other tenses express complex relations between the time interval designated by the tense and a local evaluation time, which will be utterance time for the highest tense, but may change as one goes down a syntactic tree.[26] So for Abusch as for Enc, tenses are not operators.

In perhaps the most extensive recent work on tense and sequence of tense, Ogihara (1996) adopts a formalism for representing natural language tense that uses explicit quantification over time in the object language, where tenses express relations between times. Thus, for a sentence like

17. A man died.

(when uttered at i)

we get the following representation in Ogihara's intensional logic IL:

17a. $Et \, Ex[man'(t,x) \, \& \, t < s^* \, \& die'(t,x)]$

where 't' is a time variable, and 's*' is an indexical constant denoting the time of speech.[27] It is true that in discussing why he adopts this formalism with explicit object language quantification over time to represent natural language, he gives practical reasons, saying the formalism is 'more flexible' than others he considers and can 'readily accommodate the complex temporal facts in natural language'.[28] He concludes

This choice of logical language should not be taken as an important theoretical decision ... The only important issue is whether the language has enough tools to describe the target constructions in natural language, and the reader will find that our notational system is indeed powerful enough for our purposes.[29]

---

[25] See her footnote 9.

[26] Though Abusch talks about a tense referring to a time (see e.g. p. 30), I don't see that she explains how such references are assigned. Instead, she concentrates more on the complex relations tenses specify between the alleged referent and the local evaluation time.

[27] See p. 35. I have suppressed the variable for a reference time in 17 ('t_{RT}') as Ogihara himself often does. Strictly for Ogihara, 17 expresses a relation between times (and so is represented by an IL expression of type $<i,<i,t>>$, where denotations for type i are times, and denotations for type t are truth values). But his definition of truth in a context for sentences of his intensional logic (expressions of type $<i,<i,t>>$—p. 58) assigns the one "free" time variable (really, one variable bound by a wide scope time variable lambda abstract) speech time, and existentially quantifies over the other in the metalanguage. Thus, 17a gives the truth conditions of 17. See p. 63. Ogihara comments, however, that introducing existential quantification in the truth definition in this way is 'not meant to carry a substantial theoretical claim' (p. 62), and he indicates that at least for English, the existential closure could be introduced sentence internally (i.e. with an existential quantifier in the sentence as in 17a) 'as part of the translation of the tense morpheme' (p. 62).

[28] P. 28. See pp. 26–8   [29] P. 28.

Despite Ogihara's pragmatic, almost instrumentalist, attitude I am inclined to view things rather differently. If the complex temporal facts present in natural language are most readily and easily represented by viewing tenses as involving explicit quantification over time and as expressing relations between times, that is a good reason for thinking that tenses really work this way.[30] But in any case, Ogihara certainly doesn't treat tenses as index shifting operators.

Finally, consider the proposal regarding sequence of tense due to Higginbotham (2002), who, like Enc, explicitly opposes an index shifting operator treatment of tense.[31] Higginbotham works in a neo-Davidsonian framework in which natural language sentences quantify over events (or events and states). Higginbotham assumes that every predicate contains an event argument place, which gets existentially quantified. Tenses are understood as expressing relations between events. In the simplest case, a tense expresses a relation between the event of uttering the very sentence it is in (which, of course, occurs at speech time or the time of the context of utterance) and some event or other (i.e. an event satisfying the existential quantification over events in the sentence). So an utterance of a simple past tense sentence asserts that some event prior to the event of uttering this very sentence is thus and so. Thus, it is very clear that on Higginbotham's proposal, tenses are not operators and so there is no need for temporal coordinates of indices.

Indeed, it is worth mentioning more generally that within such neo-Davidsonian frameworks in which English sentences involve existential quantification over events, it is virtually inevitable to treat tenses as in some way expressing temporal information about events, and so as in some broad sense expressing properties of or relations between events. Hence in such frameworks tenses are predicates of times or events. Thus, in Parson's (1990) extensive event-based semantics for English, tenses constrain or restrict the quantification over time that is claimed to be present in an English sentence (see p. 209), and thereby locate the event in time. So that tenses are not index shifting operators is all but inevitable in such frameworks.

To sum up the discussion of tenses and temporal expressions to this point, we have seen that there is data (10–12 above) that shows that tenses and temporal expressions do not work like the standard operators of tense logic. Second, and related to this, we have seen that virtually all recent attempts to handle complex

---

[30] Actually, Ogihara adopts the view that propositions are sets of world/time/individual triples. But that is only because, inspired by Lewis (1979), Ogihara thinks that believing is a matter of self ascribing a property and a temporal location, and that this must be reflected in the semantics of belief ascription (see pp. 108–20). Thus, the objects of belief must be world-time-individual triples. So strictly, the points of evaluation or indices for propositions have time coordinates. But the crucial point is that his adopting this view has nothing to do with how tenses or temporal expressions work, but has to do instead with his view about the objects of belief. We, by contrast, are investigating the question of whether the behavior of tenses forces us to treat them as operators, and hence requires having temporal coordinates of indices. It doesn't on Ogihara's view.

[31] See pp. 209–10.

data involving tenses surveyed above (13–16) have rejected the view that tenses are sentence operators.[32] I think that this is enough to show that tenses are not operators, or at least that that is the most reasonable position to hold, based on current theorizing. But it is important to be clear on why these points show this.

First, the issue is not one of expressive power. That is, I am not claiming that *no* version of the view that tenses and temporal expression are sentence operators could be formulated that would assign the right truth conditions to the data we have discussed. Indeed, I think that is false. Through the late 60s and 70s, there was a debate about whether all readings of English sentences with temporal elements (including tenses, expressions such as 'now', etc.) could be expressed by a language containing only tense operators, or whether e.g. one needed a language in which one explicitly quantified over time. We can put this by saying that the question was whether English temporal expressions could be understood as operators, or whether, because there were readings of English sentences that could not be expressed only with tense operators, we had to understand English as containing explicit quantifiers over time. The outcome of this debate was that relative expressive power alone does not seem to tell us whether tenses can be treated as operators, or e.g. must be understood as object language quantifiers over time. For, first, even relatively simple (single index) operators have surprisingly strong expressive powers. Hans Kamp (1968) showed that (if time is modeled as the real numbers) any operator definable in a language with explicit quantification over times, a two place 'earlier than' predicate of times, and one-place predicates of times can be expressed in a language without quantification over or variables for times that contains only his two-place sentence operators 'S' ("since") and 'U' ("until"). Second, each time someone has come up with an English sentence whose truth conditions aren't given by any formula of some language containing only tense operators (and no explicit quantification over time), new operators are introduced yielding a language that has a formula with the truth conditions in question. For example, Kamp (1971) showed that sentences such as 'A child was born which will be king' have truth conditions that are not expressible in a tensed predicate logic containing standard Priorean tense operators. The introduction of the doubly time indexed 'Now' operator allows for the expression of such truth conditions. Vlach (1973) claims that the intuitive truth conditions of sentences like 'One day, all persons alive then would be dead' cannot be expressed in Kamp's 'Now' enhanced language. But he introduces another doubly time indexed operator (K—"then") that allows for the expression of such truth conditions. This dynamic has continued with the introduction of ever more operators with ever more indices.

Now Quine (1960) had already shown how to formulate a language with the expressive power of first order predicate logic, using only predicate operators,

---

[32] Ludlow (1999) might seem to be an exception to this. See note 37 below.

and no variables or quantifiers. Thus, it seems clear that by introducing temporal operators mimicking Quine's, one could achieve the expressive power of a first order predicate logic quantifying over times in a language with only operators, and no variables or quantifiers for times. And indeed, various theorists during the 1970s working in the operator tense logic framework had begun to introduce operators that were analogues of Quine's operators (e.g. permuting time coordinates of indices, and substituting one time coordinate for another rather as Quine's 'Inv' and 'Ref' operators permuted predicate argument places, and identified them, respectively). Van Benthem (1977) is a nice summary of these developments up to 1977. Discussing the tendency of those working in the "operator tense logic" tradition to keep adding more points of time as coordinates of their indices, and adding more complex operators to manipulate these complex indices, van Benthem (1977) writes:

. . . the tendency exists to add ever more points in time at the *index* (of evaluation), which are then *manipulated* by operators without moment variables in the object language. The alternative, which should have been kept in mind throughout the discussion, is the use of predicate-logical formulas containing moment variables and overtly displaying these *manipulations*. Clearly, if one is willing to increase the complexity of the index to any extent (while adding enough operators to take profit of it), there is no need to ever resort to predicate logic *technically*, but in our opinion it is a Pyrrhic victory.[33]

What is important here for our purposes is van Benthem's point that, given the willingness to use indices with more and more time coordinates, and operators to exploit them, the expressive powers of the two sorts of languages inevitably will converge. And indeed, Cresswell (1990) formulates a language whose sentences are evaluated at infinite sequences of times (or worlds) and that contains no time (or world) variables or quantifiers over times (or worlds), but that for each n, contains an operator that can in effect substitute the nth element of a given sequence for the 0th and an operator that can substitute the 0th element for the nth. He shows that such a language has the expressive power of a language that has explicit quantifiers over times (or worlds).[34]

---

[33] P. 426.

[34] Let σ be an infinite sequence of times (or worlds) and let $\sigma(n)$ be the nth element of σ. Suppose that the interpretations of formulas of our language assign sets of such sequences to formulas, (I suppress reference to an assignment of values to variables). Intuitively, these are the sequences at which the formulas "are true" (on analogy with the assignment of sets of times to formulas in a standard tense logic, where these are the times at which the formulas "are true"). Then Cresswell's operators work as follows: for 'ϕ' a formula, σ belongs to the set of sequences an interpretation V assigns to 'Then$_n$ ϕ' iff $\sigma[n/0]$ belongs to the set of sequences V assigns to 'ϕ', where $\sigma[n/0]$ is σ but with $\sigma(n)$ in place of $\sigma(0)$. And σ belongs to the set of sequences assigned to 'Ref$_n$ ϕ' iff $\sigma[0/n]$ belongs to the set of sequences V assigns to 'ϕ', where $\sigma[0/n]$ is σ but with $\sigma(0)$ in place of the $\sigma(n)$. Here $\sigma(0)$ should be thought of as "the evaluation time", which is shifted by "ordinary" operators (e.g. in tense logic, past and future operators; in modal logic, necessity and possibility operators). See Cresswell (1990: 30, 46). So the 'Then' operators, which are a generalization of doubly indexed 'Now' or 'Actually' operators, take another time in the sequence and make it the new evaluation

Thus my claim that English tenses cannot be viewed as operators cannot be based on the claim that to treat them in this way would be to not capture the expressive power of English (since I would not claim that treating them as quantifiers over times would have this result).

Rather, the claim that we should treat tenses as e.g. involving quantification over times (and expressing relations between times) rather than as index shifting sentence operators is supported by three points: (i) as we have seen, in order to achieve the required expressive power, operator approaches must introduce something like Cresswell's indexed operators and multiply the time coordinates of indices ad infinitum. But this is just a cumbersome way of using operators to mimic object language quantification. Surely, simply doing the job with object language quantification itself makes more sense (there is a reason no one does logic with Quine's predicate operators instead of explicit quantifiers). (ii) Treating tenses as involving quantification over times allows for a simpler, more elegant, less ad hoc treatment of tenses and temporal expressions than does an operator treatment; and (iii) allows for a more plausible account of the relation between the surface structures of English sentences and the syntactic representations of those sentences at the level of syntax that is the input to semantics, which I have been calling *LF*. [35] This, in turn, explains the fact mentioned above: that virtually all current researchers trying to give a treatment of the complex temporal data in natural languages eschew an operator approach to tenses in favor of treating tenses as something like quantifying over, referring to and/or expressing relations between times. Since I have already covered point (i) above, let me briefly illustrate points (ii) and (iii) by means of a couple of simple examples.

First, point (ii). For the sake of definiteness, let me suppose that a tense quantifies over times, while putting a restriction on that quantification, and that predicates have argument places for times. So, for example, at the relevant level of syntactic representation, the following a sentences will look like the following b sentences:

18a. Maggie is happy.
19a. Maggie was happy.
20a. Maggie will be happy.
18b. $Et\ (t = t^* \ \&\ \text{Maggie be happy}(t))$
19b. $Et\ (t < t^* \ \&\ \text{Maggie be happy}\ (t))$
20b. $Et\ (t^* < t \ \&\ \text{Maggie be happy}\ (t))$

---

time, so that in the evaluation of the formula it embeds, the old evaluation time is ignored. The 'Ref' operators, which are a generalization of an operator introduced in Vlach (1973), take the evaluation time, and change another element in the sequence to it, so that it may be subsequently picked up by a later 'Then' operator.

[35] Thanks to Delia Graff Fara for pointing out a respect in which my discussion of these issues in King (2003) was misleading.

(where 't*' is a term that gets assigned the time of speech).[36] Now note how easily temporal adverbs of the sort discussed above ('yesterday', 'in 2004', etc.) are accommodated in such a representation. Letting '$\leq$' be an expression expressing the *part of* relation (between times) and supposing that 'yesterday' in the context of utterance (in part) picks out the day before the day including the time designated by 't*', the following sentence:

21a. Maggie was happy yesterday.

can be rendered as

21b. Et (t<t* & t$\leq$yesterday & Maggie be happy (t))

Thus, temporal adverbs like 'yesterday' effectively function as predicates of times, and are readily and smoothly added to the present framework. As suggested above, it is, by contrast, much less clear how to treat such adverbs if one is treating tenses as operators. At any rate, the treatment is sure to be much more complex.

Turning now to point (iii) above, consider the following pair of sentences, which are in relevant respects like sentences discussed in Kamp (1971), where Kamp argues that the presence of the temporal indexical 'now' in English, together with (alleged!) index shifting tense operators require double temporal indexing (one index to be shifted by operators, and another to be unshiftable, so that an embedded 'now' could pick it up):

22. A child was born who would be king.
23. A child was born who will be king.

Using standard tense operators, together with Kamp's 'N' ('now'), these sentences are represented as follows:

22a. P(A child: x (born (x) & F(king(x))))
23a. P(A child: x (born(x) & NF(king(x))))

Now if we take the operator proposal seriously syntactically, as we should (i.e. as claiming that tenses are really syntactically operators), 22a and 23a are the LFs for 22 and 23. The crucial point is that even though 22 and 23 appear to have

---

[36] If we think that the past tense in 19a picks out a particular past time, we could suppose that in the context of utterance the existential quantification over times given in 19b is further restricted just as happens in cases like 'All the beer is in the fridge.' Similar remarks apply to the future tense (or modal) in 20a. If we consider the contents of 18b–20b when the term 't*' is not assigned any value, we see that they will be contents that determine functions from times to propositions (i.e. they determine functions from a time t_0 to the propositions expressed by 18b–20b when t_0 is assigned to 't*'). Thus the present account allows for temporally neutral contents. And in fact I think we often talk about temporally neutral contents, as when you say 'America is the moral leader of the world' and I respond 'That might have been true ten years ago, but it isn't now.' I might have even responded 'I believed that ten years ago but I don't today.' But despite this I think that the objects of our attitudes and what we assert etc. are not temporally neutral. I hope to elaborate on this elsewhere. But my main point here is that the present account yields temporally neutral contents.

exactly the same number and sort of syntactic consistuents combined in the same ways, and differ only in the words 'would' and 'will', they have different LFs: 23's LF contains an additional operator ('N') that corresponds to no operator in 22's LF. Presumably, this operator is somehow due to the presence of the word 'will' in 23. But then when we consider a sentence containing 'will' alone, such as

23'. A barbarian will be king.

presumably it will be represented as follows:

23'a. F(A barbarian: x (king(x)))

In the case of 23', 'will' only contributes one operator to its LF, whereas in 23 it contributes two. Surely the fact that the LFs for 22 and 23 contain different numbers of operators despite the fact that the sentences are exactly similar syntactically and that 'will' contributes different numbers of operators to LFs in different cases looks ad hoc and presupposes a very messy relation between the surface structures of sentences and their LFs.

By contrast, in the tense as quantifiers type framework, 22, 23, and 23' have LFs roughly as follows:

22b. $Et\ (t<t^* \ \&\ A\ child(t): x\ (born\ (x,t)\ \&\ Et'\ (t<t'\ \&\ king(x,t'))))$
23b. $Et\ (t<t^* \ \&\ A\ child(t): x\ (born(x,t)\ \&\ Et'(t^* <t'\ \&\ king(x,t'))))$
23'b. $Et\ (t^*<t\ \&\ A\ barbarian(t): x\ (king(x,t)))$

where 't^*' is an expression designating the time of utterance. Now looking at 22a, 23a, and 23'a and 22b, 23b, and 23'b, surely having something like the latter as LFs for 22, 23, and 23' looks less ad hoc and results in a cleaner relation between surface structure and LF than does having 22a, 23a, and 23'a as LFs for these sentences. At least 22b and 23b have the same number and sorts of constituents and 'will' makes the same sort of contribution to the LFs of 23b and 23'b.

To repeat, then, the reasons for treating tenses as involving quantification over times (and expressing relations between times) rather than as index shifting sentence operators are (i) versions of the operator approach with sufficient expressive power are simply cumbersome means for mimicking object language quantification over times; (ii) treating tense as involving quantification over times allows for a simpler, more elegant, less ad hoc treatment of tenses and temporal expressions than does an operator treatment; and (iii) allows for a more plausible account of the relation between the surface structures of English sentences and the syntactic representations of those sentences at the level of syntax that is the input to semantics. As I said above, this is why current researchers on tense adopt the former approach; and this is good reason for thinking it is the correct empirical, syntactical claim about tense in natural language.[37]

---

[37] Ludlow (1999) employs an operator-like treatment of tense. Does Ludlow (1999) then constitute an argument to the effect that the correct empirical, syntactical claim about tenses is that

But if the proper way to treat tenses is *not* as index shifting sentence operators, then there is no need for temporal coordinates in indices of evaluation. This, in turn, means that we are no longer forced to hold that variable but simple semantic values are, or determine, functions from worlds, locations, standards of precision *and times* to truth values, as Lewis claimed. At most, we are stuck with the view that the variable but simple semantic values of sentences are, or determine, functions from worlds, locations and standards of precision to truth values.

they are index shifting operators? It seems to me that the answer is clearly 'no' for several reasons. First, though Ludlow's (absolute) tenses Past, Fut, Pres attach to sentences to form new sentences (actually they attach to inflectional phrases that have the form NP[I VP]) as operators do, Ludlow's tenses do not shift times in the index of evaluation, and indeed Ludlow does not have times in his indices of evaluation. The reason for this is that Ludlow believes, correctly I think, that if one's semantic theory quantifies over (past and future) times in the metalanguage one is metaphysically committed to those times (see p. 85). Since Ludlow is defending presentism and wants to avoid this commitment, he doesn't want any quantification over times in his metalanguage. But then he can't treat tenses as index shifting operators, since to do so requires quantification over times in the metalanguage (e.g. 'Past(ϕ)' is true at t iff 'ϕ' is true at some t'<t). Hence, despite the fact that Ludlow's absolute tenses look a bit like operators, they are not index shifting operators at all, and times are not elements of his indices of evaluation. Second, and perhaps even more importantly, despite some comments in Ludlow (1999) that suggests otherwise, the book cannot be seen as having defended the empirical claim that tense in natural language works in the way given by the semantics for tense he provides. For a variety of reasons, some purely metaphysical, Ludlow is trying to give a semantic account of tense that employs only what he calls "A series resources" (see p. 111). It is not as though an empirical study of the behavior of tenses suggests this constraint. This is a constraint Ludlow brings to his attempt to construct a semantics of tense. In order to account for even quite simple tense phenomena (e.g. that an utterance of 'I turned the stove off' at a given time does not communicate the claim that I turned the stove off at some time prior to that time—see p. 9, 111) given this constraint, Ludlow must make some very radical moves. He is forced to claim that all natural language sentences have 'when' clauses (p. 118). When they appear not to ('I turned the stove off'), such clauses are "implicit" (syntactically realized but not phonologically or inscriptionally realized). It is important to see here that these implicit 'when' clauses are not posited on the basis of any syntactic evidence. They are posited so that Ludlow can capture certain data given the constraints he is working under. Since these implicit 'when' clauses are an important part of Ludlow's account of tense, in order to claim that tenses in fact work along the lines of Ludlow's theory, one would have to provide independent empirical evidence of the existence of these implicit when-clauses. Though this is something Ludlow does not do, he clearly recognizes the burden to do so when he writes: 'Whereas the B-theory looks for temporal reference, the A-theory [Ludlow's] looks for implicit clausal structure . . . Whether this strategy can be carried out is an open empirical issue; perhaps the positing of this implicit clausal structure will collide with general principles of linguistic theory.' (p. 132) But then until it is shown that there is good reason for positing this implicit syntactic structure (other than that it allows Ludlow to capture certain data), it can't be claimed that Ludlow has shown that tenses work in the way given by his semantic account (which presupposes the existence of this implicit structure). Ludlow himself admits that it is an open empirical question whether this implicit structure is really there. But then it is an open empirical question whether tenses in fact work in the way suggested by Ludlow's semantics. Thus, Ludlow (1999) does not constitute an argument that tenses do work in that way. Finally, I should add that in any case, it isn't clear that Ludlow's account, even assuming implicit 'when' clauses (and implicit relative clauses—see p. 131), can handle all of the complex data discussed above. Ludlow doesn't discuss the differences between the readings had by our sentences 13 and 14 and it isn't clear to me how he would capture these differences. Further, Ludlow does not explain how he can get the "double access" reading of our sentence 16, and again it isn't at all clear to me how he would do so.

But I don't think we are stuck with this result either. Specifically, I don't think there is a good case for locations being coordinates of indices either. The reader will be relieved to hear that I shall be more concise here than I was in the case of times.

Why does Lewis think that locations must be coordinates of indices? Lewis suggests that in sentences such as

24. Somewhere, the sun is shining.

'Somewhere' is an index shifting "location" operator. He thinks that 24 is true relative to an index i iff 'the sun is shining' is true relative to some i' that differs from i only on its location coordinate.[38]

Now Lewis gives no argument that 'somewhere' is an index shifting location operator, and it seems to me that there are good reasons for resisting this view. For in a variety of ways, 'somewhere' behaves like a quantifier over places, as indeed it superficially appears to be. First, 'somewhere' appears to occur in argument position in a variety of sentences, such as:

25. Somewhere is prettier than here.[39]
26. John was somewhere.
27. Chris went somewhere.
28. Annie resides somewhere.

Though quantifiers (and NPs generally) occupy argument position in sentences ('Every woman is beautiful.'; 'Chris loves every child'), operators (e.g. modal operators, etc.) don't (*'Necessarily is beautiful.'; *'Chris completed necessarily'). Second, in such constructions, 'somewhere' allows for restriction by further predicative material, as do other quantifiers (e.g. 'Every woman *from Carnelian Bay* is beautiful'):

25a. Somewhere in North Lake Tahoe is prettier than here.
26a. John was somewhere in North Lake Tahoe.
27a. Chris went somewhere in North Lake Tahoe.

Note too that, as with other quantifiers, additional further restrictions can always be added:

26b. John was somewhere in North Lake Tahoe near Carnelian Bay by a marsh.

"Normal" sentence operators, by contrast, do not allow the addition of such further restrictive descriptive material.

---

[38] See Lewis (1980): 27 and 39.

[39] Some find this sentence a bit awkward, but I think that is because of the completely unrestricted quantification here ('something is beautiful' seems similarly, if a bit less, awkward). If this is right, such sentences should improve when 'somewhere' takes on further restriction. As 25a illustrates, this seems correct.

Third, in such constructions 'somewhere' exhibits what appear to be quantifier scope ambiguities with respect to other quantifiers:

27b.   Chris went somewhere in North Lake Tahoe every Friday night.

27b seems to have a reading on which Chris went different places on different Friday nights, as well as a reading on which she frequented one place every Friday, (to bring out the latter reading, imagine that a private investigator is attempting to determine how Chris spends her time, and having determined that she spends every Friday at the same location, utters 27b—perhaps the continuation 'and I'm going to find out where it is' helps bring out the reading). Other constructions also make clear that 'somewhere' (plus descriptive material) exhibits scope ambiguities with other quantifiers. For example:

29a.   A monitor will be set up somewhere near every volcano.
29b.   The next debate will be held somewhere that every candidate visited during the last year.

For pragmatic reasons, 29b is naturally read with 'somewhere . . .' taking widest scope, whereas the opposite is true of 29a. Of course, operators too exhibit scope ambiguities with respect to quantifiers. But the point, again, is that here 'somewhere' allows further descriptive material to restrict it as do quantifiers generally (and operators do not) and occupies argument position as do quantifiers generally (and operators do not). Thus, the fact that it exhibits what appear to be quantifier scope ambiguities here as well constitutes further evidence that it really is a quantifier.

Of course, one might claim that 'somewhere' is ambiguous, and that though it is a quantifier in 25–9 above, it is an index shifting operator in 24. However, I'm not sure what the independent evidence for such a claim might be. For example, even in 24, 'somewhere' allows for the addition of restrictive descriptive material just as it does in 25–9, and, again, just as other quantifiers do and as operators don't:

24a.   Somewhere in California near the coast the sun is shining.

Further in sentences like:

30.   John was somewhere in California near the coast, and the sun was shining.

'somewhere in California near the coast' occupies an argument position occupied by normal quantifiers, and it allows for a reading of the second sentence on which it is equivalent to 24a. So here, where the expression 'Somewhere in California near the coast' appears to be a quantifier, it affects the interpretation of 'the sun was shining' in 30 just the way the very same expression does in 24a. Surely all of this suggests 'somewhere in California near the coast' is a quantifier in 24a as well, (and that 'Somewhere' is in 24).

Now if 'Somewhere' is a quantifier in 24 (and so are the related expressions in 25–29), in order to have a semantic effect on the embedded sentence it must bind a variable in it. This means that the sentence must contain some sort of "covert" location variable. Though I don't intend to speculate on the exact nature of that variable, there are a couple of things worth saying about it. First, I am agnostic with respect to the question of exactly what sort of variable it is, (e.g. there may actually be a location variable; or it may be that the embedded sentence in 24 contains only an event or situation variable, which itself gets bound by 'somewhere' (since an event assigned to such a variable has locational properties); or it may be that 'somewhere' is a quantifier over locational *properties* of events, and so binds a variable that takes these as values, etc.). Second, whatever the nature of the variable, I am agnostic with respect to whether it is an argument or an adjunct (e.g. it may be that 'somewhere' binds the "covert" temporal variable in the covert adjunct 'at t'). And indeed, it may be that for some sentences that 'Somewhere' embeds in the way that it embeds 24 the variable it binds is an adjunct and in other cases it is an argument.

To summarize, we have seen that there is no reason to think that 'somewhere' in 24 is, as Lewis assumes, an index shifting location operator. Further, I don't think there are any other expressions that are properly treated as index shifting locational operators (indeed, 'somewhere' would probably be the best candidate). I conclude that there is no reason to think that English contains any index shifting location operators, and hence no reason to think that locations must be features of indices of evaluation.

Thus far we have argued that neither times nor locations are needed as coordinates of indices. This leaves only worlds and standards of precision. Though I won't try to argue the point in as much detail as I did in the case of tense or even location expressions (indeed, I'll be very brief here), I don't think that expressions such as 'strictly speaking' are operators that shift a standard of precision coordinate of an index of evaluation either. Hence I don't think that standards of precision are coordinates of indices either. It is certainly true that whether we intuitively consider an utterance of a sentence like 'France is hexagonal.' to be true or false depends on something like the degree of exactness or precision we expect in the context of utterance. But I seriously doubt that the proper way to understand this phenomenon theoretically is to have standards of precision as coordinates of indices of evaluation that can be shifted by alleged operators such as 'strictly speaking'. It seems to me that locutions like 'strictly speaking' are devices for commenting on what one is doing in uttering the sentence they embed.[40] One of my reasons for thinking that 'strictly speaking' is

---

[40] As are locutions like 'Frankly speaking', 'Between you and me' and 'Just so you know'. This is essentially the view of Bach (1999). He calls expressions of this sort *utterance modifiers*, and says of them that they are 'used to comment on the main part of the utterance in which they occur.' (p. 356)

not a feature of index shifting operator is that it doesn't comfortably embed in lots of constructions:[41]

31. *Necessarily, strictly speaking tomatoes are fruits.
32. *If strictly speaking lobbying were illegal, then politicians would be more honest.

If 'strictly speaking' is an operator, it should be embeddable in these cases. On the other hand, if it is used to comment on what one is doing in uttering a sentence, that would seem to explain why it isn't embeddable in these cases.

If this is correct, then indices do not need standards of precision as coordinates. Thus, the only coordinate left in indices are possible worlds. This means that variable but simple semantic values are or determine functions from possible worlds to truth values. Of course such semantic values *can* be identified with propositions, and hence Stalnaker *did* give the right reason for favoring an approach yielding variable but simple semantic values over an approach yielding constant but complicated semantic values, (i.e. we independently need propositions, and only variable but simple semantic values of sentences can be identified with them).

It remains to consider Lewis's objection to the sort of view we have developed. The fact that what appear to be index shifting operators can be reconstrued as object language quantifiers was not lost on Lewis. And thus Lewis anticipated the strategy of reconstruing all apparent index shifting operators except modal ones (i.e. world shifting ones) as e.g. object language quantifiers, thus leaving only a world as an index and so allowing the identification of variable but simple semantic values of sentences with propositions, as Stalnaker proposed.[42] This is a version of what Lewis derisively called *the schmentencite strategy*.[43] It is worth highlighting a consequence of our version of the strategy. As already mentioned, if e.g. 'somewhere' is a quantifier, then sentences it embeds (when it is nonvacuous) must contain a free variable of some sort. But this means that they are in some

---

[41] This is related to what Bach thinks shows 'strictly speaking' etc. do not contribute to what is said by sentences in which they occur. Bach thinks that such expressions don't embed comfortably under 'said'. But oddly, 'strictly speaking' can seem fine so embedded: 'John said that strictly speaking tomatoes are fruits.'

[42] I should mention that although I go on to talk as though *various* apparent operators have been reconstrued as object language quantifiers, strictly we have done this only for 'somewhere'. With respect to tenses and temporal expressions, it may be that (at least some of them) are quantifiers, but we only really committed ourselves to the view that they are not index shifting sentence operators. Of course, expressions like 'strictly speaking' have not been reconstrued as quantifiers at all, but I have claimed they are not feature-of-index shifting operators.

[43] See Lewis (1980: 33) where he discusses various versions of the schmentencite strategy, ours included. Lewis actually discusses the strategy twice, as it is put to two uses. First, he discusses the strategy as a way of trying to avoid the claim that truth of sentences depends on both context *and index* (pp. 32–3). We don't put the strategy to this use, since we have embraced the dependence of truth on context and index. He later very briefly discusses it as a way of rescuing Stalnaker (p. 39). As his language makes clear, Lewis is very dismissive of the strategy in both places.

sense not genuine *sentences* and will not be assigned propositions as semantic values. They can only be assigned propositions *relative to an assignment of values to variables*. Hence, when I claim that propositions expressed by sentences relative to contexts can be identified with Lewis's variable but simple semantic values (or compositional semantic values) had by these sentences relative to contexts, 'sentences' here must be understood to be expressions lacking free variables. On this way of using the term, the expression 'somewhere' embeds in a sentence like 'Somewhere the sun is shining' is not a sentence![44] What is being claimed can be put more conspicuously as follows: sentences without free variables can be assigned propositions relative to contexts compositionally; and so the variable but simple semantic values assigned to sentences without free variables relative to context are propositions.

So what is Lewis's argument against the schmentencite strategy? It is difficult to tell, because Lewis is so dismissive. Considering the strategy precisely as we have used it, as a way of defending Stalnaker, Lewis writes:

There is always the schmentencite way out: to rescue a generalization, reclassify the exceptions. If we said that seeming sentences involved in shiftiness of features other than the world . . . were not genuine sentences, then we would be free to say that the semantic values of a genuine sentence, in context, was its propositional content. But what's the point?[45]

Note that in effect we have done what Lewis mentions. We have reanalyzed cases of "seeming shiftiness" (apparent time and location operators) in other terms (e.g. 'somewhere' as a quantifier, which embeds a "sentence" with a free variable, and hence not a "genuine sentence"). Since the above quotation contains all Lewis says about why this shouldn't be done, it isn't clear what his argument is. But putting this together with his earlier remarks on the schmentencite strategy, I think we can reconstruct his thinking. Lewis's remarks suggest that he thought that reconstruing alleged index shifting sentence operators as object language quantifiers was a sort of ad hoc technical trick. It can be done, but it is just an unmotivated, ad hoc move designed to save a theory ('. . . to rescue a generalization, reclassify the exceptions . . . ').

The important point here is that Lewis's attitude would be justified if and only if the independent evidence available favored the view that the alleged operators in question really are operators. For suppose it didn't. Then either: 1) the independent evidence is neutral, and we should be indifferent as to how the expressions are treated; or 2) the independent evidence favors the view that the alleged operators aren't operators. If option 1 is correct, how can Lewis claim that it is ad hoc to treat the expressions as non-operators? Since there is no

[44] This is worth highlighting, because I haven't consistently used the word 'sentence' this way in the present work. To do so would have made exposition more difficult throughout and would have required tedious motivation earlier.
[45] Lewis (1980): 39.

independent evidence either way, one treatment is no more unmotivated and ad hoc than the other. Treating the alleged operators other than as operators can only amount to "reclassifying exceptions" in some pejorative sense if there is some reason for the initial classification to begin with. But on option 1 there isn't. In any case, we have argued that in fact option 2 is correct: we claim that the independent evidence available favors the view that the expressions in dispute (tense and location expressions) are not operators. Thus, Lewis's objection here carries no weight against us.

In conclusion, I have argued that tenses and temporal expressions, location expressions and expressions such as 'strictly speaking' are not operators. In turn, this means that indices need not contain times, locations or standards of precision. This leaves only worlds as coordinates of indices. Indeed, worlds can simply be identified with indices. As a result, variable but simple semantic values are or determine functions from possible worlds to truth values and so can be identified with propositions. Obviously, my own view is that they *determine* such functions. Thus, I conclude that Stalnaker *has* given Lewis a reason for favoring variable but simple semantic values over constant but complicated semantic values. We need propositions, and they *can* be identified with variable but simple semantic values but *not* with constant but complicated semantic values. We thus vindicate the view that the compositional assignment of propositions to sentences in contexts is the primary job of semantics *and* undermine the sorts of arguments Jason Stanley offers against RT and for a version of two dimensionalism. In addition, we secure the motivation for propositions offered in the Introduction by vindicating the view that propositions are both the objects of attitudes like belief and doubt and the things on which modal operators operate.

7

The Paradox of Analysis

In Chapter 2, I discussed what I consider to be various virtues of the view of propositions I have been defending in this book. I mentioned there that the view provides us with the materials to resolve the paradox of analysis and address other related problems. This final chapter of the book is devoted to these issues. I'll begin by discussing philosophical analysis and formulating a version of the paradox of analysis.[1]

Providing philosophical accounts or analyses of various notions is a central task that occupies philosophers. It is not at all unusual to read a work of philosophy in which the author offers an account or analysis of mental representation, knowledge, reference, justice or moral goodness. Some philosophers are queasy about calling their accounts analyses. When they offer philosophical accounts of notions, they deny that they are giving analyses and claim to be doing something else. Perhaps such queasiness is due to skepticism about the very possibility of producing anything that deserves the label 'analysis'. Addressing such skepticism head on is too big a task to take on here. So I will simply assume that there are real philosophical analyses and that one of the jobs of philosophers is to provide them.

Of course, even if we don't directly argue against skepticism about philosophical analyses, those of us who think there really are such things still need to explain to the skeptics exactly what they are. I believe that for an account of philosophical analysis to be a real contender, it must answer at least the following questions:

i. What are the objects of analysis (that is, what is analyzed in a correct philosophical analysis)?

ii. Under what conditions is a purported analysis a correct analysis?

iii. Why are we able to produce philosophical analyses from the armchair?[2]

iv. What is the difference between the following sorts of claims, all of which seem to deserve the label 'analysis' but each of which differs from the others in certain ways:

a. For all x, x is a brother iff x is a male sibling.

---

[1] Some material in the present chapter is drawn from King (1998) with the kind permission of *Philosophical Studies* and Springer Science and Business Media. Some of the details of the view defended here are different from the one defended in King (1998).

[2] I am deliberately staying away from the term 'a priori' here—more on this below.

    b. For all x, x is an instance of knowledge iff x is a justified true belief.[3]

    c. For all x, x is water iff x is liquid H_2O.

  v. What is the solution to the paradox of analysis?

I think questions i–iii are clear enough as they stand, but questions iv and v perhaps require additional comment. Regarding iv, though a–c all seem to be in some sense analyses, things like a are trivial in a way things like b and c aren't. Things like b are discoverable from the armchair, as is a; but things like c require empirical investigation. These differences should be explained and clarified, as should be the sense in which a–c are all nonetheless analyses. As we'll see, there are additional issues involving analyses like c. As to question v, various things have been called the paradox of analysis over the years, but despite these differences of formulation, I think there is a common structure. We begin with something that is claimed to be a correct analysis, say:

1. For all x, x is an instance of knowledge iff x is a justified true belief.

2. For all x, x is a brother iff x is a male sibling.[4]

It is then claimed that if 1 and 2 are correct analyses, we may infer that they must "mean the same thing as" or "say the same thing as" or "express the same proposition as" or "make the same statement as"

1a. For all x, x is an instance of knowledge iff x is an instance of knowledge
2a. For all x, x is a brother iff x is a brother.

(Different reasons may be given for this inference, depending in part on which of the above formulations ("mean the same thing as", etc.) is used.) It is then claimed that there is some difference between 1 and 1a, (e.g. one is informative, the other not) and 2 and 2a (e.g. one is an analysis, the other not) that precludes their "meaning the same thing", etc. The paradox is that given that 1 and 2 are correct analyses, it appears that the sentence pairs 1/1a and 2/2a must *and* must not "mean the same thing", "express the same proposition", etc.[5]

The relevant issues and problems having been outlined, I now turn to the tasks of sketching an account of analysis; showing that the account answers the five questions discussed above; and comparing the account with a couple of other accounts of analysis. The account I shall sketch to a great extent falls out of a framework that comprises three elements. I believe each of these elements can be independently motivated and is independently plausible. To my mind, that makes the account of analysis I shall offer very attractive. I begin by discussing each element in turn.

---

    [3] For present purposes, I shall assume that this provides a correct analysis of knowledge.

    [4] I'll often ignore the property of being human in this and other examples in what follows for ease of exposition.

    [5] In the exchange that initiated contemporary discussion of the paradox of analysis, Moore (1942) and Langford (1942) themselves state "the" paradox in slightly different ways.

The first element of the framework is the account of propositions I have been defending. In fact, however, only a certain feature of that account is crucial here, as I shall make clear later. Thus, so long as one accepts a theory of propositions with that feature, it is not in fact necessary to accept my *exact* account of propositions in order to accept the account of analysis I shall sketch. Still, having noted this I'll presuppose the account of propositions I have been defending here. And I'll continue to assume that names contribute individuals to propositions; that syntactically simple n-place predicates (count nouns, adjectives and verbs) contribute n-place relations to propositions; that well behaved sentential connectives like 'and' and 'iff' contribute truth functions to propositions; and that determiners like 'every', 'some' and 'most' contribute relations between properties to propositions.

The second element of the framework I intend to employ in formulating my account of analysis is a claim about properties and relations. The claim is that some properties and relations are complex, and have other properties and relations as components. To illustrate, take the property of being a bachelor. It might be thought that the properties of being adult, unmarried, and male are components of the bachelor property. The idea is that the bachelor property is a complex property that has being unmarried, being adult and so on as component parts that are combined conjunctively to form the bachelor property. In this case, the mode of combination of the component properties that form the bachelor property is something like property conjunction. But it should not be thought that conjunction is the only mode of combination. For, first, I at least would countenance a disjunctive mode of combination. But more importantly, there are other modes as well. Consider the property of being an uncle. Roughly, we might think the uncle property is to be understood as (suppressing being human for simplicity):

3. x is an uncle iff x is male and some: y(x is a sibling of y & some: z(y is a parent of z))

Here there are various modes of combination that combine the components in forming the uncle property. First, the *parent of* relation combines with the property of properties *some*. *Some* combines with an n-place relation on one of its argument places to yield an n-1 place relation. In the above case, *some* combines with the *parent of* relation on its second argument place to yield a one-place property that holds of x iff x is a parent of something. Similar remarks apply to *some* combining with the two-place relation of *x's being y's sibling where y is a parent*. I would like to have more to say about how *some* combines with a two-place relation on an argument place to yield a one-place property. But this would involve formulating a general theory of how properties and relations combine to form complex properties and relations. Doing that is well beyond the scope of the present work. So I will just assume there are various modes by means of which properties and relations combine to form complex properties and relations. My main concern now is to note that modes of combination other than conjunction are involved.

Let me add two caveats before moving on. First, in talking of complex properties and relations having other properties and relations as components, I leave open exactly what it means for one property or relation to be a component of another. As my remarks probably suggested, I myself tend to think of this in terms of the one property literally being built up (in part) out of the other, so that in some sense the complex property or relation has its components as parts. But it may be that there are other ways to think of what it is for a property or relation to be a component of another property or relation. What is important for my purposes is that a complex property or relation has the components it does, combined in the way they are combined in it, in virtue of its nature; and that as a result necessarily, the complex property is built out of its components combined in that way. Second, in claiming that there are complex properties and relations, I don't commit myself to the claim that there are metaphysically simple properties and relations. I tend to believe there are, but I'm not entirely sure why and it seems possible that there are not.

Let me now turn to the third and final element of the framework I shall employ in giving my account of analysis. This final element is the claim that there are three categories of words such that the words in a given category are all governed by the same standard of linguistic competence; but words in different categories are governed by different standards of linguistic competence. In the case of each category, I assume that words in that category express complex properties or relations. To be competent with a word in the first category, which I will call a *category one word*, one must be able to specify the components of the property or relation expressed by the word and how those components are combined in the property expressed by the word. 'Bachelor' is a paradigmatic category one word. To be competent with the word, one must know that it expresses a property that has as components the properties of being unmarried, being male and being adult and that these properties are "conjunctively combined" in the bachelor property.[6] Of course, a competent speaker wouldn't put it this way. She would just say that to be a bachelor is to be an unmarried adult male. But given our framework, we as theoreticians would describe what she knows in saying this as knowing the components of the property expressed by 'bachelor' and how they are combined in forming this property. Other examples of category one words include 'vixen', 'uncle' and 'grandparent'.

The second category is more difficult to characterize. Very roughly, I want to say that to be competent with a category two word e requires that one

---

[6] Qualification: does one really need to know *all* the components and how they are combined to be competent? Probably not. It seems in certain cases competent speakers may offer up components and modes of combination for category one words that aren't quite right. E.g. mine here allow the Pope to be a bachelor, which isn't obviously correct.

[handwritten note: by convention may change]

be able to reliably determine whether a given entity possesses the property expressed by e and to thereby know whether e applies to the entity or not.[7] More explicitly, being competent with such a word e requires that given any entity o that paradigmatically possesses the property P expressed by e or paradigmatically fails to possess P, were one to know all facts about o relevant to whether it possesses P or not, excluding the fact that o possesses P or the fact that o fails to possess P, one would correctly determine whether o possesses P and thereby know whether e applies to it or not. Roughly, this means that given an entity to which e paradigmatically applies or paradigmatically fails to apply, speakers competent with e and who have sufficient information about the entity know whether e applies to the entity or not. More briefly, speakers competent with e can reliably determine whether e applies to an object or not given sufficient information. Words like '(morally) good', 'modest', and 'knowledge' seem to be category two words. Could a word be in category one and category two given what I have said to this point? Perhaps 'bachelor' might be an example. To avoid problems this might create, let's stipulate that category two words can't be in category one as well. So if something is a category one word it ipso facto fails to be in category two.

Finally, words in category three fail to be governed by the standards of competence governing categories one and two. Indeed, I think it is hard to say what the standard of competence is for such words. Let me just say that the paradigmatic category three words are the so-called natural kind terms like 'water', 'tiger', 'aluminum' and so on.

Now it seems to me clear that there are these three categories of words that are governed by different standards of competence. To be competent with 'bachelor', you must be able to specify the components of the bachelor property and their mode of combination. This isn't true for 'knowledge'. To be competent with 'knowledge', you must be able to recognize paradigmatic instances of it given sufficient information. But neither of these is true for 'aluminum'. So there really do seem to be at least these three categories of words that are distinguished by the standards of competence governing the words in each category. I hasten to add that I am not claiming that there aren't further categories as well or that there aren't finer distinctions within each of our three categories. This may or may not be so.

Now that we have the three elements of our framework in place, let's begin to discuss analysis. First, I shall assume that analyses are stated in the following canonical form:

4. For all x, x is F iff C(x)

---

[7] For ease of exposition, I have switched from talking about properties and relations to talking only of properties. I take it is easy to see how a formulation that includes relations here would go.

where I shall assume that 'F' is syntactically simple and that 'C(x)' is a syntactically complex predicate containing free occurrences of the variable 'x'.[8] Now according to our theory of propositions, sentences like 4 express propositions whose structures are identical to the structures of the sentences expressing them. So 4 expresses a proposition that looks something like this:

4'. [EVERY: x [F*(x) IFF Ͳ(x)]]

where EVERY is the contribution 'For all' makes to propositions, IFF is the contribution 'iff' makes, and F* is the property expressed by 'F'.[9] I'll come back to these constituents in a moment. First, let me discuss Ͳ(x). Ͳ(x) is what 'C(x)' contributes to 4'. As I indicated above, 'C(x)' is syntactically complex. Since on the present view of propositions, the structures of propositions are identical to the syntactic structures of sentences expressing them, the structure of 4' must be identical to the structure of 4. This means that the structure of Ͳ(x) must be the same as the syntactic structure of 'C(x)'. As I said in Chapter 2, Ͳ(x) is a structured, complex sub-propositional constituent whose structure mirrors the syntactic structure of 'C(x)'; in general, syntactically complex predicates contribute to propositions complex sub-propositional constituents whose structures mirror the syntactic structures of the predicates contributing them. Because it is important for present concerns, at the risk of boring the reader let me refresh his or her memory of the discussion of these issues in Chapter 2 by running through a relatively simple example. Consider the complex predicate:

5. met Seth Morrison

Oversimplifying, this predicate has the syntactic structure as follows:

5'.

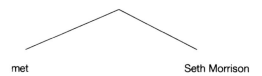

met   Seth Morrison

Now on our view of propositions, the syntactic structure of a sentence like

6. Every skier met Seth Morrison.

is virtually identical to the structure of the proposition expressed by that sentence. But this means that the contribution made by the predicate 5/5' to the proposition expressed by 6 must have a structure virtually identical to that of 5'.

---

[8] We would want to extend the account I shall sketch to eliminate the requirement that 'F' be syntactically simple. I don't see any problems with doing so in principle, but it would require a lot more complexity in various places.

[9] I don't think variables occur in "quantified" propositions (see Chapter 2 and the Appendix). But for ease of exposition, here I will talk as though they do.

As I indicated, my view is that the contribution made by the predicate 5/5' to the proposition expressed by the sentence 6 is the following entity:

7.

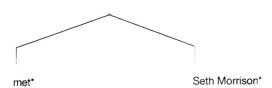

met*   Seth Morrison*

where met* is the relation of meeting and Seth Morrison* is Seth Morrison.[10] Let's call the things at the terminal nodes of entities like 7 its *constituents*. So 7s constituents are met* and Seth. Clearly, the entity 7 has the same structure as the predicate 5/5' as required. Now 7 is not the relational property of meeting Seth Morrison. Presumably, that relational property is the result of Seth saturating the second argument place in the meeting relation. That is not what 7 is. 7 is the meeting relation standing in a relation, represented by the tree structure, to Seth Morrison. The relation that holds together Seth and the meeting relation in 7 (again, represented by the tree) is of the same sort that generally holds together the constituents of propositions. Such relations were discussed in Chapter 2.

Though 7 is not the relational property of meeting Seth, as I said in Chapter 2, in the definition of truth for propositions, the sub-propositional constituent 7 must get mapped to that relational property. After all, 'Every' in a sentence like 6 contributes to the proposition expressed by it a relation between properties. Thus, 6 expresses a proposition that is true iff the properties of being a skier and the relational property of meeting Seth stand in the relation expressed by 'Every'. So in the definition of truth for propositions, the propositional constituent 7 must get mapped to the relational property of meeting Seth. And generally, complex predicates will contribute entities like 7 (except more complex if the predicate is syntactically more complex than 5/5') to propositions, and the definition of truth for propositions must map these entities to the relevant properties.[11] As I did in Chapter 2, I shall put this by saying that the complex sub-propositional contributions syntactically complex predicates make to propositions, though not properties or relations themselves, *represent* properties or relations.

Earlier I said that one of the three elements that comprise the framework that my account of analysis falls out of is a theory of propositions that has a certain feature that my account has. I can now say what that feature is. One must accept an account of propositions on which complex predicates contribute to propositions complex sub-propositional constituents that have properties and relations at their terminal nodes and that represent other properties. Of course,

---

[10] I have left out the relation that is the semantic significance of the syntactic relation in 7 as well as other features for ease of exposition.
[11] This idea is addressed briefly in the Appendix.

an account of propositions distinct from mine could have this feature. But that complex predicates function in this way is well motivated on my account; and, as I have tried to argue throughout the present work, my account of propositions has much to recommend it.

Returning to $\mathcal{C}(x)$, what I have been saying is true of it, since it is the contribution made to the proposition 4' by the syntactically complex predicate 'C(x)' in 4. Thus, $\mathcal{C}(x)$ is a complex sub-propositional constituent like 7 except perhaps more complex; and like 7, it represents a property, that is, gets mapped to the property by the definition of truth for propositions.

Having clarified the nature of the constituent $\mathcal{C}(x)$ of propositions like 4', we can say something about the truth conditions of propositions of this form. Though I've said what I take truth functional connectives and determiners to contribute to propositions, I won't bother here with details about the nature of the constituents EVERY and IFF of 4'. I'll assume we have an account of determiners and sentential connectives according to which sentences of the form of 4, and hence propositions of the form 4', are true iff everything is such that it possesses F* iff it possess the property represented by $\mathcal{C}(x)$. Obviously, then, many true propositions of the form of 4' fail to be analyses.

However, we are now in a position to say what an analysis is. An analysis is a proposition of the form 4' such that (i) the property represented by $\mathcal{C}(x)$ is identical to the property F*; and (ii) the constituents of $\mathcal{C}(x)$ are components of the complex property F*.

A few comments on this characterization are in order. First, on the view in question, what is being analyzed is a complex property or relation. In the case of 4', it is F*. The constituents of the entity $\mathcal{C}(x)$ are components of the complex property F* being analyzed. So the analysis tells us what the components are of the complex property being analyzed and how they are combined in it. If we assume, as seems very plausible and as I said we would earlier, that a complex property or relation has the components it does combined in the way they are as a matter of necessity, then an analysis will be a necessarily true proposition. This answers questions i and ii we began with. Second, turning to question v and the paradox of analysis, recall that in order to get the paradox, we need the claim that if the following are analyses

1. For all x, x is an instance of knowledge iff x is a justified true belief.

2. For all x, x is a brother iff x is a male sibling.

then they must "mean the same thing as" or "say the same thing as" or "express the same proposition as" or "make the same statement as"

1a. For all x, x is an instance of knowledge iff x is an instance of knowledge.

2a. For all x, x is a brother iff x is a brother.

But we reject this claim, because on the present view 1 and 1a (and 2 and 2a) do not express the same proposition even if 1 (and 2) is an analysis. The reason is that 'knowledge' contributes the property of being a bit of knowledge to the proposition expressed by 1, whereas 'justified true belief' contributes a complex $\mathcal{C}(x)$ type entity that represents the property of being a bit of knowledge (assuming 1 is an analysis) and whose constituents are components of this property. Thus, on the one hand, 'knowledge' and 'justified true belief' make different contributions to the proposition expressed by 1, and so we block the paradox of analysis by holding that 1 and 1a don't express the same proposition. But on the other hand, since 'justified true belief' contributes to the proposition expressed by 1 a $\mathcal{C}(x)$ type of entity that *represents* the property of being a bit of knowledge, we preserve the intuition that 'knowledge' and 'justified true belief' in some sense "stand for" the same property. So a central feature of the present view is that though 'knowledge' and 'justified true belief' make different contributions to propositions, there is a sense in which they "stand for" the same property. This will be important later when we discuss alternative accounts of analysis.

This leaves only our original questions iii and iv unanswered:

iii. Why are we able to produce philosophical analyses from the armchair?

iv. What is the difference between the following sorts of claims, all of which seem to deserve the label 'analysis' but each of which differs from the others in certain ways:

   a. For all x, x is a brother iff x is a male sibling.
   b. For all x, x is an instance of knowledge iff x is a justified true belief.
   c. For all x, x is water iff x is liquid H_2O.

First consider c in question iv. If water is indeed liquid H_2O, then this seems like an analysis in some sense. And perhaps it even satisfies our definition of an analysis. That is, perhaps 'water' expresses a complex property. And perhaps 'liquid H_2O' contributes to the proposition expressed by c a complex $\mathcal{C}(x)$ type entity that represents the property of being water and whose constituents are components of that property. I tend to think these things are so and below I'll assume that they are. But whatever its status exactly, c is not a philosophical analysis since establishing it requires scientific, and not merely philosophical, investigation. What this shows is that our characterization of analysis is not yet a characterization of *philosophical* analysis, since it would not rule out things like c being analyses. Similarly, in my view anyway, a isn't a philosophical analysis either, since establishing it doesn't even require philosophical investigation.

In order to distinguish *philosophical* analyses from these other analyses, we must return to the claims about linguistic competence made earlier. Note that one difference between a, b and c above is that 'brother' in a is a category one word, 'knowledge' in b is a category two word, and 'water' in c is a category three word. This, I believe, is the key to distinguishing philosophical analyses from other analyses like a and c. Specifically, a proposition R is a philosophical analysis relative to a linguistic community c iff (i) R is an analysis; and (ii) the sentence of c expressing R has a category two word expressing the complex property being analyzed. Obviously, this makes the proposition expressed by b relative to our linguistic community a philosophical analysis, and not so for the propositions expressed by a and c.

But it is important to see the intuitive motivation behind this characterization of philosophical analyses. It is this. Recall that being competent with a category two word e requires that given any entity o that paradigmatically possesses the property P expressed by e or paradigmatically fails to possess P, were one to know all facts about o relevant to whether it possesses P or not, excluding the fact that o possesses P or the fact that o fails to possess P, one would correctly determine whether o possesses P and thereby know whether e applies to it or not. But this means that a speaker who is linguistically competent with the category two word 'knowledge' and who knows the relevant facts about an actual or hypothetical situation in which something is or is not a paradigmatic instance of knowledge is able to correctly determine whether the thing is or is not an instance of knowledge. By exploiting this ability and considering a wide variety of such situations, a person can, in virtue only of his linguistic competence, formulate hypotheses about the proper analysis of knowledge that explain the judgments he makes about the situations in question. Of course, he may not succeed in actually formulating a correct analysis of the relevant property. His linguistic competence guarantees only that he will make correct judgments about paradigm cases given relevant information. His competence does not guarantee that he will hit on the correct analysis of the property that in fact explains his judgments. But with some hard work and luck, such a person may hit upon the proper analysis of knowledge.

The important point here is that a person can do this by considering hypothetical situations, armed only with her linguistic competence. That is, a person can do this from the armchair. Note that we now have an answer to question iii as to why philosophical analyses can in principle be produced from the armchair. They can be, because the only materials required for their production are hypothetical scenarios and linguistic competence with the category two word expressing the property being analyzed. Thus, anyone who is linguistically competent with the category two word expressing the property one is trying to analyze has a shot at formulating an analysis on the basis of judgments about hypothetical scenarios. I don't want to debate whether formulating a correct analysis in this manner would constitute a priori knowledge. That would depend in part on whether the knowledge that constitutes linguistic competence in such cases is a priori knowledge. As I've stressed, the important point is that we have explained why philosophical analysis can be produced from the armchair.

By way of contrast, suppose a linguistically competent person is considering a category one word, say 'brother', and the property it expresses. In virtue of her linguistic competence, she will *know* the components of the complex property and how they are combined to form it. That is, she will be in a position to formulate and correctly assert things like

2. For all x, x is a brother iff x is a male sibling.

Since this is so merely in virtue of her linguistic competence, any linguistically competent person in her community will also be able to do so. So in this case, unlike the case of a category two word and the property it expresses, linguistic competence *suffices* for the successful formulation of the analysis. Thus, things like 2 will seem trivial, unlike claims like 1.

Further, if a linguistically competent person is considering a category three word and the property it expresses, given something that paradigmatically possesses the property or fails to and the relevant facts about the situation, her linguistic competence alone will not allow her to correctly determine whether the thing possesses the property expressed by the word or not. Thus, she will *not* be able to consider a wide variety of hypothetical situations, and judge correctly whether the property in question is instantiated in those situations. Thus, absent such judgments, she will be in no position to formulate hypotheses regarding the analysis of the property in question that would explain the judgments that she can't make! In this case, then, her linguistic competence alone doesn't even put her in a position to form hypotheses about the analysis of the property expressed by the word. She therefore will not be able to formulate analyses of properties expressed by category three words from the armchair. In saying this, we have given an answer to question iv as to how the following differ, though they all may well be analyses:

a. For all x, x is a brother iff x is a male sibling.
b. For all x, x is an instance of knowledge iff x is a justified true belief.
c. For all x, x is water iff x is liquid H_2O.

and why only a and b are discoverable from the armchair.

The central idea of this attempt to characterize philosophical analyses is that philosophical analyses (for a given community) are simply analyses such that typical members of the linguistic community bear a certain sort of epistemic relation to the analyzed property in the analysis. Thus the appeal to words and standards of linguistic competence is simply a way of getting at the epistemic relations typical (linguistically competent) members of the community bear to the properties in question. However, it is not difficult to put the matter more directly, without what some may perceive as a detour through linguistic competence.[12] Corresponding to the different standards of linguistic competence associated with our three categories of words, we might suppose that there are (at

---

[12] I'm not sure it is such a detour since it seems plausible to suppose that the acquisition of a language significantly determines the epistemic relations one bears to the properties expressed by words of the language.

least) three different ways that typical members of a community are epistemically related to complex properties. First, typical members of the community may know the components of a complex property and how they are combined to form the complex property. Second, typical members of the community may not know the components of the property but be able to reliably determine whether the property is present or absent given sufficient information. Third, typical members of a community may be aware of the existence of a property but in general not know its components and not be able to reliably detect its presence or absence. Then we may say that a proposition R is a philosophical analysis for a community c iff (i) R is an analysis; and (ii) typical members of the community are related to the analyzed property in the second way mentioned above.[13]

Before comparing the account of analysis just sketched with a couple of other accounts, it is worth discussing a few further points about the account. First, our characterization of analyses allows for "varying depths" of analyses. This is true whether the analysis is philosophical or not. Consider, for example, the sentences

8. For all x, x is a bachelor iff x is an unmarried adult male

and

9. For all x, x is a bachelor iff x is an unmarried man.

Given what we have said, 8 expresses the following proposition:

8a. [[EVERY :x] [[x bachelor*] IFF [x unmarried*[x adult*[x male*]]]]]

Now assuming that 'man' expresses the property of being an adult male, 9 expresses the proposition

9a. [[EVERY: x][[x bachelor*] IFF[x unmarried*[x adult-male*]]]]

where adult-male* is the complex property of being an adult male, which has as components the property of being an adult and the property of being male. Though 8a and 9a are different propositions, the complex entities on the right side of IFF in each presumably represent the same property: being a bachelor. And both are analyses. However, 8a is a "deeper" analysis than 9a. For the complex entity in 8a has as constituents *more* components of the property of being a bachelor (unmarried*, adult* and male*) than does the complex entity in 9a (unmarried* and adult-male*). And of course there very likely are analyses "deeper" than 8a. Supposing that the constituents of the complex entity in 8a (unmarried*, adult*, male*) are complex properties, there is a proposition like 8a except that the complex entity in it contains as constituents the components of these complex properties. It seems to me that the fact that our account allows for

---

[13] Neither definition of a philosophical analysis for a community requires that members of the community recognize that the analysis is an analysis; and the second doesn't even require that the community have the linguistic wherewithal to express the analysis.

analyses of different depths is a very good thing, since in fact analyses do seem to vary in this way. We'll return to this below.

A second point to consider is the light our account of analysis sheds on so-called *theoretical identities* such as

10. Water is liquid H_2O.
11. Gold is the element with atomic number 79.[14]

Following Soames (2002), let's reconstrue these as universally quantified biconditionals:

10a. For all x, x is (a drop of) water iff x is (a drop of) liquid H_2O.
11a. For all x, x is (a bit of) gold iff x is (a bit of) the element with atomic number 79.

Still loosely following Soames, suppose that we thought that (if true) 10 tells us what the property of being water is and 11 tells us what the property of being gold is. If that is right, then the property of being water just is the property of being liquid H_2O. And if these properties are the same (similarly for being gold and being the element with atomic number 79), then it may seem that 10a and 11a express the same propositions as the following:

10b. For all x, x is (a drop of) water iff x is (a drop of) water.
11b. For all x, x is (a bit of) gold iff x is (a bit of) gold.

But surely 10a and 10b must express different propositions. For one thing, as Soames points out, 10b is knowable a priori and 10a isn't. We might call this the *paradox of theoretical identification*, since it closely resembles the paradox of analysis. It is in all essentials what Soames (2002) calls *the meaning problem*.[15]
It should be clear how our view solves it. I take it that it is now obvious that on our view, 10a and 10b (and 11a and 11b) express different propositions. On the right side of the proposition expressed by 10a is a complex sub-propositional constituent of the sort discussed above that represents the property of being water. It has as constituents the property of being a liquid and the property of being H_2O.[16] These, in turn, we may suppose, are components of the complex property of being water. As such 10a expresses an (scientific) analysis and a necessary truth. We have already indicated why it cannot be arrived at from the armchair. 10b by contrast expresses a trivial (and necessary) proposition that has the property of being water on both the left and right sides. Of course, similar remarks apply to 11a and 11b. Thus we solve the meaning problem.

---

[14] My discussion here owes much to Soames (2002).   [15] P. 276.
[16] There are subtleties here about how to think of the semantics of the expression 'H_2O'. It seems to me that it is itself syntactically complex, and that would mean that the sub-propositional complex entity 'liquid H_2O' contributes to propositions has more constituents than I claim it does in the text (e.g. the property of being hydrogen, etc.). I'll suppress that here for simplicity.

Soames notes a second concern about sentences like 10a and 11a and the propositions they express. Imagine that I formulate another sentence

10c. For all x, x is (a drop of) water iff C(x).

where 'C(x)' is some predicate that characterizes what it is to be a drop of water at the *sub*atomic level. But if both 10a and 10c truly say what the property of being water is, how can 10a and 10c express different propositions? Yet it seems that they ought to. This is closely related to what Soames (2002) calls *the depth problem*.[17] Again, it should be clear how the above view of analysis solves this problem. As indicated, according to the present view, on the right side of the proposition expressed by 10a is a complex sub-propositional constituent that represents the property of being water and has as constituents the property of being a liquid and the property of being H_2O, which are components of the complex property of being water. As a result, 10a expresses an analysis. On the right side of the proposition 10c expresses there is also a complex sub-propositional constituent, call it W, that represents the property of being water. Its constituents are also components of the complex property of being water. And so 10c too expresses an analysis. However, it will be a *deeper analysis*, in the sense discussed above, than is the proposition expressed by 10a. For W presumably contains as constituents more components of the property of being water than does the sub-propositional constituent on the right side of the proposition expressed by 10a. So we are free to hold that 10a and 10c express different propositions, but both are analyses and both are necessarily true. Thus we solve (a close relative of) the depth problem.[18]

Having explained my favored view of analysis, answered the five questions we began with, and discussed additional benefits of the view, I turn now to other accounts of analysis. In order to introduce the first sort of alternative account of analysis I shall consider, let me re-emphasize a feature of the account I have defended. On the view I have defended, even assuming 1 is a

---

[17] Pp. 276–7.

[18] Ways the present account of analysis can be extended are discussed in King (2000). I should add that at a certain level of abstraction, Soames' own solution to the meaning and depth problems has much the same structure as ours. On Soames' view, a syntactically simple "natural kind" predicate like 'water' contributes only an *intension I* (function from worlds to extensions) to a proposition, whereas a syntactically complex predicate like 'being liquid H_2O' contributes a *property* to a proposition. However, that property determines the same intension I that 'water' contributes to a proposition. As a result, 10a, 10b, and 10c express different propositions (Soames holds that 'C(x)' in 10c contributes a different property to the proposition expressed by 10c than 'is (a drop of) liquid H_2O' contributes to the proposition expressed by 10a). However, they are all necessarily true. So on Soames' view, there is a sense in which 'water' and 'liquid H_2O' stand for the same thing (a certain intension) despite making different contributions to propositions (one contributes the intension; the other a property determining that very intension). On the present view that is true as well: 'water' and 'being liquid H_2O' in a sense stand for the same thing (a property—'water' contributes it to propositions and 'being liquid H_2O' contributes to propositions a complex sub-propositional entity that represents this very property), despite making different contributions to propositions.

correct analysis, 'knowledge' and 'justified true belief' nonetheless make different contributions to the proposition expressed by 1. However, as I mentioned above, there is a sense in which, despite this fact, the two expressions "stand for" the same property. 'Knowledge' contributes the complex property of being an instance of knowledge to the proposition expressed by 1. 'Justified true belief' contributes to the proposition a complex sub-propositional constituent that has as constituents components of the knowledge property. But crucially, this complex sub-propositional entity *represents* the complex knowledge property in the sense that the definition of truth for propositions maps this complex sub-propositional constituent to the knowledge property. Thus, 'knowledge' stands for the knowledge property by contributing it to the proposition expressed by 1. 'Justified true belief' stands for the knowledge property by contributing to the proposition expressed by 1 a complex sub-propositional constituent that represents the knowledge property. Thus, on this account a correct analysis like 1 does not assert that *two different properties* stand in some intimate connection. There is only one property, the complex knowledge property, and a correct analysis tells us what its components are and how they are combined in it.

By contrast, some other accounts of analysis hold that what makes an analysis like 1 correct is that the *distinct* properties expressed by 'knowledge' and 'justified true belief' are related in a very intimate way, (the matter is sometimes put in terms of concepts, rather than properties being distinct, but nothing hinges on that here). Accounts differ as to what this intimate relation is supposed to be, but let me consider one prominent account, that of Diana Ackerman (1981, 1986).[19] I should say at the outset that the main thing I find objectionable about all such accounts is that they are unable to give a satisfactory explanation of the relation that they claim obtains between the property being analyzed and the distinct property providing the analysis. This will be illustrated in the case of Ackerman's account. I shall also make another, more intuitive complaint about such accounts.

Let us continue to use 1 as our running example of an analysis. Ackerman begins by noting that for 1 to be an analysis, at least two conditions need to be met. First, 1 must be necessarily true. Second, 1 must be knowable a priori. This much seems right, depending on how we understand being knowable a priori. But as Ackerman herself points out, other examples that don't seem to be analyses satisfy these conditions. For example:

12. For all x, x is 28 iff x is the second smallest perfect number.
2a. For all x, x is a brother iff x is a brother.

Neither of these seems to be an analysis, yet both are arguably necessary and knowable a priori. So some third condition is needed to distinguish real analyses

---

[19] Chisholm and Potter (1981) is another example of a view on which the property being analyzed and the property analyzing it are distinct.

like 1 from things like 2a and 12. Let's put the first two conditions Ackerman claims an analysis needs to satisfy as follows: one property or concept P analyzes another property or concept Q iff i) P and Q are necessarily coextensive; and ii) that something is Q iff it is P is knowable a priori. Ackerman's key idea for the needed third condition is this: iii) the claim that necessarily something is Q iff it is P can be arrived at and justified by "the philosophical example and counterexample method." Ackerman (1986) describes the method as follows (my emphasis):[20]

J investigates the analysis of K's concept of Q . . . by setting K a series of armchair thought experiments, presenting K with a series of simple described hypothetical test cases and asking K questions of the form "If such and such were the case, would this count as a case of Q?" J then contrasts the descriptions of the cases where K answers affirmatively with the descriptions of the cases where K does not, and J *generalizes* upon these descriptions to arrive at the properties and their mode of combination that constitute the analysans of K's concept of Q.

Roughly speaking, Ackerman's contention is that the crucial third condition required for P to analyze Q is that the claim that necessarily something is Q iff it is P can be the outcome of the sort of philosophical inquiry described.

I don't think Ackerman's account here is correct. A minor but by no means trivial worry with Ackerman's account is cashing out the modal element in her condition: in what sense is it that the claim that necessarily something is Q iff it is P *can be* the outcome of the method described? But the account has much more severe problems.

The first problem is noted by Ackerman (1986) herself, and concerns the unexplained notion of *generalization* employed in her characterization of the third condition required for an analysis. Suppose that in considering the cases K counts as Q and those that she doesn't, using a priori philosophical method I generalize from these and conclude that P analyzes Q. But now consider *any* R that is knowable a priori to be coextensive with Q and that is necessarily coextensive with Q. That is, consider any R that satisfies only Ackerman's first two conditions. The question is, why doesn't R satisfy the third condition as well and provide the analysis of Q? For all we've said, I could easily have generalized from K's responses and concluded that R, instead of P, analyzes Q. After all, nothing has been said about generalization from K's judgments regarding which cases are Q except that we have to capture those judgments. But since R is knowable a priori to be coextensive with Q and is necessarily coextensive with Q, supposing that R analyzes Q will explain K's judgments just as well as supposing that P analyzes Q will. Recall that R by hypothesis is an arbitrary property that is a priori knowable to be coextensive with Q and necessarily coextensive with Q. And recall that the whole point of adding the *third* condition involving

---

[20] P. 310.

generalization from K's responses was to prevent R from analyzing Q in any case where it is merely a priori and necessary that R and Q are coextensive. But given any R for which it is necessary and a priori that R is coextensive with Q, we haven't been told yet why R can't be the outcome of generalizing from K's responses about hypothetical cases instead of P. But then we haven't been told why, for any R for which it is necessary and a priori that something is Q iff it is R, R might yet fail to analyze Q. But telling us this was the whole point of Ackerman's third condition. So her account so far does not get beyond the claim that if P analyzes Q, it is necessary and a priori that P and Q are coextensive. But this is not yet an *account* of philosophical analyses; it is simply an obvious necessary condition on them (waiving any worries about a priority).

Even supposing we get around this first problem, there is another serious problem. This problem involves a dilemma regarding her third condition. Either the fact that the claim that necessarily something is Q iff it is P can be the outcome of the sort of philosophical inquiry described is explained by or supervenes on some *other* relation between P and Q or it doesn't. That is, we have this fact: the claim that necessarily something is Q iff it is P can be the outcome of the sort of philosophical inquiry described. Now either this fact about P and Q is explained by or supervenes on some further relation between P and Q or it doesn't. I don't think we can accept the latter disjunct. How could it be a brute fact, a fact without further explanation, that the claim that necessarily something is Q iff it is P can be the outcome of the sort of philosophical inquiry described? Surely there should be some further explanation of this fact. There should be some further relation between P and Q that explains *why* the claim that necessarily something is Q iff it is P can be the outcome of the sort of philosophical inquiry described. So suppose there is. Call this relation R. Then it seems to me that the third condition really is that P and Q stand in R, whatever R is. But then Ackerman hasn't given us an account of analysis. She has only said this: P analyzes Q iff i) P and Q are necessarily coextensive; ii) that something is Q iff it is P is knowable a priori; and iii) P and Q stand in some relation R that explains why the claim that necessarily something is Q iff it is P can be the outcome of the sort of philosophical inquiry described. Of course, until we are told what R is, we have no real account of analysis. This can be seen clearly by noting that all Ackerman has really told us is that P is a philosophical analysis of Q iff it is a priori and necessary that P and Q are coextensive, and the claim that they are necessarily coextensive can be arrived at by philosophical method. It seems to me rather unsatisfying to be told that philosophical analyses are distinguished from things like

12. For all x, x is 28 iff x is the second smallest perfect number.

by being the possible outcomes of philosophical inquiry. What is wanted is some explanation of *why* this is so.

Finally, Ackerman's account has a difficulty shared by any account according
to which when P analyzes Q, P and Q are distinct concepts or properties.
Intuitively, when one tries to give an analysis of some concept or property Q,
one is trying to say what Q *is* and not merely trying to specify another concept
or property intimately connected to Q. Just try to imagine attempting to give an
analysis of reference, or moral goodness or mental representation and ask yourself
whether this isn't so. Of course, if we became convinced that no account that
denied that when P analyzes Q, P and Q are distinct is workable, we could be
driven to the view that we must embrace this counterintuitive claim. But I have
tried to show that there is a workable account that denies this.

The final view of analysis I will discuss is a view that figures prominently
in the work of two dimensionalists such as David Chalmers (1996; Chalmers
and Jackson 2001) and Frank Jackson (1998; Chalmers and Jackson 2001). I
should preface my remarks here by saying that I do not think that Chalmers and
Jackson envisage what they call *conceptual analysis* playing the role in philosophy
that I imagine what I am calling *philosophical analysis* playing. For Chalmers
and Jackson, conceptual analysis plays a crucial role in determining whether
certain reductive explanations can succeed. After reading an earlier version of
this chapter, Chalmers told me (p.c.) that he at least does not view their
account of conceptual analysis as providing an account of what has traditionally
been called philosophical analysis. But because their account of analysis has
become well known and because I am often asked about it in the context
of discussing philosophical analysis, I think it is worth considering whether
it can be pressed into service as an account of what has traditionally been
called philosophical analysis, despite the intentions of Jackson and Chalmers
themselves.

Jackson and Chalmers work in a so-called two dimensional semantic framework. According to such a framework, expressions are associated with two
intensions, that is, two functions from possible worlds to extensions. What they
call the *primary* or *A* intension of an expression maps a possible world "considered
as actual" to the extension of the term at that world. That is, consider a world
w very much like ours except that XYZ fills the oceans, lakes and rivers of that
world, and is what comes out of faucets and is what people drink. Now suppose
that w is the actual world. That is, suppose we discover that XYZ fills our lakes,
oceans etc. Then the extension of 'water' in w is XYZ. That is, the primary
intension of 'water' maps the world to XYZ. But now let us consider w as a
way things might have been but aren't. Water is H_2O in the actual world, and
XYZ fills the lakes and oceans of w. Then the stuff in the oceans and lakes of
w isn't water. That is, the *secondary* or *C* intension of 'water' maps w to H_2O,
just as it maps every world to H_2O. So the primary intension of a term maps a
world to the extension of that term on the supposition that the world in question
is actual. The secondary intension of a term maps a world to the extension of
that term on the supposition that *this* world is the actual world. Loosely put,

the primary intension of 'water' maps a world to whatever plays the "water role" in that world; and the secondary intension of 'water' maps every world to H_2O.

Now this should make clear that in the general case, knowing the secondary intension of a term requires knowing what the actual world is like in certain ways. Knowing that 'water' maps every world to H_2O requires knowing that in the actual world water is H_2O. Not so with a term's primary intension. I can know that if the XYZ world is actual, then the extension of 'water' is XYZ without knowing what water is in the actual world.

According to Jackson and Chalmers, conceptual analysis essentially amounts to determining what the primary intension of a term is. So a conceptual analysis of water would amount to figuring out what the extension of 'water' is at possible worlds considered as actual. At the actual world, it is H_2O, at the XYZ world recently discussed it is XYZ, and so on. Two minor caveats. Chalmers is skeptical about the possibility of finding a finite expression whose primary intension is the same as that of the expression involved in the conceptual analysis. So he is skeptical about the possibility of expressing his conceptual analyses by means of sentences like 1:

1. For all x, x is an instance of knowledge iff x is a justified true belief.

Jackson is less skeptical in this regard. Second, Chalmers holds there is no reason to think that the primary intensions of terms are total functions on the set of all possible worlds. For example, some worlds may be such that if they are taken to be actual, we wouldn't know what to say about the extension of 'water'. So for Chalmers at least, conceptual analysis may not yield any neat statements like 1, nor even primary intensions that are total functions from worlds to extensions. He thinks conceptual analysis will at any rate yield a bunch of conditionals of the following form:

13. If the actual world is thus and so, then the extension of 'water' is so and so (or alternatively, water is so and so).

For ease of exposition, I will henceforth characterize the Chalmers-Jackson account of conceptual analysis as holding that conceptual analysis is the uncovering of the primary intensions of terms. Our question is whether conceptual analysis so understood adequately characterizes what has traditionally been called philosophical analysis. I do not think it does. I'll offer two reasons why not.

First, Jackson and Chalmers hold that the primary intensions of terms can vary from speaker to speaker. Jackson (1998) writes:

I have occasionally come across people who resolutely resist the Gettier cases. Sometimes it has seemed right to accuse them of confusion . . . but sometimes it is clear that they are not confused; what we learn from the stand-off is simply that they use the word 'knowledge' to cover different cases from most of us. In these cases it is, it seems to me, misguided to accuse them of error (unless they go on to say that their concept of knowledge is ours)... [21]

And Chalmers and Jackson (2001) write:

... perhaps a city dweller might use 'water' non-deferentially for the liquid that comes out of faucets (knowing nothing of oceans) and a beach dweller might use 'water' non-deferentially for the liquid in the oceans (knowing nothing of faucets).... the subjects have different conditional abilities... [22]

To say that the subjects have different conditional abilities is just to say that they associate different primary intensions with the terms. But now consider two different moral philosophers arguing about the proper philosophical analysis of moral goodness. Imagine that both are sincere, reflective and intelligent. Imagine that their analyses yield different results. That is, they entail that different things are morally right in different situations. Suppose, finally, that the philosophers have thought long and hard about the cases they disagree on and each remains firm in her opinion. If the Chalmers-Jackson account of analysis is correct, we should at this point tell these two poor souls that they aren't really arguing at all! It just turns out that they associate different primary intensions with the term 'moral goodness', just as, according to Jackson, some associate a different primary intension with 'knowledge' than the rest of us. But if this is right, then some of the central disputes in philosophy aren't really disputes at all. It is simply a matter of the disputants talking past each other because of associating different primary intensions with the key term in their debate. I think that this consequence of taking the Chalmers-Jackson view of conceptual analysis to be an account of philosophical analysis is very unfortunate.

But there is a second, more telling reason for not so taking the Chalmers-Jackson view of conceptual analysis. Suppose 1 is in fact a correct analysis:

1. For all x, x is an instance of knowledge iff x is a justified true belief.

On the Chalmers-Jackson view, this would be because 'justified true belief' has the same primary intension as 'knowledge'. But for terms like 'knowledge' and 'justified true belief' the primary intension is the same as the secondary intension. Whether we consider a world as actual or as counterfactual, the same things will count as knowledge. But then since 'knowledge' and 'justified true belief' have the same primary intension, they have the same secondary intension. This in turn means that the whole sentence 1 has the same primary and secondary intensions as the sentence 1a:

1a. For all x, x is an instance of knowledge iff x is an instance of knowledge

But then the two dimensional framework of Chalmers and Jackson has no resources for dealing with the paradox of analysis. 1 and 1a share all the

---

[21] P. 32.   [22] P. 7.

semantic values provided by the framework. Of course, one could introduce more resources. But then there is the danger of stipulating an ad hoc solution to the paradox of analysis. In any case, my point is that the Chalmers-Jackson account of conceptual analysis by itself provides no means of dealing with the paradox of analysis. And of course, I said at the outset that for an account of philosophical analysis to be a contender, it must solve the paradox of analysis. The Chalmers-Jackson view does not, and so in my view is not a contender.

Let me conclude with a bit of summary as to what I take to have been accomplished in this chapter. First, I sketched my favored account of philosophical analysis. In so doing, I described three elements that together constitute a framework for addressing the issues surrounding analysis. I claimed that my account of analysis answers the five questions posed at the outset that I think any account of analysis should answer. I tried to stress that I think that the elements of the framework can be independently motivated, in the sense that they are plausible independently of providing an account of philosophical analysis. I also claimed that my account of analysis shed some light on various features of so-called theoretical identities such as 'Water is liquid H_2O'. Next, I considered the account of analysis due to Diana Ackerman. I took Ackerman's account to be representative of accounts of analysis according to which when property P analyzes property Q, P and Q are distinct properties. In this way, Ackerman's account contrasts with my own. I claim that one problem with such accounts is specifying the intimate relation that obtains between P and Q when P analyzes Q. And I argued against Ackerman's account that she was unable to specify such a relation. I also claimed that accounts of this sort seem intuitively incorrect in that in giving an analysis of a property, one is trying to say what it is, not how it is related to some distinct property.

Finally, I considered the account of conceptual analysis due to David Chalmers and Frank Jackson. I wish to stress again that Chalmers does not and Jackson *may* not see their account as an account of philosophical analysis as traditionally understood, though others have tended to take it this way. In any case, I argued that their account of conceptual analysis cannot be pressed into service as a general account of philosophical analysis. To do so would have the consequence that some of the main disputes in philosophy are merely verbal. Also, their account does not have the resources to by itself solve the paradox of analysis.

In conclusion, I hope that my remarks have made clear why I think the account of analysis I have defended is plausible and why it enjoys certain advantages over alternative accounts.

APPENDIX

Quantification and Propositions

I illustrate here how quantification works in the theory of propositions I am defending. Let's begin with a rough statement of the main ideas, which were alluded to in Chapter 2. We first introduce the notion of *argument positions* in the formulae of the simple language we consider. These are simply positions in the formulae where names and variables occur. We then suppose that propositions expressed by sentences of our language have argument positions corresponding to the arguments positions in the formulae expressing them. Since in the syntax of sentences of natural language, which is our real concern, argument positions will be certain terminal nodes in syntactic trees, and since the structure of a proposition will be identical to the structure of the sentence expressing it, for every terminal node in the syntactic tree of a sentence, there will be a corresponding terminal node in the proposition it expresses and vice versa.[1] Thus for any sentence and proposition it expresses, we can talk of the argument position in the proposition corresponding to any argument position of the sentence expressing it and vice versa. A formula of our language Φ will express a proposition (propositional frame—see below) P, where if an argument position in Φ is occupied by a name, the corresponding argument position in P will be occupied by the bearer of that name; and if an argument position in Φ is occupied by a variable, the corresponding argument position in P will be empty. A quantified formulae Σ will express a proposition (propositional frame) Q in which the empty argument positions corresponding to the argument positions in Σ occupied by the variable of the quantifier are *linked*. This is illustrated below. Linking of argument positions in propositions (propositional frames) does the work of variables in handling the propositional semantics of quantification. From a metaphysical perspective, *being linked* is a two-place relation between empty argument positions in a proposition (propositional frame). For argument positions to be so related in a proposition (propositional frame) P is for them to correspond to argument positions in the formula(e)/sentence(s) expressing P that are occupied by the same variable or index (depending on how binding is implemented in the syntax). This is a real relation between argument positions in propositions (propositional frames), and so there is nothing artificial about exploiting it in doing the semantics of quantification. I assume that linking is symmetric and transitive.

I have chosen a language whose syntax doesn't closely resemble English for simplicity. Since the main point is to illustrate how quantification is handled on the theory of propositions being defended, so long as the method illustrated will work for sentences of English and the propositions they express, that the syntax of our simple language

---

[1] Things are slightly complicated by the fact that the functions that are encoded by syntactic concatenation occur in propositions. As a result, a proposition has a bit of extra structure not had by the sentence expressing it. See the discussion of 4b' and 4c in Chapter 2. But so long as we don't consider the position occupied in the proposition by the function that is encoded by the syntactic concatenation an argument position in the proposition, the claim about argument positions in propositions and the sentences expressing them in the text holds.

diverges from that of English makes no difference. Suppose our language contains n-place predicates ('A', 'B', with or without numerical subscripts) for all n > 0; individual variables ('x','y', with or without numerical subscripts) and names ('a','b','c', with or without numerical subscripts). Assume it also contains the one-place sentential connective '~' and the two-place sentential connective '&'. The language also contains the determiners 'every', and 'some'.

The syntax is as follows:

1. If δ is a determiner, α is a variable and Σ is a formula containing free occurrences of α [$\delta\alpha\Sigma$] is a quantifier phrase.

2. If Π is an n-place predicate and $\alpha_1, \ldots, \alpha_n$ are names or variables, [$\Pi\alpha_1, \ldots, \alpha_n$] is a formula.

3. If Ω is a quantifier phrase and Σ is a formula, then [$\Omega\Sigma$] is a formula.

4. If Ψ and Φ are formulas, so are $\sim\Phi$ and [$\Phi\&\Psi$].

Sentences are formulae with no free variables. *Argument positions of a formula* are defined as follows:

1. The argument positions of [$\Pi\alpha_1, \ldots, \alpha_n$] are the positions occupied by $\alpha_1, \ldots, \alpha_n$ in [$\Pi\alpha_1, \ldots, \alpha_n$].

2. The argument positions of $\sim\Phi$ and [$\Phi\&\Psi$] are the argument positions of Φ and those of Φ and Ψ, respectively.

3. The argument positions of [[$\delta\alpha\Sigma$]Ψ] are those of Σ and Ψ, together with the position occupied by the first (leftmost) occurrence of α in [[$\delta\alpha\Sigma$]Ψ].

An argument position of the sort characterized by clause 3 will be called a *quantificational argument position in a formula*. All others will be called *atomic argument positions in formulae*.

As indicated above, since on the present view the structure of a proposition is identical to the structure of the formula/sentence expressing it, I assume that propositions have argument positions corresponding to all argument positions in formulae expressing them. I take for granted the notion of *an argument position in a proposition (propositional frame) corresponding to an argument position in the formula expressing it.* An argument position in a proposition (propositional frame) corresponding to a quantificational argument position in a formula will be called a *quantificational argument position in a proposition (propositional frame).* All other argument positions in propositions will be called *atomic argument positions in propositions (propositional frames).* In what follows let δ be a determiner; $\Sigma, \Psi,$ be formulae; Π be an n-place predicate; $\alpha, \alpha_1, \alpha_2, \ldots$ be names or variables; and ξ be a variable. Formulae express propositional frames as follows:

1. The propositional frame expressed by [$\Pi\alpha_1, \ldots, \alpha_n$] is [$\Pi^*\underline{\alpha_1}^*, \ldots, \underline{\alpha_n}^*$], where Π^* is the n-place relation expressed by Π; $\alpha_i^* (1 \leq i \leq n)$ is the bearer of α_i if α_i is a name, and an empty argument position otherwise; and $\underline{\alpha_1}^*, \ldots, \underline{\alpha_n}^*$ in [$\Pi^* \underline{\alpha_1}^*, \ldots, \underline{\alpha_n}^*$] are the n argument positions corresponding to the n argument positions of [$\Pi\alpha_1, \ldots, \alpha_n$], where any two (empty) argument positions of [$\Pi^* \underline{\alpha_1}^*, \ldots \underline{\alpha_n}^*$]

that correspond to argument positions of $[\Pi a_1, \ldots, a_n]$ that are occupied by the same variable are *linked*.[2]

2. The propositional frames expressed by $\sim\Sigma$ and $[\Sigma\&\Psi]$ are $\sim^*\underline{\Sigma'}$ and $[\underline{\Sigma'\&^*\Psi'}]$, respectively, where $\sim^*$ and $\&^*$ are the truth functions expressed by $\sim$ and $\&$, respectively; Σ', Ψ' are the propositional frames expressed by Σ and Ψ respectively; and any (empty) atomic argument positions of Σ' and Ψ' that aren't linked in them to quantificational argument positions and that correspond to argument positions of $[\Sigma\&\Psi]$ that are occupied by the same variable in $[\Sigma\&\Psi]$ are linked in $[\underline{\Sigma'}\&^*\Psi']$.[3]

3. The propositional frame expressed by $[[\delta\xi\Sigma]\Psi]$ is $[[\delta^* \ldots \Sigma']\Psi']$, where Σ', Ψ' are the propositional frames expressed by Σ, Ψ, respectively; δ^* is the semantic value of δ; any (empty) atomic argument positions of Σ' and Ψ' that aren't linked in them to quantificational argument positions and that correspond to argument positions of Σ and Ψ that are occupied by the same variable in $[[\delta\xi\Sigma]\Psi]$ are linked in $[[\delta^*\Sigma']\Psi']$; and the (empty) quantificational argument position of $[[\delta^* \ldots \Sigma']\Psi']$ (indicated by three dots) corresponding to the first occurrence of ξ in $[[\delta\xi\Sigma]\Psi]$ is linked in $[[\delta^* \ldots \Sigma']\Psi']$ to all argument positions of Σ' and Ψ' that correspond to argument positions of Σ and Ψ that are occupied by ξ.

I call these *propositional frames* because they include things expressed by formulae containing free variables. For example:

1. $[Ax,x]$

expresses the frame

1a. $[A^*\_\_ \_\_]$

where A^* is the two-place relation expressed by 'A'; linking is indicated in the obvious way; and '$\_$' indicates empty argument positions in the propositional frame. Frames like 1a aren't truth evaluable at worlds. A *proposition* is a propositional frame in which

---

[2] The underlining in $[\Pi^*a_1^*, \ldots, a_n^*]$ is intended to indicate that *being linked* holds among the argument places as appropriate. I assume throughout that the only argument places that are linked in propositional frames are those that clauses 1–3 here require to be linked.

[3] This may appear to violate some notion of compositionality. For '$[[Fx]\&[Gx]]$' and '$[[Fx]\&[Gy]]$' express different propositional frames according to this clause (since the argument positions in the propositional frame expressed by '$[[Fx]\&[Gx]]$' corresponding to the occurrences of 'x' are linked, but those in the propositional frame expressed by '$[[Fx]\&[Gy]]$' corresponding to the occurrences of 'x' and 'y' are not). But '$[Gx]$' and '$[Gy]$' express the same propositional frame. So the left and right conjuncts of the two conjunctions express the same propositional frames, but the conjunctions express different propositional frames. But I don't think this does violate compositionality, because the propositional frame expressed by a conjunction should be a function of the propositional frames expressed by its conjuncts, the semantic value of '$\&$' and the syntax of the conjunction. But the syntax of '$[[Fx]\&[Gx]]$' is different from the syntax of '$[[Fx]\&[Gy]]$' in virtue of the different patterns of occurrences of variables. Hence, that the two formulae express different propositional frames does not violate compositionality. Thanks to Jim Pryor for discussion here.

every empty atomic argument position is linked to a quantificational argument position.[4] These are expressed by sentences.

Finally, we define truth at a world for propositions. Let o, $o^1, o^2, \ldots$ be individuals; R be an n-place relation; Ξ, Γ be propositional frames; X,Y be propositions; AND and NOT be the truth functions for conjunction and negation, respectively; and EVERY and SOME be the semantic values of 'every' and 'some', respectively. If R is an n-place relation, the *intension of R* is a function from worlds to sets of n-tuples of individuals (the members of which stand in R at the world in question); and the *extension of R in w*, $ext_w(R)$, is the result of applying its intension to the world w.

1. A proposition of the form $[R \, o^1, \ldots, o^n]$ is true at w iff $<o^1, \ldots, o^n>$ belongs to $ext_w(R)$.

2. A proposition of the form [X AND Y] is true at w iff $AND(V_{X,w}, V_{Y,w})=T$, where $V_{X,w}, V_{Y,w}$ are the truth values of X and Y at w. (Similar clause for NOT.)

3. A proposition of the form $[[EVERY \ldots \Xi]\Gamma]$ is true in w iff $\{o^1 : \Xi(o^1/ \ldots)$ is true at w$\}$ is a subset of $\{o: \Gamma(o/ \ldots)$ is true at w$\}$, where $\Xi(o^1/ \ldots)$ is the proposition that differs from the propositional frame Ξ only in having o^1 occur in it in every argument position that in Ξ is empty and is linked to $\ldots$ in $[[EVERY \ldots \Xi]\Gamma]$; and similarly $\Gamma(o/ \ldots)$ is the proposition that differs from the propositional frame Γ only in having o occur in it in every argument position that in Γ is empty and is linked to $\ldots$ in $[[EVERY \ldots \Xi]\Gamma]$.[5] (Similar clause for SOME.)[6]

In the foregoing, I did not try to implement the idea suggested in Chapters 2 and 7 that a (one-place) complex predicate contributes to propositions a sub-propositional complex entity that *represents* a property. To implement that idea formally, among other things one would have to develop a formal account of how properties and relations combine to form complex properties and relations. This in turn would require a full blown theory of the modes of combination by means of which properties and relations combine to form complex properties and relations. As I said in Chapter 7, I currently have no such theory. And that is why I did not attempt to implement the relevant idea here. But I can gesture at the way such an implementation would go. Certain propositional frames, as they occur in propositions, would be our sub-propositional complex entities contributed

---

[4] The intention is that a propositional frame containing no empty argument positions is a proposition (in virtue of vacuously satisfying the characterization of a proposition).

[5] By the argument position $\ldots$ in $[[EVERY \ldots \Xi]\Gamma]$, I of course mean the quantificational argument position following the outer most occurrence of EVERY in $[[EVERY \ldots \Xi]\Gamma]$, (which is indicated by $\ldots$). We know that $\Xi(o^1/ \ldots)$ and $\Gamma(o/ \ldots)$ are propositions, since $[[EVERY \ldots \Xi]\Gamma]$ is a proposition. Because the latter is a proposition, the only empty argument positions in Ξ and Γ that aren't linked to a quantificational argument position in them are those that in $[[EVERY \ldots \Xi]\Gamma]$ are linked to the "outermost" quantificational argument position in $[[EVERY \ldots \Xi]\Gamma]$, (i.e. the quantificational argument position following the outermost occurrence of EVERY in $[[EVERY \ldots \Xi]\Gamma]$). In $\Xi(o^1/ \ldots)$ and $\Gamma(o/ \ldots)$, those argument positions are occupied by o^1 and o, respectively. Hence $\Xi(o^1/ \ldots)$ and $\Gamma(o/ \ldots)$ are propositions.

[6] On this way of doing things, it is natural to take EVERY and SOME to be relations between sets, or perhaps between properties (in the latter case, the relation would hold between properties A and B at a world w iff the extension of A at w is a subset of the extension of B at w). I have adopted this latter view in the book, but I am open to taking EVERY and SOME to be relations between sets as well.

by complex predicates to those propositions. So we would want a definition mapping the propositional frames contributed to propositions by complex predicates to the relevant properties. To take a simple example, consider the following sentence of our language:

2. [[Every x[Ax]] [[Bx]&[Cx]]]

and the "complex predicate" occurring in it

2a. [[Bx]&[Cx]]

2a contributes the following propositional frame to the proposition expressed by 2:

2a'. [[B*__] AND[C*__]]

where B* is the semantic value of 'B' (a property) and similarly for C*; where linking is again indicated in the obvious way; and where '__' again indicates empty argument positions. 2a' needs to be mapped by our definition of (certain) propositional frames representing properties to the (complex) property of being B* and C*. In saying only this much, I don't pretend to have indicated how such a definition would go. But I do think this suggests the lines along which it would have to proceed.

References

Abusch, D. (1997). 'Sequence of Tense and Temporal De Re', *Linguistics and Philosophy*, 20: 1–50.

Ackerman, D. F. (1981). 'The Informativeness of Philosophical Analysis', *Midwest Studies in Philosophy*, V1.

—— (1986). 'Essential Properties and Philosophical Analysis', *Midwest Studies in Philosophy*, XI.

Adams, R. (1981). 'Actualism and Thisness', *Synthese*, 49: 3–41.

Anderson, C. A. (1983). 'The Paradox of the Knower', *The Journal of Philosophy*, 80(6): 338–55.

Armstrong, D. (1978). *Universals and Scientific Realism*, Vols. I and II. Cambridge: Cambridge University Press.

Bach, K. (1997). 'Do Belief Reports Report Beliefs?' *Pacific Philosophical Quarterly*, 78: 215–41.

—— (1999). 'The Myth of Conventional Implicature', *Linguistics and Philosophy*, 22: 327–66.

Bealer, G. (1993). 'A Solution to Frege's Puzzle', in J. Tomberlin (ed.) *Philosophical Perspectives 7, Language and Logic*. Atascadero, CA: Ridgeview Publishing Company.

—— (1998). 'Propositions', *Mind*, 107, 1–32.

Beaney, M. (ed.) (1997). *The Frege Reader*. Oxford: Blackwell Publishing.

Beghelli, F. and T. Stowell (1997). 'Distributivity and Negation', in Szabolcsi (1997), 71–107.

Benacerraf, P. (1965). 'What Numbers Could Not Be', *The Philosophical Review*, January, LXXIV(l): 47–73.

Bigelow, J. (1996). 'Presentism and Properties', in J. Tomberlin (ed.) *Philosophical Perspectives, Vol 10: Metaphysics.*, Cambridge, MA: Blackwell Publishing.

Chalmers, D. (1996). *The Conscious Mind: In Search of a Fundamental Theory*. Oxford: Oxford University Press.

—— (2003). 'Foundations of Two Dimensional Logic', available on Chalmers' website at: http://consc.net/chalmers/

—— F. Jackson (2001). 'Conceptual Analysis and Reductive Explanation', *Philosophical Review*, 110: 315–61 (also available on Chalmers website at: http://consc.net/chalmers/ The pagination of the version on the web is used in the text).

Chisholm, R. M. and R. C. Potter (1981). 'The Paradox of Analysis: A Solution', *Metaphilosophy*, 12(1).

Chomsky, N. (1995). *The Minimalist Program*. Cambridge, MA: MIT Press.

Cresswell, M.J. (1985). *Structured Meanings*. Cambridge, MA: MIT Press.

—— (1990). *Entities and Indices*. Dordrecht: Kluwer Academic Publishers.

—— (2002). 'Why Propositions Have No Structure', *Nous*, 38(4): 643–62.

Crisp, T. (2003). 'Presentism' in M.J. Loux and D. Zimmerman (eds.) *The Oxford Handbook of Metaphysics*. Oxford: Oxford University Press, 211–45.

Cross, C. (2001). 'The Paradox of the knower without Epistemic Closure', *Mind*, 110(438): 319–33.

Cross, C. (2004). 'More on the Paradox of the Knower without Epistemic Closure', *Mind*, 113(449).

Den Dikken, M., R. Larson and P. Ludlow (1996). 'Intensional "Transitive" Verbs and Concealed Complement Clauses', *Rivista di Linguistica*, 8: 29–46.

—— —— —— (2002). 'Intensional Transitive Verbs and Abstract Clausal Complementation.' *Linguistics Inquiry*, forthcoming.

Doepke, F. (1982). 'Spatially Coinciding Objects' in M. Rea (ed) *Material Constitution*. Lanham, MD: Rowman and Littlefield.

Dowty, D. (1982). 'Tenses, Times and Adverbs and Compositional Semantic Theory', *Linguistics and Philosophy*, 5: 23–53

Dummett, M. (1981). *The Interpretation of Frege's Philosophy*. London: Gerlad Duckworth and Company Limited.

—— (1991). *The Logical Basis of Metaphysics*. Cambridge, MA: Harvard University Press.

Enc, M. (1987). 'Anchoring Conditions for Tense', *Linguistic Inquiry*, 18: 633–57

—— (1996). 'Tense and Modality', in S. Lappin (ed.) *The Handbook of Contemporary Semantic Theory*. Oxford: Blackwell Publishing.

Epstein, S. D. (1999). 'Un-Principled Syntax: The Derivation of Syntactic Relations', in S.D. Epstein and N. Hornstein (eds.) *Working Minimalism.*, Cambridge, MA: MIT Press.

Evans, G. (1977). 'Pronouns, Quantifiers and Relative Clauses (I)', *Canadian Journal of Philosophy*, 7(3): 467–536.

Fara, Delia Graff. (2001). 'Descriptions as Predicates', *Philosophical Studies*, 102(1): 1–42. Originally published under the name 'Delia Graff'.

Fine, K. (1985). 'Plantinga on the Reduction of Possibilist Discourse' in J.E. Tomberlin and Peter van Inwagen (eds.) *Alvin Plantinga*. Dordrecht: Reidel, 145–86.

Fitch, G. (1994). 'Singular Propositions in Time', *Philosophical Studies*, 73: 181–7.

Forbes, G. (2000). 'Objectual Attitudes', *Linguistics and Philosophy*, 23: 141–83.

Frege, G. ([1923] 1977). 'Compound Thoughts', *Logical Investigations*, P.T. Geach (ed.) Boston, MA: Yale University Press.

—— (1977). *Logical Investigations*, P.T. Geach (ed.) Boston, MA: Yale University Press.

—— (1979). *Gottlob Frege, Posthumous Writings*. Chicago, IL: University of Chicago Press.

Fukui, N. (2001). 'Phrase Structure' in Baltin and Colloins (eds.) *The Handbook of Contemporary Syntactic Theory*. Malden, MA: Blackwell Publishing.

Higginbotham, J. (1983). 'Logical Form, Binding and Nominals', *Linguistic Inquiry*, 14: 395–420.

—— (2002). 'Why is Sequence of Tense Obligatory', in G. Preyer and G. Peter (eds.) *Logical Form and Language*. Oxford: Oxford University Press, pp. 207–27.

Hinchliff, M. (1996). 'The Puzzle of Change' in J.Tomberlin (ed.) *Philosophical Perspectives, Vol 10: Metaphysics*. Cambridge, MA: Blackwell Publishing.

Hoffmann, A. (2003). 'A Puzzle about Truth and Singular Propositions', *Mind*, 112(448): 635–51.

Jackson, F. (1998). *From Metaphysics to Ethics: A Defence of Conceptual Analysis*. Oxford: Oxford University Press.

Jubien, M. (2001). 'Propositions and the Objects of Thought', *Philosophical Studies*,104: 47–62.

Kamp, H. (1968). 'Tense Logic and the Theory of Linear Orders', doctoral dissertation. University of Cailfornia, LA.

——— (1971). 'Formal Properties of "Now" ', *Theoria*, 227–73.

Kaplan, D. (1989). 'Demonstratives' in Almog, Perry and Wettstein (eds.) *Themes from Kaplan*. Oxford: Oxford University Press.

——— R. Montague (1960). 'A Paradox Regained', originally published in *Notre Dame Journal of Formal Logic*,1: 79–90. Republished in *Formal Philosophy*, R. Thomason (ed.). (1974). Boston, MA: Yale University Press.

Katz, J. (1981). *Language and Other Abstract Objects.*, Lanham, MD: Rowman and Littlefield.

King, J. C. (1994). 'Can Propositions be Naturalistically Acceptable?', *Midwest Studies in Philosophy*, XIX: 53–75.

——— (1995). 'Structured Propositions and Complex Predicates', *Nous*, 29(4): 516–35.

——— (1996). 'Structured Propositions and Sentence Structure', *Journal of Philosophical Logic*, 25: 495–521.

——— (1998). 'What is a Philosophical Analysis?' *Philosophical Studies*, 90: 155–79.

——— (2000). 'On the Possibility of <u>Correct</u> Apparently Circular Dispositional Analyses', *Philosophical Studies*, 98: 257–78.

——— (2001). *Complex Demonstratives: A Quantificational Account*. Cambridge, MA: MIT Press.

——— (2002). 'Designating Propositions', *The Philosophical Review*, 111(3): 341–71.

——— (2003). 'Tense, Modality and Semantic Values', in J. Hawthorne (ed.) *Philosophical Perspectives Volume 17, Philosophy of Language*. Malden, MA: Blackwell Publishing.

——— (2005). 'What in the world are the ways things might have been?', *Philosophical Studies*, forthcoming.

——— J. Stanley (2005). 'Semantics, Pragmatics and the Role of Semantic Content', in Z. Szabo (ed.) *Semantics versus Pragmatics*. New York: Oxford University Press, pp. 111–64.

Kripke, S. (1972). *Naming and Necessity*. Cambridge, MA: Harvard University Press.

Langford, C.H. (1942). 'The Notion of Analysis in Moore's Philosophy', in P.A. Schilpp (ed.) *The Philosophy of G.E. Moore*. La Salle, IL: Open Court,.

Lewis, D. (1970). 'General Semantics', reprinted in *Philosophical Papers Volume 1* (1983). New York: Oxford University Press.

——— (1979). 'Attitudes *De Dicto* and *De Se*' reprinted in *Philosophical Papers Volume 1* (1983). New York: Oxford University Press.

——— (1980). 'Index, Context and Content', reprinted in *Papers in Philosophical Logic* (1998). Cambridge: Cambridge University Press.

——— (1983). 'New Work for a Theory of Universals', reprinted in *Papers in Metaphysics and Epistemology* (1999). New York: Cambridge University Press, pp. 78–107.

——— (1986a). *On the Plurality of Worlds*. Oxford: Blackwell Publishing.

——— (1986b). 'Against Structural Universals' reprinted in *Papers in Metaphysics and Epistemology* (1999). New York: Cambridge University Press, pp. 78–107.

——— (1991). *Parts of Classes*. Cambridge, MA: Basil Blackwell Publishing.

——— (1998). *Papers in Philosophical Logic*. Cambridge: Cambridge University Press.

Linsky, B. and E. Zalta (1994). 'In defense of the simplest quantified modal logic' *Philosophical Perspectives*, 8: 431–58.

Linsky, B. and E. Zalta (1996). 'In defense of the contingently nonconcrete', *Philosophical Studies*, 84: 283–94.

Ludlow, P. (1999). *Semantics, Tense and Time: An Essay in the Metaphysics of Natural Language*. Cambridge, MA: MIT Press.

Markosian, N. (2004). 'A Defense of Presentism', in D. Zimmerman (ed.) *Oxford Studies in Metaphysics, Vol 1*. Oxford: Oxford University Press, pp. 47–82,

Matthews, R. (2002). 'Logical Form and the Relational Conception of Belief' in Preyer and Peter (eds.) *Logical Form and Language.*, New York: Oxford University Press. pp. 421–43.

McKinsey, M. (1999). 'The Semantics of Belief Ascriptions', *Nous*, 33(4): 519–57.

McMichael, A., (1983). 'A Problem For Actualism About Possible Worlds', *The Philosophical Review*, XCII(1).

Merrill, G. H. (1980). 'The Model Theoretic Argument Against Realism', *Philosophy of Science*, 47: 69–81.

Moltmann, F. (2002). 'Nominalizing Quantifiers'. Unpublished manuscript.

Montague, R. (1963). 'Syntactical Treatments of Modality, with Corollaries on Reflexion Principles and Finite Axiomatizability', originally published in *Acta Philosophica Fennica*, 16:153–67. Republished in *Formal Philosophy*, R. Thomason (ed.) (1974). Boston, MA: Yale University Press.

_____ (1974). 'The Proper Treatment of Quantification in Ordinary English', in R. Thomason (ed.) *Formal Philosophy*. Boston, MA: Yale University Press.

Moore, G.E. (1942). 'A Reply to my Critics', in P.A. Schilpp (ed.) *The Philosophy of G.E. Moore*. La Salle, IL: Open Court.

Ogihara, T. (1996). *Tense, Attitudes and Scope*. Dordrecht: Kluwer Academic Publishers.

Parsons, T. (1990). *Events in the Semantics of English: A Study in Subatomic Semantics.* Cambridge, MA: MIT Press.

_____ (1993). 'On Denoting Propositions and Facts', in J. E. Tomberlin (ed.) *Philosophical Perspectives, 7, Language and Logic*. Atascadero, CA: Ridgeview Publishing Company, pp. 441–60.

Partee, B. (1973). 'Some Structural Analogies between Tenses and Pronouns In English', *Journal of Philosophy*, 70, 601–7.

Pietroski, P. (2000). 'On Explaining That', *The Journal of Philosophy*, 97: 655–62.

Plantinga, A. (1974). *The Nature of Necessity*. Oxford: Clarendon Press.

_____ (1976). 'Actualism and Possible Worlds', *Theoria*, 42: 139–60.

_____ (1983). 'On existentialism', *Philosophical Studies*, 44: 1–20.

Quine, W.V.O. (1960). 'Variables Explained Away', in *Selected Logical Papers* (1966). New York, Random House.

Richard, M. (1981). 'Temporalism and Eternalism', *Philosophical Studies*, 39: 1–13.

_____ (1982). 'Tense, Propositions and Meanings', *Philosophical Studies*, 41: 337–51.

_____ (1990). *Propositional Attitudes: An Essay on Thoughts and How We Ascribe Them.* Cambridge: Cambridge University Press.

_____ (1993). 'Articulated Terms', in J. Tomberlin (ed.) *Philosophical Perspectives volume 7*. Atascadero, CA: Ridgeview Publishing Company, pp. 207–30.

_____ (1998). 'Commitment', in J. Tomberlin (ed.) *Philosophical Perspectives 12, Language, Mind and Ontology*, Oxford: Blackwell Publishing.

Russell, B. (1903). *Principles of Mathematics*, 2nd edn. New York: W.W. Norton and Company, Inc.

_____ (1910). 'On the Nature of Truth and Falsehood', in *Philosophical Essays*, (reprint edn). New York: Routledge.

_____ (1994). *Philosophical Essays* (reprint edn). New York: Routledge.

Salmon, N. (1986). *Frege's Puzzle*. Cambridge, MA: MIT Press.

_____ (1989). 'Tense and Singular Propositions' in Almog, Perry and Wettstein (eds.) *Themes From Kaplan*. New York: Oxford University Press.

_____ (1990). 'A Millian Heir Rejects the Wages of *Sinn*', in Anderson and Owens (eds.) *Propositional Attitudes: The Role of Content in Logic, Language and Mind*. CSLI

_____ (1998). 'Nonexistence', *Nous*, 32(3): 277–319.

Schiffer, S. (2003). *The Things We Mean*. New York: Oxford University Press.

Sider, T. (1999). 'Presentism and Ontological Commitment', *The Journal of Philosophy*, XCVI(7): 325–47.

_____ (2001). *Four Dimensionalism*. New York: Oxford University Press.

Soames, S. (1987). 'Direct Reference, Propositional Attitudes and Semantic Content', *Philosophical Topics*, 15.

_____ (2002). *Beyond Rigidity*. New York: Oxford University Press.

_____ (2005). *Reference and Description: The Case Against Two-Dimensionalism*. Princeton, NJ: Princeton University Press.

Stalnaker, R. (1970). 'Pragmatics', *Synthese*, 22. Reprinted in *Context and Content* (1999). Oxford: Oxford University Press.

_____ (1999). *Context and Content*. Oxford: Oxford University Press.

_____ (2003). *Ways a World Might Be*. New York: Oxford University Press

_____ (2006). 'Merely Possible Propositions'. Unpublished manuscript.

Stanley, J. (1997a). 'Names and Rigid Designation', in B. Hale and C. Wright (eds.) *A Companion to the Philosophy of Language*. Oxford: Blackwell Publishing.

_____ (1997b). 'Rigidity and Content', in R. Heck (ed.) *Logic, Language and Reality: Essays in Honor of Michael Dummett*. Oxford: Oxford University Press.

_____ (2000). 'Context and Logical Form', *Linguistics and Philosophy*, 23(4): 391–434.

Szabo, Z. (2000). 'Compositionality as Supervenience', *Linguistics and Philosophy*, 23: 475–505.

Szabolcsi, A. (1997). 'Strategies of Scope Taking', *Ways of Scope Taking*. Dordrecht: Kluwer, pp. 109–54

_____ (2001). 'The Syntax of Scope', in Baltin and Collins (eds.) *The Handbook of Contemporary Syntactic Theory*. Malden, MA: Blackwell Publishing.

Thomason, R. (1980). 'A Note on Syntactical Treatments of Modality', *Synthese*, 44: 391–5.

_____ (1980, ms.). 'Some Limitations to Psychological Orientation in Semantic Theory' Available at: http://www.eecs.umich.edu/~rthomaso/

Uzquiano, G. (2004). 'The Paradox of the Knower without Epistemic Closure?', *Mind*, 113(449).

van Benthem, J.F.A.K. (1977) 'Tense Logic and Standard Logic', *Logique et Analyse*, 80: 395–437.

Varzi, A. (2004). 'Mereology', *The Stanford Encyclopedia of Philosophy*, Fall edn). Edward N. Zalta (ed) Available at: http://plato.stanford.edu/archives/fall2004/entries/mereology/

Vlach, F. (1973). ' "Now" and "Then". A formal study in the logic of tense anaphora', PhD dissertation, UCLA, London.

Williamson, T., (2002). 'Necessary Existents', in A. O'Hear (ed.) *Logic, Thought and Language*. Cambridge: Cambridge University Press, pp. 233–51. Available at: http://www.philosophy.ox.ac.uk/faculty/members/index_tw.htm (I use the pagination of the latter).

Wittgenstein, L. (1958). *Tractatus Logico-Philosophicus*. London: Routledge and Kegan Paul.

Zimmerman, D. (1998). 'Temporary Intrinsics and Presentism' in Zimmerman and van Inwagen (eds.) *Metaphysics: The Big Questions*. Cambridge, MA: Blackwell Publishing.

Index

Index